Charles F Swain

Captain Waters, and Bill his Bo'son.

A tale of the ocean and the farm

Charles F Swain

Captain Waters, and Bill his Bo'son.
 A tale of the ocean and the farm

ISBN/EAN: 9783337023508

Printed in Europe, USA, Canada, Australia, Japan

Cover: Foto ©Andreas Hilbeck / pixelio.de

More available books at **www.hansebooks.com**

CAPTAIN WATERS,

AND

BILL HIS BO'SON.

A TALE

OF THE OCEAN AND THE FARM.

BY

R. O. SAULT,

(CHAS. F. SWAIN.)

———————

———————

NEW YORK:
JOHN P. JEWETT, PUBLISHER,
180 Fulton Street.

1878.

Press of Chas. A. Coffin,
85 & 87 John Street.

CONTENTS.

CHAPTER.	PAGE.

PUBLISHER'S INTRODUCTION.

The manuscript of this work was placed in my hands, for examination, some weeks since. I took it home and read it aloud to my four boys, their ages varying from 9 to 15 years. So absorbed did they all become in the development of the story, with its fascinating descriptions of "*Life upon the Ocean Wave*," that they could not be persuaded to go to bed, without a promise from me, that I would stop where I was, and resume the reading on the following evening. Being satisfied that it could not fail to interest every youthful mind, I tested it still further upon cultivated adults, and with similar results. The work is now offered to the public, in the confident belief that it will prove to be one of the most readable works on sea life, which has appeared for many years. The reader will soon find that it is not a concoction of land-lub-ber-isms, but a veritable transcript of actualities, faithfully drawn by an "*Old Salt*;" being a history of the life-long experiences of the Captain, his Bo'son and dog. Bill the Bo'son is a phenomenon; a genuine salt upon the ocean, and *sui-generis* in navigating a farm,—especially so in his encounter with the venerable *Patriarch of the sheep-fold*. Bill will henceforth figure in Ocean Literature with "Ratlin the Reefer," "Robinson Crusoe," and other worthies of that ilk.

JOHN P. JEWETT, Publisher.

New York, Feb., 1877.

The Bo'son's Faithful Dog, Bose, Rescuing
Little Nellie from Drowning.
(See Page 37.)

CAPTAIN WATERS AND HIS BO'SON.

CHAPTER I.

THE CAPTAIN CONCLUDES TO CHANGE HIS MODE OF LIVING.

CAPTAIN Joseph Waters commenced his life on the ocean at the age of seventeen years, and without the aid of money or relatives worked his way up to the command of a ship.

After spending over forty years on the ocean and accumulating enough of the riches of this world to provide for all future wants, and allow him to select his own mode of living, he carefully surveyed the coast to find a safe and comfortable harbor where he could anchor and "ride out" the declining years of his life.

When a boy he had lived and worked on a farm. He liked it then and thought he should like it again.

Sailors often when at sea, and especially in stormy weather, talk of changing their occupation and becoming farmers, and Captain Waters had also for many years contemplated such a change.

In arranging to relinquish an occupation to which he had devoted more than forty years of his life, he felt that his first duty would be to make a proper provision for those who had been his companions on the ocean. They through many long years had been in his service, obeyed his commands and aided him in accumulating his wealth, and had become attached to him as his friends. The Captain therefore felt impelled by all the obligations, and bound by all the mystic ties of ocean brotherhood, to see them well provided for.

His old steward had sailed with him twenty-two years, had served him all that time faithfully in that capacity, and being an educated man, had rendered important assistance in keeping his books and making out his accounts. He was of foreign birth, differing in race, and also slightly in complexion, from his commander.

The stewardess had been sailing with him over twenty years. He saw her for the first time when she was discovered on board of his ship among the steerage passengers. It was her first voyage from Liverpool to New York, and in the winter season. Before reaching port her father and mother died, leaving her without a known relative in the world. The Doctor reported her sick and needing special care, and she was taken into the cabin, and tenderly nursed by Mrs. Waters until she fully recovered. At the end of that voyage she expressed a wish to remain on board, as she had neither home nor friends, and declared that if the captain and Mrs. Waters would keep her with them, she would never leave while they had a ship to float in. Ocean life, as it proved, suited her well, and she always kept her promise.

Last, but not least, among those to be cared for, was Bill Thomas, the Bo'son. Bill had sailed with Captain Waters twenty-seven years, and during the last twenty of those years the Captain would as soon have thought of making a voyage around the world without his chronometer, as without his Bo'son.

Chronometers require winding up, and sometimes change their rate at sea, and have to be corrected by lunar observations, or sighting the land ; they cannot always be depended on. The Bo'son never required winding up, and could at all times be depended on.

The Captain talked the subject over with Mrs. Waters, and she said :

"It is sheer nonsense to think of going on a farm, unless we take the whole family with us."

Their children were all grown up, married and settled in life, and Mrs. Waters meant, by the "whole family," the Bo'son, steward and stewardess, and it would have been difficult to convince her that either of them belonged less to the family then she did herself.   All the others seemed to share this feeling.

Presently Mrs. Waters added : "Captain, how are you to get along on a farm without the steward to give your orders to, when you want an early breakfast or something extra cooked? Who, I should like to know, but the old steward, can cook a duck with curry sauce to suit your taste? And who but he can get up twice laid codfish so that you can eat it? And who is to brush your coat, black your boots, tell you where your storm-hat is when you want to go on deck in a. squall, tell you how the ship heads, or hand you the spy-glass when there is a sail in sight? I am free to admit that, though I have sailed with you on every voyage for the last twenty years, and many odd voyages before that, and have lived with you at sea and on shore for nearly forty years, I have never been able to learn, as you call it, where the duck and curry out-haul leads, or where the hauser-laid codfish halliards are belayed."

"Nancy," said the captain, "do you expect that I am going to reef topsails on the farm when there is a heavy blow, or that I shall raise a sail and want a spy-glass to see which way she is headed? You have been so long at sea yourself, that you are actually salted through and through."

"If you don't want a storm-hat or spy-glass, you will be wanting something every hour in the day, and my hands will be full of milk and butter and the like, so that I can't be chasing around after you all the time."

"Well, well, Nancy, if you do chase me around with your hands full of milk and butter, I shall certainly need the steward to swab me off and make me fit to see company ; but as for duck and curry, or hauser-laid codfish, they are dishes that none but a sea-cook can properly get up. I own, my dear girl, that you are more than common in the line of good roasts, good cakes and pies, but for a sea-hash, sea-pie, duck and curry, or codfish balls, the old steward never had an equal, and if he don't go with us, I shall miss him."

"And what are you going to do, Joe, or some one to

pick up things and put them in their places, some one to receive and execute your orders? You have had the Bo'son with you so long, and been so accustomed to depend on him to do about everything, that you will be lost without him. You might as well go to sea without a compass as to go on a farm without Bill the Bo'son. In a month you would not know where to find anything, and might have some difficulty in finding yourself; and in two months you wouldn't be able to tell the points of the compass."

The good lady, whose best feelings were enlisted for the welfare of the family, had been warming up all the time, so she continued :

"As for myself, I shall never think of going on a farm or anywhere else without Lizzie. Why, bless your old heart, Lizzie has sailed with us so long that she knows all the ropes. I can't do without her any better than you can do without the Bo'son and steward ; and then to talk of breaking up our family after we have grown old together, and of cutting ourselves adrift from a crew that have sailed with us on so many voyages, braved with us so many dangers, and served us so faithfully ! And what could the poor creatures do without us ? They are getting old like ourselves, have no friends but us, no home but ours, and would you turn your back on them in their old age ? If you do, I shall be ashamed of you as an old sailor."

"Old lady, I never meant any such thing, and you have sailed with me long enough to know better. Whoever heard of Joe Waters turning his back on a friend or shipmate, or of his being unmindful or ungrateful to those who had served him ? It is for them, as well as for ourselves, that I wish to arrange a comfortable future."

"Yes, Joseph, I do know your heart, for I have summered it and wintered it, sailed with it on every ocean and sea known to navigators, known it at sea and on shore for nearly forty years, and it has been less changed by time and climate than chronometers and compasses are. I do know better than to think that you will leave the Bo'son and steward to shift for themselves ; and as for Lizzie, she is shipped for life, either at sea or ashore. The best thing you can do, old boy, is to call the family together and tell them the whole story, and hear what they'll have to say about it. I know they'll all feel badly to learn that the ' Neptune ' is to be sold, and that you and I have made our last voyage ; but the sooner it is over the better it will be for us all."

" My good woman, you are on the right tack now, as you generally are, and I'll do what you recommend, and do it this very evening, for the matter has been a heavy weight on my heart ever since I concluded not to make another voyage. It will be hard to part with the ship, but harder to part with the crew, and if we can only take them with us to the farm, we shall all be as contented and happy there as we have been on shipboard."

CHAPTER II.

THE CAPTAIN'S NEW ARRANGEMENT WITH HIS CREW.

THE ship had been in port long enough after her last China voyage to discharge the cargo, and was now lying at the foot of Rector street, New York. The officers and rest of the crew had been paid off and discharged, leaving, as Mrs. Waters was pleased to express it, " The family to themselves." They had been so long accustomed to the ship and to their own limited society, that when in port they lived on board, as they could enjoy more comforts on board of the " Neptune " than they could at any of the hotels.

In the evening the Captain called them into the cabin, and requested them to be seated, as he had something to say that would take time. After sitting a few minutes, the Captain opened the subject by saying: " We have sailed long together, and been satisfied with each other. I have made my last voyage; the ship ' Neptune ' is for sale."

It was all that he could say, and it was hard for him to

say that. It is only those who have long followed the sea, been long attached to a favorite ship, or about to leave home not to return, who can appreciate his feelings, or fully understand the effort it cost him to make that statement.

They looked at each other, at Mrs. Waters, and at the Captain, and all of them appeared astonished and dismayed.

The Bo'son was the first to speak, which he did after making an effort very much like trying to get through a hole that was a trifle too small to admit his body, and said :

"And what in the name of"—

"Hold on, Bo'son—no hard words here—remember where you are."

"I do remember where I am, Cap'n, and wouldn't use any hard words; but what in the name of the sheet-anchor is to become of us?"

"That, Bo'son, is what I wish to find out, and for that I have called you all into the cabin."

The steward and Lizzie appeared to expect the Bo'son to do all the talking and make the best arrangement he could for the whole party; and as the ship was to be given up, whatever the Bo'son did, or agreed to do, they would be satisfied with, and also do, saying, "Bill has sailed longest with you and ought to know best."

"Cap'n Waters, in the first place I want to know where you and Mrs. Waters are going to anchor yourselves for the rest of life, as a great deal depends on that, as regards what the Bo'son will conclude to do. After sailing with you twenty-seven years, and the last seven of them in the ship 'Neptune' that I helped build, and helped rig, and that I have taken so much pride in, before I will go to sea in any other ship, or with any other man or woman, I'll pull the stroke oar of a ferry-boat between New York and Blackwell's Island, and ferry over criminals."

The captain informed them that after having spent so many years on the ocean and in roving about the world, that he really wanted rest and a home on the land, and that he intended purchasing a farm, and on it spending his remaining days.

The Bo'son brightened up at once and said :

" How, in the name of——"

" Hold on again, Bo'son, what are you about ; do you forget yourself ? "

" Well, sir, I am holding on all I can, but how, in the name of old Neptune, do you expect to sail a farm without your Bo'son and steward ?   And how is Mrs. Waters to scull the pantry without Lizzie ? You will be singing out, ' Bo'son, Bo'son, where is the hand-lead and line, where is the spare pump gear ? Bo'son, call all hands and ready about ;' and no Bo'son on board to answer, ' aye, aye, sir ! ' A fine time you will have navigating a farm without your old Bo'son on board."

Captain and Mrs. Waters were much amused at Bill's notion of sailing and navigating a farm, for they knew that the Bo'son had never been three miles inland in his life. What he thought the captain would want of a hand-lead and line, or how often he expected the farm to be put about, was more than they could tell.

" You know, sir," continued the Bo'son, " that I am as good a carpenter and blacksmith as I am a Bo'son ; that I am as handy with an axe and a stick of timber, or a piece of hot iron and a hammer as I am with a marline-spike and a piece of rope ; and I can't see how you are going to do without me. For twenty-seven years I have been learning all that I could, so as to be more useful on board of your ship ; and for many voyages you have never wanted anything done that I couldn't do, nor anything made that I couldn't make, and now you talk of selling the ship, and cutting your Bo'son and steward adrift, and of navigating a farm all by yourself. Well, sir, you just go and try it once, and see where you will fetch the first tack,—if you undertake any such voyage without your steward I'll bet my best go-ashore trousers against nothing, that in less than a month you will lose your appetite and be as thin as a midshipman on board of a man-of war, or the second mate of a merchant ship ; and if you go without your Bo'son you will never find anything, and be lucky if you find yourself. The first spell of foggy weather you have, for want of a good look-out forward and a hand to heave the lead, you will run the old farm hard and fast ashore, and she will be a total loss."

The captain and his lady had a hearty laugh at Bill's idea of running a farm ashore, but observing that he and the others remained very serious, the captain said, "Go on, Bo'son."

"Yes, sir; if, after all you have done for me, you go and sell the 'Neptune' without giving me notice one voyage ahead, and then turn me adrift on dry land to starve, and no one to look after me, I'll just go and raise particular and extra——"

"Hold on, Bo'son, what are you about to say?" interposed the captain.

"Mischief," continued Bill, "and you can bet your best bow-anchor against the flyjib downhaul that I'll do it, for I'll take the image of old Neptune from the bow of the ship and burn it, scuttle and sink the ship alongside of the wharf, and then drown myself; that is what the Bo'son will do."

Bill was laboring under deeper feelings than he had ever realized before. During the many years that he had been sailing with Captain Waters, he had thought but little about the future, nor had he ever seriously contemplated the possibility of a separation from the captain, his lady, his ship, and the others that had sailed so long with him.

They all knew that the Bo'son was speaking from his heart, while he was fearing that he might be deserted and left without home or friends. His attachment to the Captain, Mrs. Waters and the others, was as strong and sincere as his true character was noble and generous.

"Bo'son," said the Captain, "I don't wish or mean to turn you adrift, or desert you, for you have been the best and truest man that has even sailed with me, and your old Captain is not ashamed to tell you so. I have done but little for you, while you have done much for me, and now you may claim and receive your reward.

Bill's eyes and face again brightened and he said;

"Yes, Cap'n, you and Mrs. Waters have done everything for me, made a man of me, you have been father and mother to me, and the only ones that I have had. When I first shipped with you I was a poor drunken sailor, without a friend or dollar in the world, and now I am a sober man, with a good account in the Seaman's Saving Bank, and all by your kindness and good treatment."

Bill's feelings were getting the best of him, and he had to put a stopper on, and there appeared to be a little difficulty in the throats of them all, so the Captain by way of relief said :

"Bo'son, you have always been at sea and know nothing about the land, and I have thought you might be unwilling to give up your occupation, and if you did you might not be contented in the country ; the work and duty on a farm is so different from what it is on shipboard, that you would have everything to learn."

"Suppose, sir, the work is all different, is that a good reason for you leaving the Bo'son ashore when you have a new ship, and are going to sail in a new latitude ? Can't I learn what I don't know ?   What are you going to do if you are struck with a squall and carry away a spar, and no carpenter on board to make another,—or part a topsail-sheet or tie, and no Bo'son ready with a coupling ?"

"Bo'son, we never have or need such things on a farm."

While the Captain was replying to the Bo'son, his attention was attracted in an opposite direction, and he heard a whisper; turning again, Bill said :

"Well, sir, suppose you part a log-chain, or want the tongue of an ox-cart fished, how then ?"

"Mutiny ! mutiny !" cried the Captain. "Mrs. Waters, you have been whispering in Bill's ear, or he would never have steered that course."

"Well, Capt'n, what if I did,—it was all for the good of the family, and couldn't I help the Bo'son along in his trouble without the charge of mutiny being brought against me ?"

The Bo'son was much excited, and showed more anxiety than he had before exhibited on any occasion, and he went on to say :

" I don't see, sir, why you want to cut me adrift and abandon me to the underwriters ? I am still fit for duty, and can earn my feed. I want no wages ; all I want is room under deck to sling my hammock, and an even chance at the mess-kid, and you might be willing to let me work my passage in a new ship, and not leave me here alone to be murdered and eaten up by the land sharks."

Captain Waters believed himself proof against being overcome by his feelings, but Bill's friendship and earnestness was more than he could well master. He left his seat, and taking the Bo'son by the hand, said :

" Bill, you old sea-dog ! when I desert you or leave you ashore with your colors at half-mast, may the chronometer run down, the compass lose its attraction, the ship leak, the pumps become choked, and the rudder unhung ; and then may I be coming on the American coast in the winter season, with thick weather and heavy head-winds. Now Bill, if you think you can live ashore, and would like to try your hand at farming, only say the word and you are shipped for a long voyage, but you must promise me never to swear while you are on the farm."

" I'll do it, sir, and take my oath never to swear without your orders, if you will take me with you, and let me carry the old dog along," was Bill's reply.

" You can take the dog, Bo'son, for we should all miss him, and he would miss us. He never had any home but the ship, nor any friends but such as he has made on board.   You will both be natural curiosities in the country,—a pair of well matched sea-dogs. You will understand that your wages will be the same on the farm that they have been on the ship. No man can serve me at sea or on shore without wages."

" What, " exclaimed Bill, " do I want of wages ? You know, sir, that I have money in the bank, and no use for it."

" You can't tell, Bo'son, what may happen. Who knows but, after learning the business of farming, you may buy a farm, get married and become a farmer yourself. Never fire the last shot you have in the locker, if you can help it."

"Hurrah!" cried Bill; "haul aft the head sheets and let her luff a little. Bill Thomas, the old Bo'son, is going to be a farmer and have a wife. Keep a sharp look-out ahead."

As all was now arranged with the Bo'son, the Captain informed the steward and Lizzie that he and Mrs. Waters were anxious that they should continue in the family and go with them to the country. They cheerfully consented, and the arrangements were completed.

The evening party separated, each feeling cheerful and happy, and all fully uniting with Mrs. Waters in the hope she expressed, "That all would have good weather and fair winds."

CHAPTER III.

THE BO'SON, STEWARD AND LIZZIE.

AFTER leaving the cabin, the Bo'son, steward and Lizzie went on deck together, as it was a lovely moonlight evening.

Bill was never before known to be so excited, or to act so much like a boy. He scaled his best tarpaulin hat forward and blew his Bo'son's call for all hands, which was answered by the old dog Bose. Bill told the dog that all hands were shipped for a long voyage, and no going aloft. He seized the old steward and danced him "fore and aft" the deck, until the poor fellow was completely out of breath; and then put his arms around Lizzie's neck and actually kissed her, a liberty he had never before taken, though they had been sailing together over twenty years.

Lizzie said: "Get away, Bill! How dare you? What do you mean, you sea-monster?"

Bill did get away, and subsided into himself again with the remark:

"I don't mean any wrong—only all hands and the dog are going in the new ship, with the old captain and his mate. Hurrah! hurrah! for the new ship and the old crew. Who says the Bo'son isn't a happy boy now?

When I was in the cabin, and thought that we were all to be discharged, and may be never see each other again, after making so many voyages together, my heart was stowed away in the lower hold, with the whole cargo stowed above it, and I didn't think it would ever be hoisted out again; so I concluded that we should all founder with no insurance on us. Now my heart is on deck again, and can be reckoned, or stowed away, as light freight."

"Can it," asked the steward, "be counted as small stowage?"

"No, steward, my heart is as large as a four-barrel cask to-night, and I think would hold as many good things, if I only had them to put in it," was Bill's ready reply.

"Is it large enough," inquired Lizzie, "to hold the love of a good-sized corn-fed country wife—such a one as the captain spoke of this evening?"

"Lizzie, you just please put your lips in the becket, and let me tell you, if Bill Thomas ever marries, it will be the most unlikely thing that has happened in many years, and the woman that he marries will know a good deal about salt water. You can hoist that on board and stow it away, and be sure that it is well stowed, or it may be damaged by heavy weather."

The three remained some time on deck, and then Bill invited them to his room in the midship-house. The room was large and well arranged with many comforts and conveniences ; a place for everything, and everything in its place. After sitting together in silence for a short time, the steward said :

"Bo'son, you will miss this room, that you have fitted up with so much care, and where you have spent so many years, and with which you have so many associations."

"Yes, steward, that is so, but I shall have a larger one in the new ship, that I can fit up like this, and possibly make some improvements on."

The steward sat a few minutes in thoughtful silence, and then said :

"I don't know how it will be, but something speaks to

my heart and says 'it is all right,' and I am satisfied that it will be so. I could not talk when we were in the cabin, and you were very nearly ashore a number of times, Bill, while you were talking with the captain ; and the lady gave you one good tow into deep water."

"Yes, Steward, that is so ; I was hard aground a number of times, because I had never sounded out the channel, and didn't know where the deepest water was ; but Mrs. Captain gave me one course by which I steered clear of some sunken rocks ; and then, somehow, I can't say exactly how, my mind was'nt clear, and my heart got shifted like a badly stowed cargo in a heavy gale of wind."

"Bill, I have been steward with Captain Waters over twenty years, and you have been seaman and Bo'son much longer ; and Lizzie came on board only one year after I did, and together we have been sailing many times around the world, and across every ocean, visiting all the principal commercial ports, until we began to think that we should never be separated. Without any warning we were called into the cabin and told that there were no more voyages to be made,—the ship was to be sold, and the question came up with us all, 'What is to become of us ?' I could never go to sea with any other man than Captain Waters, because he is the only one that knows my history and would treat me accordingly. I hope I am a Christian, and if I am, Captain Waters and his lady have been instruments in making me such, and I owe them much. I have in my room many valuable books, some in English, some in French and some in Spanish, and I have read them all. With a perfect knowledge of these languages, I have served him twenty-two years as steward, and all that time I have been a man, and the captain has recognized and treated me as a man, and for that he will ever have my esteem."

Bill replied to the steward: "I know that you have been kindly treated by the Captain and his wife, and so have we all, or we should not have sailed so long together, but I know nothing of your early history. I only know that you have been a good steward, that you have always had the meals ready at the hour, the cabin in order, and that you have been a man of few words and many deeds ; and that Captain Waters believes you one of the best cooks that ever made a sea-hash."

Bo'son, there is nothing in my early history that I need be ashamed of, but much that saddened a youthful heart. Some of the reasons why I have preferred remaining steward with our captain, must, for a time, remain as secrets. It is enough that I am strongly attached to him and his lady, that they know my history, have been very considerate with me, have taught me to look on the brightest side of life, and never to doubt the power and goodness of God."

Lizzie asked if either of them could tell her "what there was about Captain and Mrs. Waters that forms so strong a tie to bind us all to them ?"

Bill answered, " In the first place they understand themselves, and something of human nature. They don't think because they have made and saved some money, that the whole world belongs to them, with all that is in it. They have minds to understand, and hearts to feel, and they believe others have : They have a kind and pleasant word for everyone, and never an unkind word for anyone. They never boast of what they have, or what they have done, but keep doing something every day, to help somebody, and make everybody love them,—that is the secret, Lizzie."

" I believe," said Lizzie, " you are right Bill, and since it is arranged that we are all going on the farm, there is but little chance of our being separated in this world, except by death. We shall have much time in the country to talk of the past, and as it is getting late, we had better say to each other good-night."

CHAPTER IV.

BILL THOMAS, THE BO'SON.

BILL Thomas was born somewhere in England, but where, he couldn't say, nor did he know exactly when. All that he could tell was, that when a very small boy, and as early as he could remember, he was living at a Sea-port, and in a building called the Work-House. He had no knowledge of a father, mother, nor of any relatives. He thinks he must have been about ten years old when he was put on board of a small brig called the "Sunderland," that had discharged a cargo of coal at the port where he had been living, and that he never afterwards visited, nor could he remember the name of the place, if he ever knew it.

He went to New Castle and loaded with coal for London, and continued nearly three years in the coal trade. He was called Bill, and that was the only name he had until the captain took charge of another vessel, where there was an older boy named Bill, and after that they called him Tom.

While he was on board of each of those two vessels—and during all that time he was treated with great cruelty by the master, his mates and men,—he was told that he was an apprentice to the captain, and if he attempted to desert he would be put in prison.

When he was about sixteen years old he went in the vessel to the Island of Fayal. On that voyage a new man was shipped, whose name was Joe Western. Joe was the first friend that Bill had ever known, and their friendship then formed was renewed and enjoyed at a later period.

Joe could protect Bill from ill-usage by the men, but not from the cruelty of the master, and he advised and assisted Bill to run away. He arranged with a native to take Bill up on the mountain and keep him there until the brig sailed, and then made the captain believe the boy had fallen overboard and been drowned.

After the brig had sailed, Bill came down and shipped on board of a New Bedford whaler. When asked his name, he said "Tom," and when his other name was called for he answered, "Bill, sir." The captain asked him which was his first name, and he said "Bill." "Is your name," said his new captain, "Bill Thomas?" "Yes, sir," answered Bill quickly, pleased to find that he actually had two names to go on the Shipping Articles, and that was where and when he was christened Bill Thomas, a name he has ever since borne.

Bill made a number of whaling voyages from New Bedford, rising to the position of "harponeersman," and acquitting himself to the satisfaction of his superior officers. The history and particulars of those voyages will be related by himself, and in his own language, at a proper time.

He served three years on board of a man-of-war, and was also on board of a number of merchant ships before he sailed with Captain Waters; always sailing under the American flag, after running away from his first captain. He had been about all over the world, and in most of the ports known to commerce.

When the captain shipped him at Honolulu, Sandwich Islands, he must have been about twenty-three years old, and at the time of selling the ship he was fifty years of age, though he did not look to be over forty. Bill had at the time of shipping been long sick in the hospital, and was not really fit for duty, but the captain was short-handed, men were scarce, and he concluded to take him.

The captain had not been long at sea before he discovered that Bill had peculiar traits, and was a superior man. For personal cleanliness, industry and order about everything, the captain had never seen his equal among sailors. He was then a good sailor for one of his experience, but not the full and perfect seaman that he was twenty-seven years later.

His great ambition was to learn anything and everything that was worth knowing, or that would make him more useful on board of a ship. He was, when first sailing with Captain Waters, always pleased to assist the carpenter or blacksmith of the ship, because, as he said, "he could learn something every time."

One of the strongest traits in his character was that of good nature. Few circumstances, however annoying, could divest him of it, and he would often be highly amused with things that very much disturbed others. Nothing but a positive and unprovoked insult would call forth and show to others that he possessed the finest feelings of right and wrong, and when he was once aroused in the justice of his own or the cause of others, punishment was sure to be inflicted on the offenders.

His love of innocent fun was inate, and with him irresistable. He would go without his dinner, and do without sleep to enjoy it. He has often been heard to say that "I can live and grow fat on good fun, provided it harms no one."

He was never known to have a difficulty of his own with any of the officers, or with any of his shipmates; but he often interfered in the quarrels of others, to take the part of the weak, or to protect the right. No sailor could harm a boy where Bill Thomas was, and his great delight was to show a young sailor how to do a piece of work, and help him in his duty, until he could do it himself.

He would "steer the trick," or stand the look-out of any shipmate that did not feel well, and help any one that was in trouble. He was generally the first man on deck when his watch was called; the first aloft when there was duty to do, and Bill's "Aye! aye! sir," was always heard when an order was given. He could not fail of being a favorite with his officers, for he must indeed be a very bad officer who would misuse an extra good seaman.

Bill, when first sailing with Captain Waters, would have and drink his grog, and often drink too much, but even then, when he was "three sheets in the wind," and a little too drunk for duty, he was respectful to his superiors and kind to his equals. He was so good-natured when under the influence of drink, and his love of fun was so fully displayed, that no officer could possibly feel out of humor with him. It was when under the influence of strong drink on shore, that he would foolishly part with his hard-earned money, and even his clothing, without receiving any fair consideration for them. He was never cured of his love for drink until after the captain became convinced that it was useless to have liquor at sea, and shipped his crews with the understanding that no grog would be served or allowed on board. Bill found that he could do without grog at sea, and concluded that he could on shore. He soon discovered that the captain and all hands were better off without their grog, and at the end of the first voyage on which it was not used, he joined the New York Marine Temperance Society, and ever since has been a sober man.

Bill was also a great swearer when he first sailed with Captain Waters, and never quite got over it ; and he had some new-coined expressions of his own that he used on occasions, and that were very forcible in themselves, and when fully understood, were very appropriate. He never appeared to swear at anybody, but, as he expressed it, he "would let out at times, and couldn't help it. What is the difference between swearing and meaning no harm, or praying and meaning no good ? I think I must have taken to swearing naturally, because it comes so easy to me and at times appears to be a part of my duty."

Among Bill's many other qualifications, that of telling good stories should not be forgotten, and will not be, if his friends have patience to listen to him. He could neither read nor write when he first joined the ship, nor for many years afterwards. When the steward went on board, Bill found him to be well educated, and spent much time in hearing the steward read, and from him learned himself to read and write.

Bill was five feet five inches high, and stout built in body, with limbs well proportioned, and calculated by nature for hard labor and great endurance. He stood erect, and when he moved he did so with ease and in a style peculiar to many sailors, and especially so to him. His head was round, and well covered with dark, curly hair ; his neck short and stout ; his eyes small, dark and very bright. He wore side-whiskers, following the line of the jaw and rounding up towards the corners of the mouth.

He always had a pleasant, cheerful face, that was a fair index of an honest and noble heart within. He was ever clean in his dress, but discarded with disgust all articles of dress used generally by landsmen. He never owned a coat and said he "never would wear one ;" he never had a fur or silk hat, because they were more for show than use, and looked worse than a tarpaulin hat, after they had been once well wet. "Give me," said Bill, "a hat that will stand water and be as good as new."

Bill Thomas, the Bo'son, in dress and action united in himself all the elements and character of a well salted son of the ocean. The sailor could be seen in his walk, for he always kept his feet well apart and toes a little out, a habit acquired at sea in catching the roll and motion of the ship.

CHAPTER V.

BILL THE BO'SON.

AFTER Bill had made a few voyages with Captain Waters, and the captain had found out his good qualities and corrected some of his bad habits, he wanted to make a second mate of him, but Bill said "No, sir; for then I shall be called mister, and when on shore have to wear a ring-tailed jacket (coat), and that will never do for Bill." He finally consented to be Bo'son, and soon became not only pleased with the position, but so useful and so efficient, that on a voyage he would have been as much missed as one of the higher officers.

After sailing with the captain for a number of voyages as Bo'son, the captain learned to trust much to him and the steward, and to depend on them to see that everything needed for a voyage was on board before sailing from a port. Each succeeding voyage increased his confidence in the Bo'son, and he depended more on him. After Bill had become a good carpenter and blacksmith, he was still more useful, and always kept himself busy about something.

He had the rare faculty of getting much work out of the men, when extra duty was to be done; and at the same time, of keeping them all good natured, by infusing into them a portion of his own happy disposition.   If there was a bad man among the crew, Bill would make a good one of him if possible; if not, keep him at such duty by himself as would prevent him from exercising any material influence over the rest of the crew.

There were always, when at sea, two mates on board of the ship, each occupying a superior position to that of the Bo'son, and yet Bill so faithfully performed all his duties, without assuming anything to himself that did not belong to his office, or ever presuming to interfere with the duties of his superior officers, that not a single complaint ever came to the captain; but, on the contrary, each and all of the officers would say, at the end of a voyage, that their duties had been lessened and made more pleasant by the efficiency of the Bo'son.

It sometimes happened that the second mate would be a very young man, nothing but a boy in years to Bill, and often taken from among the crew that had sailed under the Bo'son; but that made no difference,—Bill would be as respectful, and as ready to obey his orders, as though they had never changed positions.   Many a young officer has had great cause to be glad that such a Bo'son was on board, to quietly instruct and assist him in his duties. Some of Bill's mottoes were : " Show a young officer his duty, teach him what he don't know, and do both privately. How can a man know what he has never learned? Every officer and man to his own duty.   Obey orders if you break the owners."

Bill was a natural mechanic, and could make anything that he had ever seen made, and a great many things that he never had seen made.   He could do most anything that he had ever seen done, but sometimes he thought he could do things that he found it very difficult to accomplish, and in a few instances he had attempted impossibilities.   It was one of his common expressions : " Show me something that looks, or is like what you want, and I think I can make it,—at any rate I will try."

In speaking on the subject once, he said : "I have attempted things that I couldn't do. I once attempted to 'shin up' (climb) a well 'slushed' (greased) flag-staff for five dollars. It was on a fourth of July, in Boston, late in the afternoon, and I had been drinking pretty freely, and I couldn't do it. I didn't know that it had been well slushed when I offered to 'shin up,' and reeve the signal halliards, but I soon found it out, when I tried and heard the people laugh, and then I felt spunky and tried all the more, and the more I tried the more the people laughed, and the more I couldn't do it. I came very near doing it, and believe I would have done it, if the staff had been a little larger, and I hadn't been drinking so much bad rum. After getting my hands and trousers well slushed from the staff, I rubbed sand over them and would work up a piece, hang on as long as I could, and then come down and get more sand, and try again ; each time going a little higher, and each time that I came down all the people would laugh, and I would help them. After many efforts, and the use of much sand, I got up where the staff was very small, and there was no chance for sanded trousers or sandy hands, and I owned up I couldn't do it, but I got the five dollars for my spunk, and the fun they had.

"At another time I attempted to scull a boat, with a line from a vessel to the wharf, at Nantucket, with a crooked oar, and I couldn't do it ; but no man ever has, or can scull a boat with a crooked oar.

"I never have tried to make a Bo'son's whistle out of a pig's tail—I don't think I could do that."

When Captain Waters contracted for the building of the " Neptune," by " day's work," he told the builder that his Bo'son was a carpenter, and arranged for him to be employed on the ship. Bill commenced when the blocks were laid for the keel, and continued to work until the ship was launched.

When the midship-house was to be arranged for the crew, the cook's galley, store-room, sail-room and Bo'son's room, the captain left the arrangement with Bill—first, because he was a good mechanic, and knew what room was necessary for each department, and second, that he might have just such a room for himself as he wished.

———

CHAPTER VI.

THE BO'SON'S DOG.

BILL'S dog, "old Bose," was as much of a character as Bill was himself, and as great a favorite "fore and aft" the ship. He was a noble fellow, black, with curly hair, and long ears. Bill obtained him from a whaling ship in the Pacific Ocean when he was a small pup. He never knew of what particular breed the dog was, or how mixed his pedigree might have been. Judging from his appearance and actions, he must have descended from the most ancient families of noble dogs, that had never disgraced themselves by mingling their blood with any inferior race. He may have had some relatives, however remote, either living at, or that emigrated from, Newfoundland, and also some from the interior and mountainous countries of Europe. It is barely possible that he had some slight relationship with the noble dogs of the ocean, as he took very naturally to the water, and was as much at home in it, as on the land.

Before he became the property of Bill, some cruel and greasy whaleman had divested the dog of a small portion of his tail. It did not injure the appearance of Bose, as he had parted with only a very small piece of his tail, and that was compensated for by a bunch of curly hair.

When first obtained he had never been on shore, and Bill liked him all the better for that, because he was a true son of the ocean. Bill had taught him many things, and it was difficult to determine which felt the greatest pleasure, Bill in teaching or the dog in learning. He possessed far more than the common intelligence of dogs, or he could not have learned and fully understood, all that he knew.

Bose, before he was a year old, would set on the top-gallant-forecastle and keep as good a look-out as any of the men, and he could be depended on to give notice of a sail, or the appearance of anything unusual. He would first scent, and then see land from the deck, before any of the crew could. If whales or porpoises were near the ship in the night, Bose was sure to know it, and give the alarm.

Whenever it was calm, Bose had his sport in the water, and if allowed, would spend hours overboard. Whatever was thrown from the deck he would bring to the side of the ship, and assist in getting a rope fast to it, that it might be hauled on board again. When he was wanted, or it was thought that he had been long enough in the water, Bill would call him to the side of the ship, lower a rope with a " bowlin " taken in the end of it, and the dog would work his forefeet through the bowlin, then take hold with his mouth, above the knot, and be hauled on board.

He was partly taught, and in part seemed to possess the knowledge by nature, how to assist a man in the water and prevent him from drowning. In some instances he would take hold of the man's clothing, as near the throat as he could, and keep his head above the water, and at other times he would allow a man to put his arm over his back, and so swim to the ship with him.

Sometimes, for amusement, in a calm, one of the men would fall overboard on purpose, and the cry would be raised, " A man overboard! A man overboard! " The dog very soon understood it, and would be overboard after the man. Once, in the night, a man did fall overboard. The cry was raised, and the dog went after him. The man fell from aloft, was injured, and would have drowned before the boat reached him, but for the dog. He would go aloft as high as the " futtock shrouds," and down again to the deck with as much ease and confidence as one of the men. The Bo'son used to say, " If I could only teach him to get over the rim of the top, he would be handy to assist in reefing topsails." Nothing delighted the dog more than to " give a pull " on any rope with the sailors. Bill would say to him, " Bose, give me a pull here on the royal-halliards, and let us sway it up taut by the leeches." The dog would take hold of the rope with his mouth, and hang his whole weight on it, until he heard the word "belay," which he understood as well as did any of the men.

Whenever the dog saw any of the men pulling on a rope, he was sure to get hold somewhere and have a pull himself. At the fall of a "jig-tackle," a rope used at the "windlass" or "capstan," as an extra hand to "hold on behind," the dog was equal to a good man, and better than two lubbers. He always took hold with a will, giving all his weight and strength to the work, and never eased up, or let go, until he heard the order. There was but little duty or work done on the ship that Bose didn't have a part in.

He would go into the midship-house where the men slept, when "eight bells" were called, and bark until every man was out of his berth, knowing as well as the men did that the watches always changed at every "eight bells," and that those that had been sleeping must take the deck.

The dog was never on shore except at some of the uninhabited islands, so that he had seldom seen one of his own species, having always lived on shipboard, and really belonged as much to the ocean, as his master did. He had a little training at the island of Socora in catching wild hogs, and at the Falkland Islands, in catching young cattle for ship's use; and performed so well that the Bo'son said: "It is a great pity that the education of such a dog should have been so neglected; as who can tell what he might have been with a finished education?"

Bose, like his master, sometimes attempted impossibilities. Once, in a light wind, he was sent overboard after a small sea-turtle, which he seized by the fore-flipper and held until a boat was lowered, and secured the turtle. At another time he went for one that was larger, which he fastened to in the same way, but the turtle headed down, and being the heaviest of the two, took Bose under water with him. The dog soon relinquished his hold and came to the surface, and after shaking his head and snorting a few times, he looked about him for the turtle without seeing it, and then headed for the ship. "Ha! ha! old dog," said Bill, "you couldn't fetch him. Never mind, old fellow, it is just as well for you to know that there are some things that you can't do, as it was for your master. Don't be discouraged, because there are a great many things that you can do, and you are a very good dog. You couldn't hold a turtle on top of the water, that was three times your own weight, any easier than your master could shin up a well slushed flag-staff, or scull a boat with a crooked oar."

Bill was in the habit of talking to the dog as he would to a human being, and in most cases the dog appeared to understand him, and would look humble or pleased, as the case might be. His character and habits were known "fore and aft" the ship, and all hands were his friends. Sometimes Bill would send him to the steward for some article that was in the cabin, and the dog would give no peace until the article was named, when he would give one bark, receive the article, and take it to his master. There were only a few articles in the cabin that the Bo'son had occasion to use and that the dog could carry, so it didn't take the steward long to run over the catalogue, and as he fully understood the dog, he generally gave him what was wanted.

CHAPTER VII.

CAPTAIN WATERS SELLS THE SHIP AND BUYS A FARM.

CAPTAIN WATERS offered the "Neptune" for sale, and directed the steward, with the assistance of the Bo'son, to make an inventory of articles on board to be sold with the ship. The Bo'son knew what there was on board, and where everything was that belonged to his own department—also about the ship and cabin stores. Whatever would be useful on the farm they were directed to reserve, pack and have ready for shipping. Captain

Waters had been so long accustomed to the steward and
Bo'son for carrying out in detail his directions, that his
orders in this instance, as usual, were only given in general terms. He could always depend on their judgment
and discretion for doing properly whatever he directed to
be done.

It may be that the captain had become a little indolent
or indifferent about small matters connected with his
ship, from the fact that others had long looked after them
for him. Be that as it may, it would only be natural for
an old salt that liked his ease and comfort, and that was
in possession of wealth enough to gratify every wish, and
knew that he could always have his own way when he
wanted it, to let others have their way, when in doing so
his interest would be well looked after and his cares lessened. Certainly no man ever had two assistants that
were more faithful in the discharge of their duties, or
more earnest to comply with the wishes of one they had
long served, more from esteem than for the wages they
received.

Captain Waters gave his directions to the Bo'son and
steward, and then left the ship with Mrs. Waters to visit
the country and purchase a farm. He found and purchased one near the Hudson River, a short distance above
Bemisc Heights, which was a portion of the old Saratoga battle ground.

On the farm that the captain purchased there was a
substantially built house, recently modernized by a citizen
of Troy, who had owned the farm for the two previous
years, and spent more money about the buildings than he
had realized from the land, and found out that to be a
gentleman farmer, required an income independent of the
farm.

There were all the necessary out-buildings on the farm,
and some that were not actually necessary, and that might
be considered as fancy buildings; there was also a good
farm or tenant house. The buildings were all in general
good order, but a change of owners usually causes some
changes in the management of things, and most likely did
on and about the farm of Captain Waters.

Mrs. Waters was highly delighted with everything, as the one great desire of her heart had been a farm, and just such a one as her father and grandfather had when she was a young woman, and where she lived until she was married. She thought that the house, with a good cleaning and painting on the inside, and some alterations in the kitchen, that Bill could make, would be just what she wanted.

The captain hired a farmer and his wife to take charge of the farm and occupy the farm house, and also a young man to assist them on the farm, and left all in their charge, and returned to New York, to complete his arrangements there.

The ship was sold, and the articles on the inventory were sold with the ship, and sold at the full price asked.

The captain chartered a canal-boat to go alongside of the ship and receive what was to be taken out, and also to receive such other freight as he might wish to put on board, and land it all at Wilbur's Basin, near the farm.

Bill had carefully packed, boxed and marked all that was on the ship, and, as he and the steward had been three weeks in preparing, all was in perfect order and readiness for shipping and moving. Neither the captain nor his lady knew what articles had been sold with the ship, or what had been packed to go on the farm; all that had been left to the Bo'son and steward.

Captain Waters and his lady having for some years contemplated such a change as they were about making, had in different parts of the world purchased such articles as would be both useful and ornamental in housekeeping, some of which had been stored until wanted, and others were on the ship at the time of purchasing the farm; so that they had a fair outfit to begin with. Whatever more was required to furnish the house was purchased—also carriages and provisions for the family, all of which were shipped on the boat.

The Captain had arranged that the Bo'son, steward and Lizzie should go on the boat, with the things, and be landed near the farm; and that he, with Mrs. Waters,

would follow them in a few days by steamboat, railroad
and private carriage to their new home.

All the arrangements having been completed, they had
nothing to do the next morning but to deliver the ship to
the new owner, and leave for the farm.

On the evening of the last night that they were to spend
on board, the Captain again called them into the cabin,
where they had all so often assembled before, and where
they were never to meet again.   Not a word was said of
the past, and nothing of the future except what related to
business.   The Captain only wished to learn if all not sold
with the ship had been taken out, and if everything was
shipped on the boat.   Being satisfied that all was right,
he gave some instructions in regard to what he wished
them to do when they reached the farm, and then said
" good night."

In the morning the Bo'son went through the ship with
the new owner and new master, and pointed out to them
every article on the inventory, and heard them say that
all was correct and satisfactory.   While the Bo'son was
performing this, his last duty on the ship, the steward and
Lizzie had removed a few light articles from the ship to
the boat lying in the same slip, near the head of the pier,
and had left the ship for the last time.

The old Bo'son, considering that all his duties were
ended on board of the " Neptune," went by himself
through every part of the ship below, and to each mast-
head, up one side of the rigging and down the other,
then out on the fly-jib-boom ; returning, he stood a few
minutes on the topgallant-forecastle, looked first aloft, and
then fore and aft the ship, after which he went down on
the main deck, walked to the gangway, where both captains
and Mrs. Waters were standing, took off his hat, bowed
to each of them, whistled to his dog, and left the ship
without speaking a single word.

When the Bo'son was gone the new captain said : " I
wish we had bought your Bo'son with the ship, for I have
met with no such man before."

Captain Waters replied : " You couldn't have him, sir ;
because he has sailed with me for twenty-seven years, and

will never go to sea with any other man.　He goes
to the country with me from choice, and I think from
what he considers his duty, to take care of me, though he
don't say so, but we know each other well.　He believes
and says 'That without him I can't navigate the farm,
and that I'll get ashore.'　Very likely he is more than half
right.　Now, sir, the ship 'Neptune' is yours, and may
you always have good freights and fair winds."　The two
captains shook hands, and the new one waited on Mrs.
Waters over the side of the ship, and thus they parted.

CHAPTER VIII.

THE BO'SON AND DOG LEAVE THE SHIP AND SAVE A CHILD.

WHEN the canal boat left the slip in tow of a steamer,
Bill was standing aft on the boat, with the dog sitting at his side.　He laid his right hand on the head of
the dog, took off his hat with his left hand, and in silence
bowed to the ship.　He continued in that position, with
his eyes fixed on the ship, while large tears were following
each other down his weather-beaten cheeks, until the
boat, in sheering in on the New York side, was about to
hide the ship from his view, when, for the first time, he
spoke, and said :

"Good-by, old 'Neptune;' we part, never to meet
again."

The old Bo'son was no longer himself, and the faithful
dog appeared to understand it ; for when Bill sat himself
down on the cabin of the boat, after the ship was out of
sight, and made no effort to hide his flowing tears, the dog
laid his head on the knee of his master, and looked earnestly, and with affection in his face, as though he fully
sympathized with him in all his sufferings.

Bill understood the dog, and fully appreciating his sympathy, patted him on the head, and said to the steward :

"That is the last of the 'Neptune.'　That ship grew up
under my eyes.　I helped lay the blocks for the keel, and

then helped lay her keel; saw every stick of timber of which she was built, every plank when it was put on, every bolt when it was driven, and every butt when it was bolted. There is no bad timber nor want of proper fastening about that ship. When the ship was finished and launched, all the rigging was fitted and put in its place, under my care. How could I help loving her? I have sailed seven years in that ship, and she has never damaged a bale of goods, never carried away a spar, and never been a dollar of expense to the underwriters. She was my sweetheart, and has been to me a wife and child. I have loved her better than I have ever loved anything else, and now I have forever lost her, and am a—what do you call a man, steward, when his wife is dead?"

"A widower," said the steward.

"Yes, yes," continued Bill. "I am a widower, and shall never again be married to such a ship, for they can't build another like her; the model is lost, and all of that kind of timber and fastening was used up when the 'Neptune' was built. I have looked after that ship as a mother would after her child. Her rigging has never chafed aloft, nor her lanyards in the 'dead-eyes,' and when her sides have been bruised by the fenders, I have rubbed them with a jack and applied a plaster of paint. That ship was born to me, and I was the first to dress her, fitted her first stays, put them on and laced them myself. She never wore a dress that I did't cut and fit, and now I have buried her without any service being read."

Bill sat some time in silence, and then continued:

"It was hard to decide between the ship and the family, but what would any ship be to me without the family? I gave up the ship to remain with the family, and be Bo'son of a farm. I have a good many of them—what do you call things people keep to put them in mind of what they can't think of?"

"Mementoes," suggested the steward.

"That is exactly it, mementoes, and I have some that will astonish the captain and all hands when they are unpacked, and that will keep us all from forgetting the 'Neptune.'"

Bill was startled from his reflections and remarks by the loud scream of a woman, and the single bark of the dog, that had left his side and was in the water in an instant. Bill comprehended at once that somebody was overboard, and he followed the dog, leaving his hat and shoes on the deck of the boat. It was a little girl, six years old, daughter of the captain and owner of the boat, who had accidentally fallen overboard. The dog saw the child fall, followed her overboard and under water, and when he came to the surface he had the child with him, holding her firmly in his mouth by the dress, near her throat, and in such a manner as to keep the child's head above the water. Bill was quickly at his side; taking the child from the dog, and facing the boat he raised it in his hands high above the water, and shouted: "All right! Little one not hurt! Come with the small boat; Bose and I will take good care of the child until you get here. Don't be frightened!"

All on board of the boat shouted in turn or together, "Is the child dead? Is the child alive? Is the child drowned?"

Lizzie told the almost frantic mother, who was a picture of despair, "that no child could ever drown where the Bo'son and dog were," and that "her little darling would be safely brought back to her."

The engine of the steamer that had the boat in tow was immediately stopped, the father of the child and the steward took a small skiff belonging to the steamer, and went to the rescue of those in the water.

After Bill had raised the child up and shown it to the anxious friends on the boat, he took it in one arm, and putting his other arm over the back of the dog, headed up stream against a strong ebb tide, and was as unconcerned about his own safety, or that of the child, as he would have been on the deck of a ship, or under a cherry tree on a farm.

The little child had been under water so short a time before old Bose brought it to the surface, that it was more frightened than injured, and soon recovered so as to reply to Bill, who assured her that " papa is coming for us all in a small boat, and will soon be here."   "Yes, yes," said the little one, " I can see him coming now."

When the father and steward reached them, and the father saw his little daughter safe and sensible in the arms of the Bo'son, and the dog rendering such efficient aid, his heart was overjoyed, and he said to Bill :

" You and your dog have done a noble deed, but I am afraid we shall upset the boat in getting you in."

" No fear of that, sir; you just take the baby first—she is all right, as you see by her little talk—and then you sit very still in the dory, and leave the rest for me to manage, and you will see what an old salt can do."

The father took the child, and was glad enough to have it again, and then Bill told the dog to go around on the other side of the boat, which he did, and putting his fore feet over the side of the boat, under the direction of his master, hung his whole weight on one side of the boat as a balance, while Bill got in over the other side, without any danger of upsetting the skiff.   Bill then told the dog to let go and follow the boat; he obeyed, and they were soon all safe on the deck of the large boat.

Bill and Bose changed characters, for they were no longer a Bo'son and a dog, but were pet lions.   Neither of them thought they had done any very great things, though others differed from them.   The father and mother of the little girl were loud in their praise of both Bill and his dog: The father wanted to buy the dog, and offered one hundred dollars for him.   Bill gave a little history of the dog, and informed the father that the dog could not be bought.   He then offered Bill the hundred dollars for saving his child, and that was respectfully declined with the remark : " Bose and I never take money for saving life; we always try to do our duty, and all we want is kind treatment from those we assist."

When the canal was reached, and the horses hitched on, Bill said :

" This is one way of navigating—no making nor taking in sail, no compass to steer by, and I can't see the use of a pilot.   It can't be much trouble to get her ashore or keep her afloat; no course to steer, and all the orders given are : ' Low bridge, lay her over to the heel-path, or lay her over to the tow-path,' and neither of them are hard to do."

On arriving at the junction of the Erie and Champlain Canals, at the first lock, the bowman of the boat was injured and disabled. Bill volunteered to take his place, an offer that was readily accepted, and he astonished all on board with his knowledge of locking, when he informed them that he had never before seen a canal. He acquired his knowledge in locking ships in and out of the tide-docks of England and Europe. After towing some distance on the sixteen-mile level, the driver, by sheer carelessness, and brutally whipping his horses, parted the towline about ten fathoms from the boat. Bose jumped into the canal, seized the end of the rope in his mouth, took it ashore, and dragged it up the towpath toward the horses. The driver dismounted, and when taking the line from the dog struck him a heavy blow with his whip. Bose fetched one gulp, and looked to the Bo'son for orders what to do in the case, for it was the first blow the dog had ever received.

Bill jumped ashore, stepping quickly toward the brute of a man that had struck his noble dog, and with one blow of his open hand laid him his length on the ground, and seizing the whip, applied it so forcibly on his person that his cries were heard for miles along the waters of the "raging canal," and he hopped about like a toad on a hot gridiron.

The captain of the boat was soon with them, and, taking the whip from Bill, was about to repeat the flogging, when the Bo'son said :

"No, no, sir ; when Bill Thomas, the Bo'son of Captain Waters, whips a man, which he don't often do, the man can't stand, and don't want any more whipping that day. I would have served the rascal right if I had let the dog have a chance at him, for the dog is only waiting orders from me to shake him limb from limb, and I have a mind to let him do it."

"Boo ! hoo ! hoo ! boo !" blubbered the driver. "Please don't let your dog bite me, and I'll never do so again. I didn't know it was your dog when I struck him."

"Well, you know it now, and had better look sharp, for the dog never forgets an injury, nor deserts a friend ; do you, Bose ? Are you satisfied, old dog, with the flogging I gave this fellow ?"

The dog appeared to fully comprehend his master, and, putting his paws on Bill's shoulders, licked his face, and then laid his head against the cheek of his master.

"All right, old dog," said Bill ; "you keep your eye on that chap, and if he ever strikes you again, shake him."

The captain of the boat and father of the child told Dick, the driver, that the dog had saved the life of little Nellie the day before, by jumping into the river and diving after the child, and that he had offered one hundred dollars for the dog, and that was ninety-nine and a half dollars more than he would give for such a brute of a driver.

Bill and the dog were treated with distinguished consideration for the rest of the passage,—little Nellie and her mother feeding the dog with all that was good to eat on the boat, and the dog watching Nellie to prevent her from again falling overboard.

Bill said to the mother : "You needn't fear, marm, that the child will fall over again while Bose is on board, for you see he never leaves her alone, and would have her by the clothes, before she could fall over the side of the boat."

CHAPTER IX.

THE BO'SON UNDERTAKES TO MILK, AND SALT SHEEP.

THE boat landed all safely at the Basin, and while the freight was being put ashore, the driver kept out of sight, fearing the Bo'son or his dog might have another account to settle with him. He told another driver "that the old Bo'son was extra heavy in using a whip, and would make a good driver with dull teams."

The farmer met them at the Basin, and with him were many of the neighbors, with their wagons, to assist in taking the things to the farm. All were pleased with the Bo'son and his dog, for Bose always recognized as his own, all the friends of his master, and never failed to respect them.

When the things were all landed, and the " Rotary " was about to continue her way up the canal, Captain Williams, his wife and the little girl Nellie, stepped ashore, and called to Bill, as they wished to again thank him and his dog for saving the child. Captain Williams wished to learn where the farm was, as he should visit it on his next trip up. Bill received the additional thanks, and the dog the additional caresses, with their usual modesty, and Bill wished them a safe passage, and that the flogging he had given the driver might do him good, and make a better man of him.

The saving of the child by the Bo'son and his dog, becoming known, was greatly magnified each time it was told by one to another of the plain farmers, until it was reported that they had saved a whole crew of shipwrecked men, women and children, on a very stormy night, on some foreign coast, whose name none of them could remember.

All the neighbors that assisted in taking the things from the boat to the farm were astonished at the quantity, and the number of boxes, large and small, and wondered what they could all contain. Such articles of costly furniture, and much of it of foreign make, they had never seen before. Some of them said " the captain must have an amazing sight of money to buy so many things."

Bill made a friend of the farmer, and induced him to stow away in one of the barns, and cover with hay, a number of boxes that he didn't wish the captain to see until the time came to unpack them.

After all was landed at the farm, Bill examined every building and everything with great care, and then said to the steward :

" Whatever isn't right on board of this ship, can be made right in time ; but there is plenty to do, and for me a great deal to learn, and you see if I don't learn it before the voyage ends, because my heart is in it."

Bill took possession of a story-and-a-half building, twelve by twenty feet in size, standing on a line, and about forty feet from the mansion, which he called the "Midship-house," and in it he placed his personal effects, and slung his hammock. He told the steward that "the Bo'son's house could be fixed up when they had more time, and that all hands must work on the main cabin, and have it ready for the captain and his lady when they came on board."

Captain and Mrs. Waters arrived on a Saturday afternoon, five days after the others had reached the farm, and found things comfortably arranged for them at their new home, for all had worked faithfully.

The captain, after surveying things, said: "How do you like farming, Bo'son?"

"I haven't tried my hand at it yet, sir. I have been working all the time in the house; but I think I shall like it, when I learn and get used to it," was the Bo'son's reply.

The next morning, the farmer and his assistant being engaged at the back of the farm, in consequence of some cattle having broken into one of the fields, there was no one to milk, and the steward said: "Bo'son, if you will milk one of the cows, so I can have some milk, I will make you a sea-hash for your breakfast."

"I'll do it, "replied Bill; " show me a bucket that will hold the juice of one cow, and I will show you how a Bo'son can milk."

Bill had watched the men when they were milking, and thought it very easy to do. It being Sunday, Bill had shaved and dressed with white trousers and a light blue shirt, which, with his tarpaulin hat, shoes and stockings, constituted his whole dress. Bill unbuttoned his shirt-sleeves, and rolled them up above his elbows, showing the Goddess of Liberty supporting a staff, from which floated the American flag, with a cluster of stars above it on one arm, and on the other a whale with a boat fast to it, and a ship in the distance—all of which had been imprinted with India ink in a masterly way. Bill took his pail and stool, and with the expression "Now for it," seated himself at the side of the cow and seized her teats, as he would have done a half-frozen jib-sheet to get it aft in a heavy blow. In an instant, Bill, his milking-pail and stool were ten feet behind the cow, and Bill was singing out "A man overboard ! a man overboard ! haul aback the main-yard!"

Bill picked himself up, and walked to where the captain was standing, and said:

"Capt'n Waters, will you please allow me to swear a little, sir?"

"No, no, Bo'son, it can't be done on the farm, according to agreement."

"Very well, sir; then if you want that cow, or any other cow on board of this ship pumped out, you must set a hand at it that understands rigging and working cow-pumps better than the Bo'son does, or it can't be done."

"Never mind, Bo'son," said the Captain, "you go and put on some clean clothes, and be ready for breakfast; I told you the duty was different on a farm, and that you would have to learn some things."

"Aye, aye, sir; I will change my clothes, and you see if I don't learn something yet," was Bill's reply.

Notwithstanding Bill's "unsuccessful milking voyage," as he styled it, the steward made him a sea-hash, which he relished so well that he was fully restored to cheerfulness.

After breakfast the Captain said: "Bill, I wish you to get some salt, and go over in the next field and salt the sheep."

"But they are not butchered yet, sir," was Bill's reply.

"I know that, Bo'son; but I want you to give it to them to eat."

"Will sheep eat salt, sir?"

"Yes, Bo'son; all the stock in this fresh water country must have salt once a week, or they do not thrive. You will find some pieces of board inside the fence; strew the salt on the boards, and the sheep will lick it off. You needn't be afraid of them; they will not hurt you."

"Aye, aye, sir; I'll do it; I don't think I have been all my life at sea, to be afraid of sheep."

Bill went as directed, and while stooping over to place the salt on a board, an old buck made a running butt at him, taking him square in the stern, and landing him on his hands and knees, fully ten feet from where he had been standing. Before he could gather himself up, the old ram was at him again, Bill making a motion like the leap of a frog, and shooting ahead some six feet, landing again on his hands and knees, with his face turned so as to look over his shoulder, and a shout of "Avast there!" The old ram went for him again, extra heavy, and Bill made another leap of about eight feet, landing in the same way, and with a shout that sounded very much like improper language.   The old buck was at him again and again, never giving Bill time to get on his feet, and each time the Bo'son landed he used an expression.

Bill afterwards always said : " If I did use any improper words, they were knocked out of me end-ways by the ram."

The Captain saw the whole affair from the beginning, and as the readiest way of giving assistance, sent the dog to his aid.

Bose caught a glimpse of Bill in his second leap, and was off over fields and fences, and just as the ram backed for the seventh butt, the dog took him by the throat, rolled him over and held him as in a vice. Bill gathered himself up, and went over the fence quicker, as he said, " Than I ever went over the rim of the ' Neptune's ' top, to overhaul the halliards and ride the topsail-yard down for reefing, in a squall."

The dog, seeing Bill on the other side of the fence, gave the old buck one severe shake, and followed his master, thinking possibly there might be more trouble, and his assistance again needed.

Bill walked toward the house with a motion not exactly natural to him, and going up to the Captain, who had a peculiar smile on his face, said :

"Capt'n Waters, will you just please let me up a little on my promise about swearing, and let me ease my mind on that ram, or I shall explode ? "

" Bill, it can't be done, you must abide by the articles ; " was the Captain's reply.

"Very well, sir, you have the agreement, and if you don't let me up I must keep it ; but tell me, sir, if that is what you call a battering ram in this part of the world ?"

"I should think that he might be called one of that kind, Bill."

"Do you believe, Capt'n, that there is any hereafter for rams ?"

"What do you mean, Bo'son ?"

"I mean, sir, another world, where rams go after they have done butting in this world."

"No, Bo'son ; certainly not, there is no hereafter for rams."

"I am sorry for that, sir, because if there was, I would wish the whole family of rams in a place so hot that they would all be roasted brown, in less than ten minutes."

"Bo'son, you shouldn't be hard on them ; it is natural for them to butt, and they don't know any better."

"That is all very well, Capt'n, for you to think so, but if you had been in my place over in the field there, you might not be so great an admirer of nature in rams, and especially in their heads. I'll tell you, sir, if I had known how duty was carried on here, and how dangerous the navigation is, I would have been sheathed and coppered before I left port, and fully insured against partial and general loss. I will learn all about this coast before I leave it, or own I am not fit for a Bo'son, and I will get square with that ram before the voyage ends. I know him by his black legs, and will settle with him one of these days."

"Bill, you will not injure anything on the farm that would be a loss to me ?"

"Certainly not, sir ; but you must remember, only for the dog you might have lost you Bo'son at the beginning of the voyage, and I will do no more harm to the ram, than the ram has done to me ; but I shall do it in a different way, for he can out-butt me, anyhow. I shall always remember that ram, and after a little, that ram will always remember me."

"You shouldn't mind trifles, Bo'son," said the Captain ; "I admit that you have not had much luck in milking, or in salting the sheep this morning, but you will do better next time."

" I never mind trifles, sir, and as for milking, I can do that if you will let me do it in a seamanlike manner."

" Well, Bo'son, tell me how you would milk in a seamanlike way?"

" Yes, sir; I'll tell you, Captain: in the first place, I would moor the old cow head and stern in the stable, put a pair of slings under her and lash her up to the beams overhead, put some ringbolts in the floor, a strap over her shoulders, and another over her hips, and lash her down; put ranging guys on her hind legs, and if necessary set them up with a gun-tackle purchase,—and then, sir, if she had any milk on board I would hoist it out, and have no trouble or kicking about it."

" I think if you had no trouble to discharge a cargo of milk from the cow, you would have considerable trouble in getting ready to discharge," was the Captain's reply.

" That is so; but I only wanted to convince you that the Bo'son could manage to milk if it was necessary."

" I have no doubt of it, Bo'son, for you generally manage to do things when you set about them. Now, Bill, go and change your clothes again and be ready for meeting."

" Aye, aye, sir," was Bill's response.

Bill had met with two mishaps that morning, and yet his good nature was not as much disturbed as his language would indicate. He could enjoy a joke, or a piece of fun, even at his own expense.

CHAPTER X.

THE BO'SON DRESSES AND GOES TO FRIENDS' MEETING.

BILL was pleased at the idea of going to Friends Meeting. He had seen Quakers in England, Baltimore, Philadelphia and New York, when they had been on board of the ship to receive or engage freight. He liked them, and was glad of an opportunity to attend one of their meetings. Captain Waters explained to the Bo'son that there were no "paid preachers" among them, and that they sometimes had silent meetings, in which all in silence did their own preaching and their own praying.

"I have seen enough of them," said Bill, "to know that I shall like them. There were some of them that helped take the things from the boat to the farm, and when the steward offered to pay them, they said : ' No, friend steward, we never receive pay for neighborly acts; thou canst tell friend Waters that he is very welcome to the little assistance we have rendered him.' "

As Bill was in a new place, and among a new people, he determined to bend his best suit of sails. He had his third suit of clothes on that morning, as the first suit was damaged on the milking voyage; the second on his salt voyage, by colliding with a battering ram, and the third suit was put on afterwards.

Bill was well supplied with clothing, and said to the steward : " I can stand a kicking from every cow, and a butting from every ram on board, and have a clean suit for them all, and not break out the ground-tier of my clothes-bag or chest."

Bill had always done his own washing at sea and in port, because he believed he could do it better than any woman, and have as many clean suits as he wished to wear, and give no extra trouble. Lizzie did his ironing by special contract, understood only by them. It was one of Bill's peculiar traits of character to be always neat and clean in his personal appearance. He was what might be called a fancy sailor, and all his clothes were cut and made in sailor style, of which he was as close a follower as any young dandy could be of the fashions of the day.

On the present occasion he opened a small chest composed of camphor-wood, one of his own making, and in which he kept his best clothing. From the many suits he selected one that he thought was most suitable, and commenced dressing himself in white linen duck trousers, with the legs wide at the bottom ; a very light blue shirt, made with a wide collar to turn over on the shoulders, the edge of the collar bound with white, and a small white star on each corner of it ; a dark necktie, in a fancy sailor knot ; a navy blue broadcloth jacket, with pearl buttons on both sides, set close to each other, and six smaller pearl buttons on each sleeve, near the hand ; brown stockings, and low long quartered shoes ; a hat of his own make, that had cost him many days labor at sea, to plait from the unbleached leaf of a foreign tree, and then to make up with a medium brim and low crown, having on it a wide black band, tied with long ends, hanging at the side, and " Neptune " in gilt letters on the front of the band. In this suit, with a " Bo'son's silver call," suspended by a fancy lanyard from his neck, and placed in the fob of his trousers, so that about one-third of it could be seen ; and an India silk pocket handkerchief in the outside breast pocket of his jacket, the Bo'son was dressed for any great occasion, or any extra company.　　Suspenders, vest and gloves were never included in a full dress of the Bo'son.　He always regarded them as useless, and belonging more to the land than the sea service.

When thus dressed, Bill Thomas was in appearance what he was in reality, a sailor in dress, as well as in character and action.

He wore his hat a little on the back of his head, showing the dark curly hair over his forehead and temples, and was the picture of a perfect and happy sailor.

Bill watched with great interest the young man, Josh, while he was harnessing the horses and placing them before the Captain's new family carriage, but kept himself at a very respectful distance, saying :

"I have had a little misunderstanding this morning with a cow, and another with a ram, and have not now a suit of sails bent, that are suitable for going into action ; and not knowing the weight of horse metal, will keep out of their range until I learn their mode of fighting."

Captain and Mrs. Waters occupied the back seat of the carriage, Josh and Bill the front seat, Josh driving, and as they were passing the field where the sheep were, Bill shook his finger at the ram with black legs, and winked with one eye at the driver.

The old Saratoga Friends Meeting-house, built in the year 1770, was a quaint old building, without paint on either the inside or outside of it. It had been standing there so long, and in it so many marriages had taken place, that there were many sweet associations connected with that old meeting-house.

It stood on elevated ground, on the west side of a road running north and south, towards the Quaker Springs, and about two miles south of that small village. Standing in front of the meeting-house, and looking towards the east, the high land of Washington County, including Willard's mountain on the opposite side of the Hudson River, was in full view, and a more lovely picture in nature it would be difficult to find, in any part of the world, during the summer and autumn seasons. Rude in its appearance, and without form or comeliness in its shape, the old meeting-house was surrounded with such beautiful scenery, and hallowed by so many associations, that it will be remembered with interest, until the last that worshipped in it have passed from the earth.

In it the most gifted and favored of their public speakers have proclaimed the pure but simple doctrines of Quakerism and truth ; and from it many a sincere, silent and vocal prayer has ascended to the most High.

It was a beautiful summer day, and early for meeting, when the captain and his family arrived, and many of the Friends, old and young, were standing around, outside of the house. They all extended a cordial greeting and friendly welcome to the new neighbors, though some appeared a little surprised at the Bo'son and his very peculiar dress ; yet many of the Friends, both old and young, shook him warmly by the hand, and a little surprised the Bo'son to find that they should do so, without any previous acquaintance. He found afterward that it was their friendly way, and usual form. Some of the elder and most substantial members of the Society said to the captain :

"We are glad to see thee and thy family come to sit and worship with us, especially as thou art not a member of our society."

" I am not a member of any religious society, but have at times attended all the different ones, and trust I am a Christian. I like your simple form, and shall esteem it a privilege to worship with you," was the captain's reply.

Welcome Goodwin, one of the oldest and most active members of the society, having long been one of their approved ministers, took it upon himself to reply to the captain, and said :

" Friend Waters, thou hast come with thy family to reside near us. The doors of our meeting and dwelling houses will ever be open to receive thee and thy family, and in them you will be welcome at all times. Our form of worship is, as thou sayest, simple, but we trust acceptable to our Heavenly Father ; the seats of our meeting-house are all free, and now let us go in."

The Bo'son saw that many of the Friends sat with their hats on, and concluded that it was one of their forms of worship. It was not a silent meeting, for after they had been sitting some time in silence, a woman Friend arose, and taking off her bonnet said, in a low, clear and sweet voice :

" There is a Divine power, and a Divine spirit in, and acting on, the hearts of us all, and if we are only willing to be led and guided by it, we shall be preserved from the evils of the world, fitted for every duty in life, and prepared for the great change at the close of life ; which we shall leave in the full assurance of a blessed immortality, in a world beyond the grave. Our pathway through life is beset with many dangers, many temptations ; and we are often led from the right, and from the truth, by yielding to our own natural desires and inclinations, instead of being governed and directed by the Divine Spirit within us. We sometimes become careless of our words and our actions, and say or do things that injure others. I desire, my dear friends, and especially you who are in the morning of life, to call your earnest attention to the light and power of God in your own hearts, and to entreat you to listen to its teachings and its wooing, that it may be well with you in this world, and well with you in the world to come. Hold no unkind feelings, one towards another ; injure no one by word or act ; do all the good you can, and guard yourselves at all times against doing evil; love one another in gospel truth, and let peace, good will and earnest friendship ever abide with you. All these blessings will be our rich inheritance while here on earth, if we are are only willing to be led and guided by the Divine Spirit."

At the close of the meeting, Welcome Goodwin said to the Bo'son :

"William, I should like much to see thee where we can talk together."

"My name is Bill, if you please, sir, and I should be glad to talk with you at any time, when convenient to you," was the Bo'son's reply.

"Well, I will call thee Bo'son now, and we will talk about thy name some other time, as I am going to call on friend Waters ; he has invited me to do so. Farewell, William," said friend Goodwin, shaking Bill by the hand.

"Good-by, Mr. Goodwin; please remember that my name is Bill."

On the way from the meeting to the farm, the captain asked the Bo'son what he thought of Friends as a society, and of their meeting.

"I have never before," said Bill, "been at one of their meetings, and for the first time have to-day heard a woman preach. I liked what she said, because I could understand it, and her words went to the right place in my heart. If what the lady said is true, and I fully believe it is, then there are a great many sailors who are Christians, and don't really know it themselves, and never have any credit from the world for being such."

"Do you think, Bo'son, that you are a Christian ? "

"No, Capt'n, not exactly, but Bose and I are both of us trying to do all the good we can, and as little harm as possible,—and here we are at home."

CHAPTER XI.

SHIP "NEPTUNE," CAPTAIN WATERS, THE BO'SON AND SOME TAR.

WHEN the ship "Neptune" was built, Captain Waters being sole owner, and intending her as a home on the ocean for himself and family, had her cabin arranged for the greatest possible comfort and convenience. It was a deck cabin, and divided into three compartments, known as the forward, middle and after cabins. In the forward cabin, on each side, were state-rooms for the officers, the steward's room, store-room and pantry; also spare state-rooms for friends that might be passengers, or spend a night on board. In the middle of this cabin, and extending nearly the whole length of it, was the dining table, with room to seat twenty-two persons. There were seats at the sides of the table, secured to the floor, to keep them in position in a sea-way. They were cushioned, covered with hair-cloth, and had shifting backs. The middle cabin was fitted up as a parlor, or drawing-room. It extended from side to side of the ship, with large windows on each side, composed of heavy thick glass, capable of resisting much force from the waves, and shutters on the outside, that could be closed in a gale of wind. The furniture, curtains, mirrors, and every article in it, were of the richest and most costly kind, and all arranged in good taste. There were two state-rooms in the forward cabin, that opened into this parlor cabin. One was occupied by Lizzie, the other kept as a spare room, and often used by special friends, or some one of the grandchildren that were invited to make a short voyage in the ship. The after cabin was the sleeping apartment, bath-room, and the captain's private office; all arranged with great taste, and every convenience that could be suggested or desired. All three of the cabins had large skylights, in addition to the air-ports or windows at the sides, so that they were well lighted and well ventilated in all kinds of weather. In the whole arrangement, great care was successfully bestowed, for comfort and convenience.

The "Neptune," when at sea, was not only a floating palace, but also a floating empire The captain was an absolute monarch, and reigned supreme. Mrs. Waters was empress, and shared the throne with him who held the sceptre. The chief mate or executive officer was prime minister, the other officers holding lower positions in the general government; the B'oson being a sort of master of horse, and the steward chief chamberlain, valet, etc.

In the household of the empress, Lizzie was first maid of honor, and filled other important positions, with great credit to herself and advantage to her royal mistress, and to all the subjects of the realm.

The "Neptune" was one of the largest freighting ships sailing under the American flag, and the captain always carried a large crew for such a large ship, saying, "There is nothing saved by being short handed at sea."

Over his empire, officers and subjects, the monarch held his sceptre so firmly, and at the same time exercised his power so mildly, that he fully controlled his people, and while they obeyed, they loved and esteemed him.

The empress and her maid of honor were ever ready and active in visiting the sick, and in contributing to the comfort and welfare of the whole people. Thus all uniting to make the empire prosperous and the people happy.

The captain not only owned the ship, but frequently the cargo, purchasing a cargo in one part of the world, taking it to another and distant part of the world, and there selling it and purchasing again. In this way, for many years, he sailed around the world, and over every ocean navigated by ships, and that without meeting with any serious disaster, or being shipwrecked on any coast.

Captain Waters was a perfect, a finished seaman, and a proficient navigator, and it could hardly be otherwise with one of his experience. He was also a man of great executive abilities, as his success in life, his uniform quick passages, and continued good discipline on board, were sufficient proofs.

In retiring from the sea, and going on a farm, it was not

to make money. The captain had enough of that already, but it was to have something to occupy his mind and time, gratify a long-cherished desire, and furnish a good home for those who had long been his companions on the ocean.

A few days after Bill's misunderstanding with the sheep, there was an occasion to use the ox-cart. It needed greasing, and the captain called :

"Bo'son! Bo'son!"

"Aye! aye, sir!" was Bill's answer.

"Go ask the steward if he has any slush, to slush this ox-cart."

"Plenty of slush on board, sir, without going to the steward."

"If that is so, Bo'son, bring it along, for Josh is in a hurry."

Bill went into the midship-house, and soon returned with a tin can that contained about fifteen pounds of good, clean ship slush. When the captain saw it, he said:

"I wish we had some tar to mix with it."

"Hold on, then," said Bill; " there is plenty of tar on board. How much do you want, Capt'n?"

"O! only about a quart."

Bill went again to his house, and returned with a regular ship's tar-bucket, containing the required quantity of Norway tar, and bringing with him a tar-brush.

"Where did you get that tar?" asked the captain.

"Brought it from the ship with me," was the Bo'son's answer.

"How much have you of it, Bo'son?"

"Fifteen gallons, sir—about half a barrel."

"Now, Bo'son, tell me what put it into your head to bring tar to a farm? for I never thought of it, and I ought to know more about it than you do."

"Capt'n, I have never been anywhere since I was a very small boy that tar wasn't used, and you can't do a good job at anything without it. If you want to set up the rigging, or strap a block, you need tar; if you want to put a handle in an axe, put some tar on the handle where it goes into the eye, drive and wedge it, and it is sure to stay there. We don't any of us know when we shall die, or where we shall be buried; but, if I am ever buried on the land, I want the box I am put in tarred on the inside, and then no small insects will get in there to bother and disturb me, for they can't live where there is tar. I knew tar would come handy for something up here, though I didn't know it was used on ox-carts."

"We don't intend burying you at present, Bo'son, but I'll remember the tar, if I am on hand at the time; and now I want you to tell me how much paint and oil will be wanted to paint the house inside and outside, and for what painting is needed on the other buildings, as I am going to New York this evening on business, and I will send it up."

Bill replied by saying: "We have plenty of paint on board, sir, for all the painting you want done."

"How much have you, Bo'son?"

"One hundred and fifty pounds of pure English white lead, ten gallons of raw and five gallons of boiled linseed oil, five gallons of spirits of turpentine, and all the different colors and brushes needed."

"Bo'son," said the captain, "how is it that you thought to bring paints, oil, brushes, and tar to the farm, when I never told you that they would be wanted here?"

"I knew, sir, that you had long depended on me to have at hand everything you called for, and I knew that you would want all the buildings, fences, carts and wagons on the farm painted and kept in as good order as you have been accustomed to have the ship kept. We had all kinds of paints on board of the ship, and you left it with me to bring such articles as I thought would be useful on the farm, and I have done so, hoping that I have made no mistake. When you call for anything wanted on the farm, that was on the ship, and the Bo'son don't produce it, then you may say you are sorry you brought your Bo'son with you."

"I think, Bill, you were right when you said ' I couldn't navigate a farm without my steward and Bo'son,' for I find you both so useful, and so much in your places, that I should be short-handed without you."

"You must remember, Capt'n, that we are not used to this ship yet, and that everything is new to us, that we have not had time to put things in their places, but in ten days more, when you return from New York, we will have the whole cargo stowed away, the decks cleared and washed off, and with us you will feel at home. There are a great many things here that will be useful beside the Bo'son, and we are sure of a good voyage."

"Yes, yes, Bill;" said the Captain, "I am satisfied that I have done right in selling the ship and coming to the country, and I am also well pleased that you and the others are with me."

"Thank you, sir," said the Bo'son, touching his hat.

———

CHAPTER XII.

BLACK-EYED SUSAN AND HER FRIENDS.

THE Captain had not been gone long from his home, and was hardly out of sight from his door, where Mrs. Waters was still standing, after bidding him good-bye, and wishing him a pleasant time and a safe return, when Bill walked up to her and touching his hat (which was his invariable custom when he spoke to any one in a position of life above his own), said :

"Mrs. Waters, will the Captain bring black-eyed Susan up with him ?"

"Yes, Bo'son ; that is fixed on ; she wants to come and we want her."

"Will the flying sky-sail come with her ?"

"Who do you mean by the flying sky-sail ?"

"I mean, marm, Julia Fizzlebob."

"I think you must mean Julia Fizzlebaugh."

"That," said the Bo'son, "is the one, but what a name ? I can never get it right, and it is no great matter, as she is of but little account."

"I am surprised, Bo'son, to hear you speak so of Susie's friend, because you are not apt to judge anyone unjustly or unkindly."

"No, good lady; I am not much given to expressing my opinion about people, but that Julia has neither head nor heart, and if you and black-eyed Susan don't know it the Bo'son does."

"You can never see anything good in others, when Susie is around. If you were a young man, Bo'son, I should expect you to fall in love and marry her; but why do you call her friend the 'flying skysail?'"

"Because she will be of no account, when 'set,' to help any one along, any more than a flying sky-sail helps a ship through the water, and if furled, would be in the way of furling the royal; that is a bigger and a better sail."

It is only proper that the reader should learn who these girls are, as they will frequently appear, and act conspicuous parts.

Susie Morton was a grand-daughter of Captain Waters, and at the age of eighteen years she had made a number of voyages in the ship; first, when very young, in company with her mother, and one to Europe without her mother. Since leaving school, Susie was a great pet and favorite of the Captain's, and if possible, in still greater favor with Bill the Bo'son.

Susie was a lovely girl, possessing nature's richest gifts, both in body and mind; of medium size, and having a well-formed person, a fine head covered with black hair, large black eyes, beautifully arched with heavy eyebrows, and fringed with long eyelashes. A single glance at her eyes told a close observer that she had a heart that could love deeply and constantly; that it might be indifferent towards individuals, but never harbored hate. She acquired knowledge from books with ease, and in less time than her classmates, and when once in possession of knowledge on any subject, ever afterwards retained it. Her disposition was mild and cheerful; she was firm in opinion and action when believing that she was right, and industrious in all things that would be of use to herself and others. An early riser from early childhood, often when others of the family were sleeping, Susie would be up, and when not engaged with her lessons, would be gliding about her father's house, so gently as not to disturb the sleepers. Mornings, when the only member of the family that would be up, except the servants, she would busy herself in various ways; sometimes in attending to her flowers and plants, sometimes in arranging and dusting the parlors, and sometimes in the kitchen and dining-room with the girl, always putting her hand on the right thing, and putting it in the right place.

Her father and mother were very much opposed to her being with the servants, or doing anything that belonged to the servants to do; but Susie was so good-natured about it that she managed to laugh them out of what they told Susie was "propriety." Susie, with a joyous laugh, would say: "Never mind about proprieties, a little wholesome exercise in the morning, to give a young girl an appetite for breakfast, and some knowledge of household duties, are in value worth a whole ship load of what you call proprieties."

"There now, you learnt that expression from your grandfather Waters," said her mother.

"Yes, mother dear, it is very likely I did, and what you are pleased to call an expression, conveys an important lesson that I wish all young girls would learn and practice; that is, to rise early, and learn at home, while young, what it will be necessary for them to know, when housekeepers themselves; I pity young girls who go out into the world with no knowledge, except what they have gained at school, and from books, and pity still more the men that they may be united to in marriage."

Julia Fizzlebaugh was cousin to Susie, on the side of Susie's father, and in no way related to Captain Waters or his family, except to his son-in-law. Julia was a dashing girl, an only child of parents with limited means, who had found it extremely difficult to meet the expenses of educating their daughter, and in keeping up such appearances as would enable the daughter to match herself with a fortune. Her education was only superficial, but suited, as they thought, to their purposes. She could sing, play on the piano, and dance; had read all the popular novels, attended the operas and concerts of the day, and considered herself an accomplished young lady. She was incapable of turning her hand to a single useful occupation, nor had she one correct idea of the duties or the responsibilities of life. Some thought her handsome, but it was only those who admired light hair. That she made a good appearance in company, and was attractive, none of her acquaintances ever denied, although some difference of opinion existed in regard to her being beautiful. She was strong-minded on one subject—that of a rich husband. On all other subjects, her mind was very unstable.

Susie and Julia had been companions and schoolmates from childhood, and, though differing widely in every respect, mind, habits, taste and feelings, they always seemed to live agreeably together, and certainly never interfered with each other, about young men visitors.

Julia was idle and listless in her habits, cold in her affections, and selfish in her nature. If she could only be gratified in idleness and luxury, she cared not how the means of her indulgence were obtained. She showed no sympathy for the struggles and privations of her parents, and would lie for hours on the parlor sofa, with a novel in one hand, and petting a cat with the other hand, while her aged grandmother was attending to household duties, and her feeble mother in the kitchen, washing and ironing her summer dresses. She would sit all the early part of a night in one easy chair, with her feet in another, reading some new work, and in the morning be ready for her breakfast, sometimes after all the family had taken theirs. She was never known to be ready for breakfast, when breakfast was ready. Rising early was unknown to her. She was a great eater of good things, and when there was anything good to eat, she expected two shares, no matter how it was procured, or who had to go without. Her parents loved her, and wished her to be conspicuous, and obtain a rich husband. To accomplish that, they had made great sacrifices and great exertion, without seeming to realize that they had assisted nature in making a finished nothing of their daughter, and been paving the way to her worldly misery in the future.

Frank Livingston and George Wilson were a couple of young men, differing as widely in character, habits and position in society, as Susie Morton and Julia Fizzlebaugh did.

Frank Livingston was left with a large fortune, that he came into full possession of at the age of twenty-one years. He was master of his fortune and of himself, with no one to control him, and no one with sufficient influence over him to direct him rightly. He had received a good education, and with his means and family influence, moved in good society. He used his money freely, and for the first few years after coming of age, had no occasion to encroach on the principal, his interest being sufficient for all his wants. After a while, his expenses increased, and he indulged himself at fashionable games; sometimes played when excited with stimulants, and he became a heavy loser, although it was not generally known.

George Wilson was the son of a sea-captain. His father was lost at sea when he was only a lad, leaving his mother, himself and sister to fight their way in the world, and with very limited means to do so. George was carefully educated by his mother, notwithstanding her limited means, and it was a mystery to many how Mrs. Wilson managed to keep her children well dressed, and at the best of schools.

George dearly loved his mother and sister, Laura, only two years younger than himself, and he made great exertions to increase the comforts of their home, and render them happy.

At the age of seventeen years his education was completed, and it was necessary for him to choose some occupation, that would increase the means for supporting the family; at least George so considered it. Notwithstanding his father had been lost at sea, that circumstance did not prevent him from choosing the ocean as an element on which to battle for bread and honor. George's father had sailed with Captain Waters, and was a number of voyages his first officer. Captain Waters received George on board of his ship as a boy, placed him under the special care of Bill the Bo'son, giving him, as the son of an old friend, better wages than he could have obtained with a stranger.

George and the Bo'son were soon warm friends,—the Bo'son anxious to teach, and George anxious to learn, so that the young lad in time, became an able and perfect seaman. Captain Waters took a great interest in the young man; taught him navigation, made him third, and then second officer of the "Neptune," which position he held on the last voyage made by Captain Waters and his family.

George Wilson was the pride and boast of Bill Thomas, and idolized almost as much as the ship was. More about "black-eyed Susan's" friends will appear in future chapters.

CHAPTER XIII.

CAPTAIN WATERS RETURNS, AND IS WELCOMED BY A SALUTE.

CAPTAIN Waters had long depended on his steward and Bo'son when at sea, and feeling sure that all his orders would be obeyed, he left the farm with orders to make such alterations in the house as the lady might wish, and then to paint, inside and outside, and he was certain it would be properly done.

Being new neighbors, and supposed to have plenty of ready money, there was no difficulty in obtaining the necessary assistance, as all appeared to feel a great desire to learn particulars about Captain Waters, his family, and all the strange and curious things that he had brought from other countries, and also to become acquainted with the old Bo'son.

According to Bill's account, "such works had never been known in that latitude before." Alterations were made in the house, and especially in the kitchen; carpets cut and fitted, every part of the house painted, some of the rooms papered, and all the furniture properly arranged.

Work at the same time was going on outside, such as changing fences, and of painting all the buildings, and of putting every thing in perfect order.

The Bo'son was every where, doing, as the men said, "more work than any two of us can, and finding work for all the rest of us to do." The Bo'son had for many years been accustomed to lay out work, and see that others did it; so that it was all natural to him. After getting the other work well along, he turned his attention to the midship-house, and the necessary improvements and alterations to be made there. He fitted the lower story to look as near as possible like his room on board of the "Neptune," only it was much larger, and his own berth wider and better arranged; also a berth on the opposite side, to be used by any friend that might be on board, visiting the Bo'son.

The second floor was fitted up to be used as a sail-room and rigging loft, where was to be stored all the canvas, coils of rope and other articles used on board of a ship, and that Bill had taken from the "Neptune."

The Bo'son had built a locker for paints and brushes, and another for such articles as are generally used about the rigging, and kept in the "Bo'son's locker" of a ship.

When the midship-house was finished, and painted inside, Bill unpacked his stores, and put things in their places. There was nothing ever taken to sea in a ship, and that could be used on a farm, that the Bo'son hadn't with him, and many things that could not be used on a farm for the same purposes that they had been used at sea. Such as a hand lead and line, a deep sea lead and line, and a ship's log line; but they could be used on a farm, or at least some of them, for other purposes than they were designed. There were, however, many other things that would be useful, such as carpenters' and blacksmiths' tools, signal lanterns, water buckets, hickory brooms, and many small articles.

The midship-house stood end to the road, and near the gable the Bo'son built something in the form of a ship's bows, and on it placed an exact image of "Neptune," as represented on the ship. He made a bowsprit, and secured it on the ridge of the house, over the head of his friend " Neptune," and run a spar through the roof at the ridge for a mast, on which he put shrouds and stays, and from which he sent up a top-mast, shrouded and stayed in the same manner. He then built outside, and in front of the house, a platform of heavy timbers and planks, on which he mounted a nine-pounder brass cannon, that he took from the ship, and then said: " The midship-house is now ready for paint on the outside," and it was so painted, being the last of all the buildings on the farm that received the touches of the brush.

Bill next turned his attention to erecting flag-staffs on the house, barn, and on all the farm buildings, which he finished on the third of July, the day before Captain Waters was to return to his country home.

On the morning of the fourth, Bill was up bright and early, for it was a great day for Bill Thomas the Bo'son.

At sunrise he run the American flag up at the main,—that is from the mast at his house,—and fired a salute of as many guns as there were then States in the Union. The Bo'son was aware that thirteen guns are considered a morning salute for the fourth of July, but said :

" Give every State in the Union a gun this morning."

Bill was more than usually patriotic, as he was fully aware that he was on the Saratoga battle-field, and where so many heavy guns hadn't been fired since the day when the American army, under General Gates, defeated the British army, under General Burgoyne, and turned the tide of war in favor of the Americans.

The quiet Quakers in the neighborhood were a little disturbed at first, but didn't appear much displeas d at the noisy display of the Bo'son's patriotism. The society of friends are friends to their country and to good order.

· At eight o'clock the Bo'son fired one gun, beat the drum and set all his colors. The display of bunting that Bill made was very great, and Mrs. Waters, Lizzie and the steward, though all pleased, were all much astonished that he had so many flags with him on the farm.

Every building had one or more flags hoisted over it, and the Bo'son's house had them streaming from masthead, down each side, as near as they could be displayed on the halliards ; and also from the mast-head to the end of the bowsprit : it was a glorious sight to see.

About noon it was expected that the captain would reach home, and with him his grand-daughter, Susie.

As the time drew near, the Bo'son seemed much excited for one so usually self-possessed. Whether it was because the captain was coming home, or because " black-eyed Susan " was coming with him, was more than any of the family could tell.

The carriage had been sent to meet the captain, and the Bo'son had stationed himself on the mansion house, with a spy-glass, and was on the look-out. He was observed to close the glass and come down with haste, go to the gun and fire it off, and then load and fire as fast as he could, keeping tally with a piece of chalk, and fired the twenty-first gun as the captain arrived at the gate.

The Bo'son took off his hat, gave three cheers, and was ready to meet his captain and Susie. The greeting between the captain and family was affectionate and hearty, and equally so between the captain and his Bo'son. The women folks took charge of Susie, after she had shaken Bill by the hand, and bestowed a warm kiss on his sun-burnt cheek, which he received and returned with interest, as due and to be paid.

The captain again took the Bo'son by the hand, and walked with him towards the midship-house, and the first words he said were :

" Bo'son, what does all this mean ?"

" It means, sir, that the ship is ready for sea, and the capt'n on board."

Captain Waters, when he reached the midship-house, relinquished the hand of the Bo'son, and surveyed all with pride and satisfaction ; but there was in his countenance the evidence of great anxiety. The Bo'son noticed it, without being able to judge the cause, and while he hoped that his captain would approve of all that he had done, he feared that something was wrong ; that he had done too much, or not enough, in preparing for and welcoming his captain and black-eyed Susan on board of the new ship.

Captain Waters pointed with his finger at the image of "Neptune" over the door, and said:

"Bo'son, where did that come from? Did you take it from the ship in your madness and folly, and disgrace me by disfiguring the ship?"

Bill's face underwent as many changes of color as would a struck dolphin, but after a few minutes' reflection, answered:

"No, sir; the Bo'son never disgraced his capt'n, nor his ship, and would have fought hard before anyone should have taken the image of 'Neptune' from the bow of the ship. You, sir, were the last of the family who left the ship, and when we were towed out of the dock on the canal-boat, the last object that I looked upon was old 'Neptune,' on the bow of the ship, still holding firmly his trident."

"Where, then, did you get this one from, that looks so much like the original?"

"I made it, sir," was the Bo'son's reply. "It has taken me seven years to do it. I thought I might some day be 'hauled up in ordinary,' and want something to remember the ship by; and so I worked on this many hours, when no one saw me, and always kept it under my berth, and it was never seen by any person but myself, until yesterday, when I took it out of the box. Don't it look like old 'Neptune,' sir?" Bill took off his hat and bowed to the image, as he asked the question.

"Yes, Bo'son," said the Captain, "it looks so much like the original, that I at first feared that you had stolen it; but I ought to know better. How is it that you have that gun and all this bunting you are flying?"

"That gun, nor this bunting, were not on the list of articles sold with the ship; I left colors enough on board, and left the iron gun, but not the Bo'son's 'bull-dog,'" was Bill's answer.

Captain Water's face had lost every appearance of anxiety, and was lit up with joy and satisfaction at the conclusion of the Bo'son's reply, and taking Bill by the hand, he fairly shook him with his right, while he slapped him over the shoulder with his left hand, and such slaps as few shoulders could have stood without being unjointed. At length the Captain said:

"You are my old Bo'son yet, and nothing can change you; but what in the name of 'Neptune' did you want of all these flags?"

"To set on such a day as this; don't they look fine, sir?"

The Captain was willing to admit that they did look fine, and reminded him of old times, but he was still more astonished when he visited the inside of the midship-house, and saw the quantities of rope, canvas, paints, buckets, brooms, lanterns, tools, and about everything used on shipboard, and all so arranged that any article could be taken out without removing others. The Captain knew that it would be useless to remonstrate with the Bo'son about having such things on a farm, as the Bo'son would constantly reply that "they will all come in use before the voyage ends," so the Captain left his Bo'son in all his glory, and went to the house, full as much delighted as Bill himself was.

CHAPTER XIV.

SUSIE'S FIRST MORNING AT THE FARM.

SUSIE Morton was in one of her gayest moods, and knowing that she was a favorite with every member of her grandfather's family, made her feel very happy to be at the farm. After grandmother came Lizzie, then the old steward for her attention, and to offer to her a warm welcome, and last, but not least, the old dog Bose, that had been using every means to secure her attention; that is, as far as he could without neglecting what he considered his other duties. The dog would dance and jump about Susie, and then run out to where the Captain and the Bo'son were, fearing that he might be needed, or that something would be done and he not be there. When Susie was at liberty, after having received the caresses of all the other members of the family, taken off her hat and sat down, then old Bose walked to her, laid his head in her lap, and looked her earnestly in the face, manifesting a depth and strength of affection equal to any ever exhibited by a human being. Susie returned his kindness by patting him on the head, smoothing down his hair, and talking to him as she had heard the Bo'son talk.

When the Captain joined the family in the sitting-room, after he had been over the whole house, inspected the improvements, and found them satisfactory, he was in the finest possible spirits, and after talking a little to the dog, said:

"Bill Thomas must be Bo'son, no matter where he is, and has almost made a ship of the farm before the first crop is harvested. What he will do ' before the voyage is up,' as he calls it, is more than any of us can tell, or when he expects the voyage to end, is more than he can tell himself. The Bo'son enjoys it, and I am willing that he should, for he seems very happy. How, Nancy, has he got along since I have been gone?"

"You have had the Bo'son so long with you, Joseph, that I should think it hardly necessary for you to ask that question. You know the Bo'son always gets along with whatever he has to do, and can accomplish whatever he undertakes."

"Hold on, mother," said the captain, "you must except milking, and salting the sheep."

"That is so; but such duties were new to him, and, with time, he could learn them. There are now other duties for us all; dinner is ready, and the steward is laboring under the belief that the captain has had nothing fit to eat since he left home, and you are sure to be well provided for to-day," was Mrs. Waters' reply.

"I shouldn't wonder," said the captain, "if that son of ' Neptune,' the Bo'son, gave us a dinner salute, as he is bound to make a noise to-day. If he has ten tons of powder stowed away somewhere, it wouldn't be any more strange than that he should have old 'Neptune' for seven years under his berth. There goes the gun. Well, let him fire, and we will eat."

Bill did fire, and, in doing so, called about him all the

young men of the neighborhood, some that were advanced in years, and also some of the young women, who came to see the flags, hear the gun, and to see the Bo'son and his dog.

After dinner, the captain desired the steward to provide a lunch for all that were about the farm, and then he invited them all in to partake of it, and asked them to visit any part of the house that they wished, and to examine whatever was worth their attention.

Both invitations were accepted. Great was the satisfaction of the neighbors present, great the marvels, and great the stories told to those not present.

At sunset the Bo'son fired his last salute, hauled down all the flags, put them away, and considered the duties of the day ended.

The family, including every member, by special invitation of Captain and Mrs. Waters, spent the evening in the family sitting room, where they enjoyed a social evening until a late hour, when all retired.

All of the Waters family were early risers, but on the next morning Susie was the first that made her appearance. She looked as bright as a happy human being could look. Her dark hair hung in curls all over her head, and down on the back of her neck; her dress, a dark calico, with short sleeves, displaying arms that any warm-hearted young, or even old man, would like to have around his neck, fitted a person that was faultless in form, and made her look what she really was—a lovely young girl. She wore slippers, had on a plain white collar, with a dark stripe in it, and a large tow-cloth apron, that must have been her grandmother's.

When Susie found that none of the family were astir, she commenced singing, " I am a merry mountain maid," and her sweet, clear voice was heard ringing through the whole house, which aroused the family, and brought the Bo'son to her side.

If ever one being loved another with all the strength, purity and fervor of a noble and generous heart, Bill Thomas loved Susie Morton. It was the kind of love that a father feels for a child, strong enough to induce him to watch over her happiness in every step that she took, and to have sacrificed all in life, and life itself, for her good. Susie esteemed him as one, that by nature and habit, was very noble and very good. They had known each other ever since Susie was a child, and she had confided in, and trusted the old Bo'son with the secrets of her own heart.

The Bo'son entered the room with his hat in his hand, and as he advanced to meet her, his face beaming with smiles, he said:

"Good morning, Beauty and Sunshine."

"Good morning, Bill; but you mustn't call me such names, or I will call you old Blow-hard, Whistling Bill, Spun-yarn, Barnacles, and anything I can think of," and she laughed, joyously and heartily.

Bill also laughed long and loud, and then said:

"All right, Morning-glory, but tell me about Julia Fizzlebob. I thought she was coming with you, and am glad she didn't."

"Bo'son," said Susie, assuming a seriousness that she really felt, "Julia Fizzlebaugh will be here all too soon, and with her Frank Livingston; but here comes grandmother, and I'll tell you all about it the first chance I have."

Mrs. Waters looked at Susie and could but admire her simple dress and lovely appearance, and then asked her why she was so dressed?

"I am going, grandma, to learn how to make butter and cheese, and how to cook and make cake, pies and puddings as you do. Pa and ma are very unwilling that I should do anything about the house, fearing that I shall stain my hands, or enlarge my fingers; but we differ in opinion, and you have taught me better lessons, and I don't mean to forget them."

"Good girl," said Mrs. Waters; "come with me to the milk-room, and Lizzie and I will give you the first lesson in butter making."

They went to the milk-room and there Susie saw, for the first time in her life, shelves covered with bright tin-pans filled with milk, and saw Lizzie skim those that had stood long enough for all the cream to rise, saw the cream placed in the churn, and the pans emptied and washed. Susie was still uninformed how the butter was to be made, but concluded to wait and learn from seeing, rather than to ask questions.

When all in the milk-room but the butter was finished, the steward rung the breakfast bell, and all repaired to the dining-room.

Susie took off the apron worn in the milk-room, and put one of a different kind on, before going to the table.

Captain Waters looked at, and almost worshipped Susie, as the little idol of his heart, which she really was. During the time occupied in partaking of the morning meal, there was a continual fire of infantry and light artillery, or something that might be compared with them, going on between the Captain and Susie Morton, in which Mrs. Waters sometimes joined, always going to the assistance of whichever party appeared to suffer most in the fight. The forces opposed to each other were so nearly equal, that Mrs. Waters, most of the time, had to remain neutral, not being able to determine on which side to place her own reserves. What Susie lacked in age and experience was made up in wit and good nature, so that the two were well matched.

After breakfast the Bo'son appeared at the door, touched his hat, and said :

"Does Mrs. Capt'n want the butter pump rigged ? .

"Yes, Bo'son ; we have to churn to-day," was the lady's answer.

"Ay! ay! marm," said Bill, with another touch of the hat, and away he went.

The Bo'son had watched them churning by hand, and had assisted, but found the work too hard for the women folks, even with a small dairy, and set himself about to find some easier way of converting cream into butter, than the old-fashioned one. It didn't take him long, because he fully understood the difference between a hand-pump for water casks, and a pump worked by a brake. He rigged the churn to be worked by a brake, in the same way that pumps are worked, and thus lessened the labor necessary to produce butter, as he had a lever, instead of a direct power. The Bo'son called it the "butter pump," and considerered it under his direction and management, believing that no one could work it properly but himself.

Susie went with him to the milk-room and saw the churning, and there arranged with the Bo'son to visit the fields in the afternoon, and gather flowers.

CHAPTER XV.

SUSIE MORTON TELLS THE BO'SON SOME LOVE STORIES.

SUSIE Morton wished to visit the fields, but not to gather wild flowers, though she might return with some as an excuse for her long absence. There were pent up in her young, pure heart, feelings such as few at her age had experienced, or at least she thought so. Bill the Bo'son was the only one that she could make a confident of,—the only one, as she believed, who could advise her rightly.

Those who knew the Bo'son slightly, or judged him from his rough outside, would have thought him the very last person that a young girl, just out of school, would have told her love affairs to; but Susie was not of the every-day family; she seemed to possess the intuitive power of penetrating the hearts of others, and learning that the Bo'son had a warm and tender place in his heart, she sought and found a passage to it. She knew his heart was warm; she believed his judgment was sound; and as she could confide in the one, she was willing to be governed by the other.

William Morton, the father of Susie, was a merchant of the city of New York. He was not rich, according to the standard of wealth of his day, but he had a good, safe business, something invested out of his business, and an income that more than supported his family in a good position in society. He and his wife were proud, and had received into their heads, and cherished in their hearts, the idea of rich relations, family connections, higher circles, best society, making a good appearance, and of occupying a high place in the fashionable world, which always costs more than it ever comes to. They both dearly loved their daughter, and by her were dearly loved in return. The daughter was considered a powerful lever, by which they and the family would be raised higher in the fashionable world. Entertaining such views and hopes, they had obtained a promise from Susie that she would not marry without their consent, and that promise was given when she was too young to think of marrying at all.

Frank Livingston had been a frequent visitor at the house of her father, and had become attached to the daughter, but had made no offer of marriage to her, though he had asked and received permission of the father to do so.

The subject had been spoken of in the family, and Susie informed of the wishes of Mr. Livingston, and an attempt made to draw from her what her answer would be. The parents told her that if she married Frank, she would gratify them, and hold a high position in society.

Susie said: "It will be time enough for me to decide when Mr. Livingston makes the offer, and until then please say no more about it."

Susie knew the ruling passion of her parents, and how difficult it would be to overcome it. She also knew more of the character and habits of Frank Livingston than her father and mother had been able to learn, because they were satisfied to receive him into the family, in consideration of his position in the fashionable world, and his family connections.

Such was the character of Susie Morton, and such had been the schooling and training of her own heart and mind, that the coming struggle did not greatly disturb, or interfere with her happiness. She knew her own strength as well as she did the weakness of her parents, and with the assistance of the Bo'son, expected to meet and overcome every difficulty.

She could not love, and would not marry, Frank Livingston, but didn't wish to pain her parents by telling them so, before any offer of marriage had been made to her; and she was fully aware that every effort on the part of her father and mother would be made to induce her to accept the offer. But from her grandfather she had inherited, not only a large portion of good common sense, but also a firmness of purpose and decision of character that could not be shaken, nor changed by ordinary events.

In the afternoon, the Bo'son and Susie took their way to the fields, for the expressed object of gathering flowers; but for the real object, on the part of Susie, of gathering strength, and of fortifying herself by the assistance of her friend, and of preparing to resist an attack that she felt certain would be made upon the citadel of her future happiness; and, on the part of Bill, of collecting information, and of giving assistance.

They went to Burgoyne Hill, and there found comfortable seats under the shade of a noble old oak, that had been growing and standing there since the day when General Frasier fell near the spot, and the American army, under General Gates, gained a victory.

Seating themselves comfortably, Bill took off his hat, laid it beside him, and said:

" Now, black-eyed Susan, tell me all you have to say—which way the wind is, whether it is fair or a head, if you are looking for a storm, and from what point of the compass you expect it—and the Bo'son will, if he can, give you a course to steer that will keep you clear of it."

Susie Morton laid one of her little hands on Bill's shoulder, and the other on his large, rough hand, and looking him earnestly in the face, said:

"I know, Bo'son, that you will aid me, because you love me, and have carried me about a ship's-deck in your arms, when I was a child, and steadied me with your strong arm when I have been walking the deck in rough weather, since I was a young woman. Now, again, I want your willing heart and strong hands, or I shall founder."

The Bo'son placed the " call " in his mouth, as though he was about to " pipe all hands to action," but Susie took it from him, saying, as she did so:

"Bo'son, the time has not come for action—it is only talk we want to-day."

"I know it; but when you talk of foundering, it is time to make, or take in sail," was Bill's answer.

"Bo'son," said Susie, with the same seriousness that she had shown in the morning, when they first met, and when she was speaking of Frank and Julia, which the Bo'son then observed, and knew was caused by some deep and unusual feelings, "hear what I have to say, and then tell me what to do."

"I'll do it, Rosebud; you can trust the Bo'son in a storm, no matter how hard the gale blows, nor which way the wind comes from."

"I know I can, or I shouldn't have asked you here to listen to me. In the first place, Frank Livingston wants to make me his wife, and my father and mother are pleased with the idea, and hope it will be accomplished."

While Susie was saying so much or so little, the Bo'son had watched her closely, put his hat on and taken it off twice, had his whistle a number of times in and out of his mouth, which didn't in the least disturb his companion. After thinking for a moment, he said:

"Who is Frank Livingston, and what is he? Do you love him, and want to be his wife?"

Susie had undergone a change; the ice was broken, and she could speak freely, notwithstanding that her own feelings, and the wishes of her parents, were so opposed, and that she knew they could not be reconciled. She answered:

"Frank Livingston is a gentleman of family, and of fortune; an orphan, left with more money than he knows how to use; is highly educated, and moves in the first circles in the city. He is handsome in person, polished in manners, lives in fine style, keeps plenty of servants, horses and carriages, is very welcome wherever he goes, and is just such a man as most any young woman would love and like to marry."

"You have told me," said the Bo'son, "who and what he is; but you have not told me if you love him, and wish to be his wife."

"No, Bo'son ; I do not love him, and will not be his wife, unless I am forced to marry him," was Susie's answer.

"Why can't you love such a man, and who will force you to marry him against your will ? " asked the Bo'son.

"I cannot love him, because he is not worthy of my love ; he has no heart, or no such heart as would be a fair exchange for mine.   His wealth may leave him, and when it does, he will have nothing to fall back on ; will be wretched himself, and make all around him equally so. He is a gambler, and loves wine. So anxious, and so earnest are my parents that I should marry into some old and rich family, that they are willing to overlook all little irregularities of conduct, and seem to consider family connections and riches a fair equivalent for every virtue and noble quality of the heart ; and for my good, as they believe, they would, if necessary to accomplish it, force me into a marriage with Mr. Livingston. Do not, Bo'son, for a moment think that my father or my mother have any object at heart but my good ; they do love me dearly, but in judgment they are at fault, and are so determined that it will be difficult to change them ; and now what is your advice ? "

The Bo'son thought earnestly for a few minutes, and then said:

"Susan, you can't be forced to marry a man you don't love ; to stop it, we'll 'call all hands.' You have told me enough to satisfy me what sort of a man Livingston is, and that you will never be his wife. It is better to fight than run from an enemy that you must meet again. Let Frank Livingston ask you to be his wife, and then tell him no ; and if he persists, and your parents back him, we'll find means enough to more than match him, no matter what course he steers. Have you told the captain and Mrs. Waters about it ? "

"No, Bill, I have not ; I wanted to talk with you first, and have you tell me what to do in the matter."

"Nothing," said the Bo'son, "can be done by you until Livingston fires his first shot. Then it will be time to reply. It is well enough to load our guns, and 'call the men to quarters.' You need have no fears, Beauty ; we are too many for 'em. There is, in first place, the captain and Mrs. Waters, and I would just like to see the chap with guns enough to take 'black-eyed Susan' from their 'convoy;' and then there is Lizzie, and she mounts a heavy battery in a good cause; the steward, the old Bo'son, and the dog; either of them a fair match for a common man, but when acting all together, they can prevent any mischief intended for you. When the captain finds out what is in the wind, they'll all have to look sharp. You just lie quiet at anchor, as you are now in a good harbor, and wait until Livingston 'hails' you, and then shape your course. "

"Bill, it is not every young girl who could fully understand you, but I do, and thank you for what you have said. It has taken a heavy load from my heart, believing, as I now do, that my grand-parents will help me better than I can help myself. When the time comes I will tell them all."

"Now you are all right yourself; tell me, little singing bird, about Julia Fizzlebob."

"Bo'son, why do you call her Fizzlebob? that is not her name."

"It is as near it as I can get; but tell me about her," said the Bo'son.

"Julia has not changed in any way, unless it is to be more in haste than formerly to be married to a rich man. She wants Livingston, and I think Frank would marry her but for me, and may do so when he finds there is no hope of Susie Morton ever being Mrs. Livingston. Strange as Julia may appear to some, I love her too much to wish her the wife of Frank Livingston Julia is vain and foolish in some things, but has a good heart."

"A good heart is a good thing, but it wants a head to steer by to reach a safe port," was Bill's reply.

"Now, Bo'son," said the fair one, " we have been from home some time, and I have told you a long story about myself, and when the time comes you can help me—you have now helped me by telling me how to act. In a week or so Frank and Julia will be here, and after that cometh other things, to be seen and talked of, and I may just as well tell you some of them now as at another time: Livingston will be trying to win and marry Susie; Julia will be trying to win and have Livingston to marry her; Livingston will be in no doubt at first, and when refused, will be vexed, and believe, with the assistance of my father and mother, that in the end he will succeed. Julia will believe at first that I am anxious to marry Mr. Livingston, and she will be vexed, and when she finds to the contrary, will love me more because I love Frank less, and her hopes will be brightened and her prospects increased."

The Bo'son was pleased and amused to hear Susie talk again like herself, and felt that he didn't care much what course Frank and Julia steered, if they only kept clear of Susie.   He said:

" Julia Fizzlebob would be just the kind of a wife for such a man, and Livingston would be just the kind of a husband to suit Julia; I wish they may have each other, and from what you say, like enough they may.   When they are married I'll fire a salute."

" Now, Bo'son," said Susie, " let us gather some flowers and go to the house."

CHAPTER XVI.

MRS. GOODWIN VISITS THE WATERS' FARM.

WELCOME Goodwin being called from home before he found an opportunity of seeing Captain Waters and his family at their home, and Mrs. Goodwin learning that the family was settled, considered that it was a friendly duty to visit their new neighbors.

Mrs. Waters received her visitor with kindness and great cordiality, and after they had sat and conversed for a time together, Mrs. Waters ask her if she would like to see the house and its arrangements.   Receiving an affirmative answer, the two started on a tour of inspection.

There is no woman who has, and loves a home, but feels

a pleasure in making it comfortable for her husband and family; no matter how humble that home may be, she will be proud of it, and happy in showing it to her friends. With such a home as Mrs. Waters had, containing all that could make it dear and desirable, such a home as she had long wanted, but not before possessed, where she expected to spend with her husband her remaining days, and where she hoped to receive and enjoy the society of her children and grandchildren, it was only natural for her to feel a pleasure in showing visitors through the house.

Notwithstanding Mrs. Waters had spent many years at sea with her husband, in doing so she had also visited all the principal ports of the world, had freely mingled in the highest circles of society, and was herself an educated and accomplished lady. It was true that when she and Captain Waters were by themselves, they often used a language belonging as much to the ocean as to the land; but when in the society of others, that was dropped by Mrs. Waters, and nothing appeared in her language and manner but that of an accomplished lady. No one could be long in her society without discovering that she was a person of superior mind, and of refined manner, and Mrs. Goodwin didn't fail to fully comprehend it.

Mrs. Waters and Mrs. Goodwin passed from the sitting-room to the parlors, that were fitted up in what appeared to the visitor to be Oriental splendor. The carpets, curtains, mirrors and furniture, were all new of themselves, and new in style to that part of the country.

Mrs. Goodwin asked : " Hast thou been much in the company of those who worship with the Society of Friends, and speak the plain language of the Scriptures ? "

" I have been much in their company, both in this country and in England, and have had them as passengers in crossing the ocean.   I fully understand their customs and their language," was Mrs. Waters' answer.

" I am glad that such is the case, because we shall fully understand each other," said the visitor.

Mrs. Waters added : " I am also aware that members of your society are not pleased where others, not of the society, attempt to use their language in conversation with them."

" That is very true, friend Waters; it is best for us all to speak the language that we are accustomed to use. How beautiful all these thing are, and how neat they look ? It requires money to buy them, and time to keep them in order, which farmers and their families do not all have, or I have no doubt some of them would gratify themselves, and enjoy the gratification of having such handsome and costly things."

.Mrs. Waters could offer no reply to the last remarks of her visitor, but calling her attention to some Chinese ornaments on the mantles, asked if she had ever seen any like them ?

"I have not; where did they come from ?"

"We obtained them all in China, when we were last there, and also many other things that are very useful in housekeeping."

" Thou and thy husband have had many opportunities of seeing the world, and of procuring articles useful and ornamental in housekeeping."

"Yes, Mrs. Goodwin ; for forty years we have been sailing the ocean, and visiting other parts of the world, not always together, for our children sometimes kept me at home, but for the last twenty years I have made every voyage with him."

" It is not then strange that you have so many beautiful and costly things."

" During the last seven years," said Mrs. Waters, " we have been preparing to settle on shore and furnish a house, and consequently have purchased, in different parts of the world, whatever we thought would be useful ; but let us pass to other parts of the house."

They passed from the parlors to the kitchen, where Mrs. Goodwin was more astonished than she had been in the parlors. The old steward was there, dressed so neat and clean, with a white linen apron on, and every part of the kitchen was equally clean ; the copper sauce and stew pans scoured, and turned bottom up on a shelf used for no other purpose, the tin-ware equally bright, and such a quantity of it, as well as of copper and iron cooking vessels, and of everything that could be made useful, that they and the cooking-range (the first one used in that part of the country) were well calculated to astonish. Mrs. Waters introduced the steward, who was very polite to the visitor, and showed her the pantries and store-room, with all that they contained, which pleased and called forth expressions of delight from Mrs. Goodwin. Mrs. Waters then led the way to the milk-room, where Lizzie was found, not at work, but just looking to see if anything needed attention. What was seen in the milk-room was equally satisfactory, and then Lizzie was introduced, and there was seen the Bo'son's "butter pump," considered by the visitor as a great improvement on the old plan of churning, and also a great curiosity. The sleeping apartments on the second floor were visited, and the furniture, much or nearly all of it having been made in foreign countries, called out additional expressions of admiration.

After Mrs. Goodwin had seen the whole house, she was preparing to leave, when she was invited to remain, and with the family take tea, which invitation was accepted.

Soon after returning to the sitting-room, Susie made her appearance, a little browned with the sun, but looking as bright and as blooming as a young lady possibly could look. Mrs. Waters presented her, and said :

"She is the wildest and merriest girl, I think, that can be found in the country. Susie and the old Bo'son are as much together as they can be ; sometimes I fear that there is a love-match between them, only I have thought the Bo'son had another attachment. How is it, Susie; are you in love with the Bo'son ?"

"Yes, grandma, I am in love with Bill Thomas the Bo'son, and have been for many years ; but not the kind of love that leads to marriage. If I do marry, I hope I may have as good a man."

"So do I, pet ; the Bo'son is a good and true man," said Mrs. Waters.

Mrs. Goodwin asked, "Will I be likely to see that Bo'son I have heard so much about ?"

Susie answered, and said, " Yes, he will be at the house soon."

The three spent a pleasant hour in conversation, when the captain arrived from the field, and joined the party, and soon they were summoned to tea.

The captain talked for a while with Mrs. Goodwin, joined occasionally by his wife and Susie, and they were all three pleased with the plain, practical, good common sense and knowledge of things exhibited by Mrs. Goodwin.

After a time, the captain said: "So, Sue, what have you and the Bo'son been doing this afternoon ? You two and the dog ought to be together on some desolate and uninhabited island, and then you would be happy."

" In that event, grandpa, you would desert the farm, buy a ship, and sail around the world, navigating every ocean and sea, until you found and rescued us. Grandma would go with you, for you would both be unhappy without us."

"I know it, I know it," said the captain ; " I couldn't spare the Bo'son and dog."

"Nor the Bo'son's black-eyed Susan," was the reply.

"Well, let it be so ; I'll own up, pet."

At the table Mrs. Goodwin praised the food, and it was worthy of praise.

Mrs. Waters told the visitor that "the steward must have all the praise, for he had made and cooked all that is on the table. Lizzie and myself have been so engaged for the last week, that we have had to leave all to him."

Mrs. Goodwin had made up her mind not to be again astonished while at the house ; but this came very near it. The steward, when he came into the room, would pass around the table so quietly, and hand things so gently, that she thought him very convenient, and that he acted more like a gentleman than like a waiter. She also observed that he and Lizzie were spoken kindly to by all.

When the steward was out of the room, Mrs. Goodwin said :

"Seeing that you are so kind to those whom you have brought with you, I wonder that you do not all eat at the same table, as is our custom."

The captain answered, "It is not our custom, and that prevents it. The Bo'son has been with us twenty-seven years, the others over twenty years. We have always sat at different tables, We cannot change. None of us wish to."

After tea, the Bo'son was called in, and the lady had quite a lengthy talk with him, and said that Welcome, her husband, had expressed a strong desire to see and talk with him also.

"I remember him," said the Bo'son. "He called me William, and thought that was my name."

Bill asked Mrs. Goodwin to visit the midship-house, for, like his mistress, he wished his house to be seen, and possibly to be admired.

The invitation was accepted, and all three of the ladies, escorted by the captain, went to the Bo'son's midship-house. In that house were things that Mrs. Goodwin had never seen before, and did not know the use of; but all was so neatly arranged, that she was much interested, and separated from the Waters family, entertaining nothing but kindly feelings towards them, that she felt would ripen into mutual friendship.

CHAPTER XVII.

MRS. GOODWIN VISITS MRS. MOORES'.

IN a rural neighborhood, occupied by plain and honest farmers, mostly belonging to or worshiping with the religious society of Friends, which was the case in that part of the country into which Captain Waters had moved, it was very natural for the people to be interested in all that related to new comers. The new neighbors differed so materially from the old residents, in habits, customs, and mode of farming and living, that a deeper and more lively interest was felt in all their sayings and doings than was usual.

It was very generally believed that Captain Waters had at his command all the money he might wish to use, and consulted only his taste and desire in the amount that he expended.

It was evident to the farmers around him, that the captain did not expect the farm to support him ; or, if he did, he would be doomed to a very sad disappointment. Things were too nice,—too much time was used in keeping them so, and there was too much hired help, for any profit to be realized, was the general opinion expressed by all. Some of the neighbors, in their sincere desires for the good of the captain and his family, and without wishing in the least to interfere, had ventured some suggestions on the subject of farming at less expense, but found that the captain very respectfully declined all advice. It was very hard for so many well-disposed neighbors to witness such extravagance, and have no means of preventing it, when they would have gladly done so.

All of the neighbors freely admitted that the captain and his family were kind and courteous to all; that none of them seemed " stuck up," or thought themselves better than other folks ; " but why can't they be advised for their own good ? " was frequently asked.

There can be found in every community, individuals perfectly willing to aid their neighbors with any quantity of good advice, always having it on hand, some of which was received from others, and never used.

The day after Mrs. Goodwin was at the Waters' farm, and took tea with the family, she called on Anna Moores, the wife of a farmer living in the neighborhood. Anna had not received a very liberal education, was not in early life among Friends, but had been received into that society " by request," and afterwards married one of its members. Anna possessed some peculiarities, and among them was an indifference about personal appearance, and a fixed determination not to waste time in cleaning, scrubbing, sweeping, and dusting her house. She was a great snuff-taker, often saying that she could do very well with two meals a day, but not without snuff.

Mrs. Goodwin found Anna in the kitchen, it being her baking day. The kitchen looked very different from the one she visited the day before, at the house of Captain Waters. There was nothing bright in or about Anna's kitchen. The tin baking pans were as black as the stove in which they were used, and that article appeared not to have been cleaned or blacked since it left the foundry where it was cast. The floor, that wore no appearance of having of late been scrubbed, or even swept, was partially covered with tubs, pails for both water and milking, wood, arti- cles of children's clothing, men's boots, women's and children's well-worn shoes, and a few used-up chairs, some with wooden and some with flag-bottoms. There were two large pine tables in the kitchen, the tops of which, like the floor, gave no evidence of a recent scrubbing, and on one of the tables were many unwashed dishes, such as are used at family meals, and hung up around the room were articles of men's and women's clothing, old hats, bridles, halters, whips, an old white- wash brush, and a tin dinner - horn. The other table was occupied with what Anna was preparing to bake, and the dishes to be used in baking. Anna had in some way managed to get inside of some articles of dress, and among them a pair of blue-yarn stockings; the tops of which were not exactly in their places, nor were the heels of her shoes.

For want of time, or some other cause, she wore her dress so loosely that it was difficult to tell whether it was originally intended to button at the back, or pin in front. Her hair was done up at the back, with a small comb and large string; and to complete her apparel, she wore a large tow-cloth apron, of chocolate color, made so by snuff, grease, dust, and other coloring matters that it had encountered. The two half-dressed, unwashed children, aged four and two years, were unsatisfactorily mixed up with other articles about the kitchen floor, and in various ways and tones expressed their dissent.

Anna saw Mrs. Goodwin as she approached the house,

and met her at the door, giving her a kindly welcome, and saying :

" Thee must come right into the kitchen, for I am baking to-day."

Anna led the way to the kitchen, followed by Ruth Goodwin, and when there, Anna shoved a tub out of the way with one foot, and a pail out of the way with the other—she took a wooden bottom chair, and after wiping it with the chocolate colored apron, said :

" There, Ruth; thee can sit down there and not dirt thy dress. How glad I am to see thee ; I have been hoping that thee would call, but didn't look for thee to-day, as it is thy baking day as well as mine."

Anna having said this much, took a large pinch of snuff, and wiped her thumb and finger on the chocolate apron, blowing her nose immediately afterwards on the same article.

Mrs. Goodwin replied : " It is my baking day, but I always bake in the forenoon, and thought that thou wouldst have also been done with baking."

" I am later to-day than usual," said Anna. " I took up Dicksons' All of a Twist, after breakfast, and the story so interested me that I finished it before I laid it down."

" I think that thou must mean Dickens' last work, Oliver Twist ?"

" That was it, Ruth; I recollect now thee speaks the name, but I think so much about a story that I always forget all the names. O ! how that dear little boy suffered, and all because his mother died ?"

" Thou hast no idea that there is any truth in that story ?"

" Why, certainly, it must have been true, or it wouldn't have been put in the book," was Anna's answer.

" Now let me tell thee, Anna Moores, that those stories are all made up, and when a farmer's wife leaves her baking until afternoon, to read one of them in the forenoon, the time is very poorly spent. They are well enough for leisure hours and evenings, but not for mornings in a farmhouse."

Anna took a large pinch of snuff, wiped her fingers and

nose on the apron, and commenced mixing her bread. When the bread was partially mixed, she took her hands out of it, worked the soft dough from her hands, took a pinch of snuff, wiped her fingers and nose again, and went on with the bread mixing, saying at the same time :

"Has thee seen or heard directly from the Waters' lately ?"

"Yes ; I was there yesterday afternoon, went all over the house, saw all that was in it, was made acquainted with the steward, Lizzie, the old Bo'son, and his wonderful dog. The house is beautiful, and so are many of the things in it. The kitchen is a model one, with every convenience desired, and the steward, who has charge of it, is a pattern of neatness and order. The milk-room, and indeed every part of the house, are perfect and in order. I staid and had tea with them, and such bread and cake I have not often partaken of, and it was all made by the steward."

Anna had finished her bread, and when Mrs. Goodwin had done speaking, she walked to her and said :

"Did thee eat bread and cake made by a man ? I couldn't have done it, I should have been afraid of being 'pisened' with nastiness. I am very particular about what I eat and who cooks it."

Anna took a pinch of snuff, wiped on the apron, and began to put her bread in the pans to bake, saying as she did so :

"I use self-rising flour, because it saves time and work, and can be put in the pans to bake right away after it is made, and I don't have to get the dough off my fingers, and then get it on again."

"I don't know how much dirt it would take to poison thee, but it must be a very small quantity, if it could be found in any part of the house of our new neighbors."

"Well, Ruth Goodwin, I can tell thee that I hate nastiness above all things in this world, and as for eating anything that a dirty man had cooked, I know I should die first,—I couldn't anyways do it."

Anna again took snuff, and again used the apron, at the same time saying:

"Thee is now here, Ruth, and never having taken tea with me, I want thee should stay and take tea with me this afternoon. I am going to make some cake and some gingerbread before I wash my hands of this dough, and we will have a nice supper, that thee can eat with a good heart, knowing that everything is clean."

Then Anna took snuff, and used the apron.

Mrs. Goodwin thought that she would need a good, stout heart, to eat what she had seen cooked, notwithstanding Anna's hatred of nastiness, and so she declined, saying:

"It is not well to be two days in succession from home at tea-time, and I am hoping that Welcome may return this afternoon from Yearly Meeting."

"If thee can't stay to tea, tell me more about the Waters' before thee goes."

"Anna, they are a nice, pleasant family, every one of them, and that steward is a jewel in a kitchen, and looks and acts more like a gentleman than like a cook. He was dressed yesterday with brown pants and vest, white shirt, cravat and stockings; his shoes shone like polished black marble, and he had on a white linen apron and jacket when he waited on the table."

"Well, I do say for it, how funny; then they don't all eat at the same table?"

"No; the Captain and his family eat at one table, the steward, Bo'son and Lizzie at another; all of the farm hands live in the other house, with the farmer."

"Are the people that they brought with them from New York willing to live with the family, and not eat at the same table?" asked Anna.

"Certainly they are, and have done so for more than twenty years," was the answer.

"I should like to see the house and all the things," said Anna.

"Go there, then; but, Anna, let me kindly say to thee, not to read such books as thou hast been reading to-day; rise early every morning when in health, and when thou dost visit the Waters', take time to wash and dress thyself first."

Anna received what was said, as it was intended, kindly, and to say it, was the object of that visit by Mrs. Goodwin.

We would not have our readers understand that Anna Moores is a representative character among the society of Friends (sometimes called Quakers), for she is not. In that religious society, all, or nearly all, are noted for cleanliness in their houses and about their persons. The contrary is the exception, not the rule. Anna had not been brought up and educated among Friends, and reflects no discredit on the society for being what she is. Her heart was all right, but she " needed to carry a little more sail, and have a head to steer by," as the Bo'son would say.

CHAPTER XVIII.

THE BO'SON SOAKS THE BUTTS OUT OF A RAM.

THE Bo'son, after assisting in the repairs and improvements, in and about the house, and having arranged his own apartments to suit him, had turned his whole attention to farming matters, determined to learn how to do whatever was to be done; and being ready and willing, he learned very fast.

One of the first things that he desired knowledge of was milking. He thought that he could milk, when he first arrived at the farm. He tried, and didn't succeed. Under the teachings of the young man (assistant farmer), Bill had become a good milker, and he told the captain, when he returned from New York, all about it, saying:

" Captain Waters, the Bo'son can rig and work the cow-pump, and discharge a whole cargo of milk without any accidents."

" I am glad to hear it, Bo'son. How about salting sheep ?"

" The Bo'son hasn't tried that but once, sir ; and then he was struck with a squall, and knocked on his beam-ends," was Bill's answer.

"I think, Bo'son, that you will learn all about the duty of this ship, after a little time. And how do you like this country life?"

"Very well, sir. It is easier than ship's duty,—less hands to work, and no night watches."

Captain Waters was just one of the happiest men that could be found at sea or on shore. He had all that he wanted,—a good farm, well stocked, and around him, besides his wife, those who, for many years, had sailed under him. He could ask for nothing more than he possessed.

The Bo'son, now that the new ship was fully rigged, and in perfect order, felt that all his accounts in this world were squared, excepting with the ram, that "knocked him on his beam-ends." That account must soon be settled.

His mind had not been fully free from the subject since its occurrence, and he had determined how to settle it.

He had been down to the river, and saw a neighbor wash sheep. He knew the sheep of the farm were to be washed soon, and that would be his time.

The Bo'son had not long to wait. A few days later, Captain Waters gave orders for washing the sheep. When they were being driven to the river, where they were to be washed, the Bo'son followed, with the dog at his side, and there appeared to be a perfect understanding between them, that something unusual was about to take place.

The captain, with his best horses, and the every-day carriage, took Mrs. Waters, Susie and Lizzie to the river, to see the sheep washed, as neither of them had before been present on such an interesting occasion.

The Bo'son had arranged with all the men engaged in washing, that none of them should touch the ram with black legs, and that he only should have the handling of that animal. It was not the intention of Bill to wash "butts" early in the day, because he first wanted to get a little accustomed to sheep-washing.

Captain Waters had obtained a promise from the Bo'son, at the time of his first introduction to the ram, or directly afterwards, that he would not injure him, nor any other animal on the farm, and knew that he could depend on that promise ; but he also knew the Bo'son so well, that he expected some kind of fun, and told the women folks to be on the look-out.

Being in the water suited the Bo'son, and he washed more sheep, and washed them better, than any of the old hands, because he regarded it as good fun. He would take a sheep on his back, walk into the water, and wash it in less time than any of the other men. He saw that some of the men, when they had walked in up to their knees, would lay a sheep on his back, and draw him into deeper water. Bill tried and practised that mode of getting sheep into deep water, with good success.

The dog Bose appeared to enjoy the sport as well as his master, never leaving him, but going in and out of the water with the Bo'son, and watching all that took place.

About noon the Bo'son asked the man in the pen to catch "butts," and bring him to the gate. The man did so, and as usual helped lift him to the Bo'son's shoulder. In the meantime the dog was active, and ready to render any assistance that might be necessary.

When the Captain saw that the Bo'son had the ram with black legs on his shoulder, he said to his wife and others in the carriage :

"Now look out for sport, the Bo'son has what he calls ' old butts ' on his shoulder, the dog at his side, and they are all going to a watering place. Look at Bill's face— isn't it comic ? There is fun, joy and satisfaction, in every feature, and if that sheep isn't well washed before he comes ashore, then the face of the Bo'son is not a true index of his purpose, and the Bo'son himself has changed his character."

When the Bo'son had the sheep well on his shoulder, and was moving towards the water, he first addressed the dog, and said to him : "Now is our time, Bose." Bill walked with the sheep on his shoulder a little way into the water, and then let him slide from the shoulder, turning him at the same time on his back, and in that position taking him into deep water, saying :

"Old butts, the Bo'son has you afloat, not in blue water, but it will answer just as well. Look sharp, old Bose, we both owe him some, and this is settling day. Let me see you butt, black legs, will you ? Ha, how do you like that? Butt if you like,—do you want more salt, and will you sail for Bill's counter again ? "

During this time Bill was continually dipping the head of the sheep under water, and holding it as long as it was prudent, and washing him with a will ; then again putting his head under, and when it was above water talking to the sheep, which seemed a great satisfaction to him.

"This, old butts, is my play; I know what I am about when on the water, and you can't get the best of me. I thought a day would come when I should square that little unsettled account, and it has come. I remember you, and if you ever reach land again, you will remember me ; and should you butt me again, and I get you afloat, that will be the last of you ; mind now I tell you so."

The dipping and washing continued for full half an hour, and until the Bo'son discovered that the ram was growing weak, when he desisted and said :

" Bose, you hold him here till I get ashore."

The dog took the sheep at the side of the neck and held him fast. Had the sheep been fresh instead of being nearly drowned, he would have been no match for the dog in the water; but weak as he was, Bose found no difficulty in keeping him afloat, and from approaching the shore.

The Bo'son worked his way to the shore, having the same joyous and satisfied countenance that he left it with. When a little distance from the edge of the water, he dropped on his hands and knees, in the same position that he was when he received the second and succeeding butts from the ram, when they first became acquainted with each other ; he then called to the dog and said :

" Let him come, Bose, I am ready for him."

The dog did let him come, but came also with him, to be ready for whatever might take place. Bill kept his eye over his shoulder as the ram neared the shore, which he did very slowly, and when on land could scarcely walk from weakness. With his head near the ground he passed the greatest possible distance from the Bo'son, and joined his washed companions.

Bill jumped to his feet, took off his hat, swung it around his head and shouted: "Hurrah! hurrah! hurrah! I've soaked all the butts out of that ram."

Captain Waters and the ladies had watched the whole proceedings with interest, and seemed to enjoy it nearly as much as the Bo'son did. The other men that were engaged in sheep washing, stopped work before the Bo'son finished washing "butts," and also watched him, and listened to what he was saying to the dog and the ram, as all had understood from Bill that the washing would do him good.

When Bill took off his hat, and shouted forth his hurrahs, Captain Waters stood up in his carriage, and did the same. Mrs. Waters nodded to the Bo'son, Susie shook first her sunshade, then laid it on her lap, clapped her hands, and laughed with unfeigned joy; Lizzie took off her sunhat, and imitated the Bo'son's motions with his, as nearly as it was possible for her to do, and she also made an effort to shout hurrah!

Mrs. Waters was the least demonstrative of any of the party, and yet, in some way, she showed that she also enjoyed the Bo'son's triumph. She said:

"Joseph Waters, you are almost as much of a boy as the Bo'son."

"That's so, Nancy; but who can help being amused at the odd doings of Bill Thomas, the old Bo'son? I couldn't get vexed with him if I tried, and it does my heart good to see him look so satisfied. I wouldn't have minded if he had drowned the old ram, only I knew there was no danger, because he is a good judge of how much water it takes to drown an animal. He said at the time the ram butted him, 'that he would settle with him,' and now he has done it, and will laugh himself to sleep many a night thinking of it."

After a little time, Bill went to the side of the carriage, and touching his hat, said:

"Captain Waters and ladies! the account between the Bo'son and the ram is settled. It has stood longer than

I generally let my debts stand, but I was not in a condition to settle.   All right now."

Bill again touched his hat as he left, and Captain Waters drove home with the carriage.

CHAPTER XIX.

FRANK AND JULIA ARRIVE

THE long looked for event of the coming of Frank Livingston and Julia Fizzlebaugh at length occurred. They arrived at the farm, and were kindly received by each and every member of the family.

Captain and Mrs. Waters hadn't the least idea that Frank Livingston visited the farm with any other object in view than that of spending a few days in the country, and of being the traveling companion of Julia.

Every one present, and some that were absent, had an object in view, and one that they much desired to obtain, and to accomplish it required great tact and energy on the part of some of them.

Captain and Mrs. Waters' only object was to see that all enjoyed themselves, and lacked nothing that would contribute to their happiness.

Frank Livingston's object was to offer himself in marriage to Susie, and receive, as he felt certain that he should, a favorable answer ; and, after spending a few days at the farm, to take up his residence at Saratoga Springs, only twelve miles distant from the farm, and from there visit his affianced wife frequently, enjoying in her society the pleasures and comforts of a country life.   Julia Fizzlebaugh's object was to secure by any possible means Frank Livingston for a husband, and be to him what he wished to make Susie.

The father and mother of Susie and Lizzie were very anxious for the success of their daughters, and though employing different means to obtain it, had the same object in view; but their object was unknown to each other.

The Bo'son's object was to be ready for a severe engagement, if necessary, to defend Susie, and prevent her from being "cut out of the fleet" by the ship of an enemy. His ideas were not very clear as to what duties he had to perform ; but whatever they were, he intended to be prepared for them by keeping a good look-out, and having the dog always at hand.

Before going up, Frank had sent some of his horses, carriages and servants to Saratoga Springs, that they might be ready there for his use. He directed his coachman to meet him at the cars, and take Julia and himself to the farm, and after arriving there, sent him to the Springs, to return early the next day, with a pair of fancy horses and a light buggy wagon.

Susie Morton and Julia Fizziebaugh retired to rest, both occupying one room. It being early, and they having much to say to each other, they did not immediately take to their beds. Julia was the first to speak of the subject nearest her heart, and say to her companion :

"Susie, you don't know how much I want Frank Livingston for a husband, nor what lengths I would go to attain my object ; and I want you to understand that I am fully aware that you also want him as a life-long companion."

"Cousin Julia, I do not want Frank for a husband, nor shall I ever marry him. My parents are anxious that I should be his wife, but that isn't a sufficient reason for me to marry him."

" Has he offered himself to you ?" asked Julia, her voice trembling enough to betray her feelings.

" No," answered Susie, " he has not ; but I presume he will the first opportunity he has, for I believe that is his object in coming here."

" And shall you give him a decided answer, declining such an offer ?"

" I shall," was Susie's reply ; " but he will not be satisfied with it, and will seek the assistance of my parents to aid him in securing me for his wife."

" Will your father and mother give him the required assistance ?" again asked Julia.

"Yes," said Susie; "they will, and do all in their power to encourage him, and persuade me to become his wife. They would force him upon me as a husband, if they could, believing it for my good; but it will be of no use."

"Then your mind is firmly made up, not to be altered?"

"Yes, Julia, on that subject it is; and however much my parents may desire it, I cannot gratify them at the expense of my own happiness; and besides, they do not know him as I do, or they would not wish him to be my husband."

Julia fetched a long breath, as if relieved of a heavy burden, that had rested on her mind, and then said:

"Cousin, I have been deceived, because I really believed, that should Mr. Livingston seek your hand in marriage, that he would be an acceptable offering to you"

"You are now undeceived, and will give me some credit for my candor."

"Yes, Susie, I will, and be equally candid with you, by saying that when Frank Livingston finds he can't marry Susie Morton, he may be disposed to offer himself to Julia Fizzlebaugh."

"In that event," said Susie, "I hope Julia will also decline the offer."

"Not I; I should only be too glad to receive such an offer, for Frank has all the requisites I wish a husband to possess."

"Julia, as you value your happiness, do not entertain such ideas. Frank cannot, will not make you happy."

"Never you mind that, cousin; I know better. You are well acquainted with me and my wishes—you know that I am determined to have a rich husband, and Frank Livingston is the man, if I can only, in any way, secure him."

"Julia, take my advice, and give him up, and give up all desire of having him for a husband. He is unworthy of you, or any other woman of high principles and affectionate feelings."

"High principles and affectionate feelings may be given to the dogs, for what I care, so far as marriage is concerned. Give me a rich husband, for I want life, company, best society, high living, costly dresses, rich jewelry, horses, carriages, servants, comfort and ease for myself, and money alone will procure for me my wants.

"I am very sorry, Julia, to hear you talk so. I had hoped that the time passed since you left school, about two years ago, had been so spent by you that you would see the world as it should be seen, and have learned that true happiness consists not in fashion and high-life, but in a congenial companion, and a proper discharge of domestic duties."

"I can tell you, Susie that I hate domestic duties, and don't mean to spend my life in scrubbing, sweeping and dusting a house, not I; I don't make my own bed now, nor take care of my room; mother does it all, and I am sure I shall do no such thing after I am married."

"How then, Julia, do you spend your time? You have no servant except the little black girl that answers the door bell, and your mother must have more to do than she is really able to perform. Do you never help her?"

"No; I have not been brought up to it, and am not going to begin now. I'll tell you how I spend my time. I am out a great deal to balls and parties nights, and don't return home until near morning, so that I seldom leave my bed before ten or eleven o'clock in the forenoon, and then ma always has a hot breakfast for me, and after eating it I don't feel like doing anything, and I lie down on the sofa, and in warm weather fan myself and read. If the weather is not warm, I read without fanning. O! it is such a luxury to read a good novel, and think of a rich husband."

"Who washes and irons your light ball dresses?"

"Ma does all that; you don't know what a considerate mother I have,—she does everything, and I have nothing to do. She makes many of my dresses, and all my other clothing. If I have a pocket handkerchief to hem I take it right to ma, and no matter what she is doing, she will stop and hem it for me. After lunch, I do my shopping and make my calls, and that is the time ma takes to do up my dresses."

"Julia, you have a false notion of life and its duties, and I fear that you will have to suffer for it. I think your parents are much to blame in so bringing you up and educating you, that you cannot fully comprehend life and its responsibilities, and have only one idea in your head, and that is a rich husband, believing that all other things necessary will be added."

"Give me the rich husband and I'll take the chances," was Julia's reply.

"Do you know, Julia, that Mr. Livingston is a gambler, and a wine drinker, and may soon waste his large fortune?"

"No, Susie; I do not know it, and cannot believe it. He is a gentleman, and has a large fortune. I know nothing of his gambling, and don't believe it. I know that he sometimes drinks freely of wine, but what of that? I would sooner put him to bed every night drunk, than marry a poor man."

"Is it not possible, Julia, for me in some way to change you, or persuade you to think no more about marrying Mr. Livingston? Are you willing under any circumstances to accept of a man that I reject? Have you no pride, no self-respect, no higher aims, no nobler aspirations than a rich husband, no matter what else he may be?"

"That is all, cousin; because I expect, with the attainment of a rich husband, to be put in possession of all other things that my heart so ardently desires."

"What will you do with such a man as Livingston, if he becomes poor? He has no profession, has no knowledge of business,—nothing to fall back on by which he could support a family."

"That is something I don't think of; that, if it comes at all, must come in the future, and the present is what I want to enjoy, and let the future take care of itself."

Susie finding that for the present she could make no favorable impression on the mind of her cousin, concluded to leave that part of the subject, and trust to circumstances and the future for greater success. Susie had told Julia more about Frank than she had communicated to any one else, but entertained no fears that Julia would betray any secrets or say a single word that would be against the character and good standing of Frank Livingston. Susie had no idea what course Julia would pursue, and it is possible that Julia herself had not fixed in her mind how she would act.

Susie told Julia that an arrangement had been made for a visit to the Springs on the following day; that Frank had invited her to ride with him, and that she had accepted the invitation, that he might have an opportunity to say all he wished.

Julia was not displeased to find that Mr. Livingston would soon know his fate,—so far as his proposal to Susie had anything to do with his fate,—and after that she would trust to favorable circumstances for the accomplishment of her own object.

Susie retired to rest and to dream of the future; Julia took a book and seated herself at the shaded lamp to read and scheme of the future and of Frank Livingston; and so for the present we leave the young ladies.

CHAPTER XX.

FRANK LIVINGSTON OFFERS HIMSELF IN MARRIAGE, AND IS REJECTED.

AT the usual hour in the morning the family assembled in the breakfast-room of the country-house, but Frank and Julia did not appear.

Julia continued to read and think many hours after Susie was asleep, and as was her custom, had no inclination for early rising in the morning. Susie had called her, but she declined to get up.

Frank Livingston, knowing the Captain's temperance habits and principles, had provided himself with wine, and after all the family had excused themselves and wished him a good-night, he went out on the piazza with a bottle of wine, glass, and some fine Havana segars, and there remained drinking, smoking and thinking until near morning. It was a lovely summer night, well calculated to invite and keep a person in the open air, but it was not in this case the lovely evening that kept Frank from his bed,—it was the force and power of habit. For years Frank had not retired to rest before two o'clock in the morning, nor had he left his bed before ten o'clock. Susie Morton, as usual, was up and dressed at sunrise, assisted her grandmother and Lizzie in arranging the rooms and dusting the furniture, and was as cheerful and apparently happy as though no unusual event was about to take place. Such was her self-command, and so confident did she feel in her ability to meet and overcome in the contest about to be entered into, that she was not in the least disturbed.

Captain Waters made it a rule in his house to inform visitors at what hour the meals were on the table, and when that hour came the meals were always there, and partaken of; there was no waiting for absentees.

Visitors sometimes appear to forget that there is no authority in the code of hospitality that warrants or excuses a disregard of the well-established rules of a family.

After they were seated at the table, Captain Waters asked if the visitors had been called in time to dress for breakfast, and being answered in the affirmative, said:

"They both know my custom; we will not wait. I think but little of people that can't get up in time for breakfast; they never amount to much."

Susie felt that her grandfather would be a powerful ally in case of a long siege, and it would be to her interest to secure an alliance with all who could aid her.

Noon is the general dinner time among farmers, and the Captain having been accustomed to dine on shipboard at that hour, continued to do so on the farm.

About eleven o'clock Frank and Julia made their appearance, and as it was so near dinner-time, concluded not to take any breakfast, though Julia said:

"It is very strange that Aunt Nancy didn't have some warm breakfast ready for me; mother would."

The Captain and Bo'son both heard the remark; the Captain said:

"She needs something besides a warm breakfast; a smart whipping would do her good."

The Bo'son said: "She aint worth counting; no good about her."

Immediately after dinner the party prepared for a visit to the Springs. Mr. Livingston offered his coachman to drive the Captain's carriage, and as the Captain was unacquainted with the road, the offer was accepted. Mr. Livingston and Susie rode together; the Captain, Mrs. Waters and Julia, with the coachman, filled the family carriage.

The old Captain couldn't exactly understand why Susie was with Frank, and he asked Julia why it was.

Julia answered: "Uncle Joe, men have their likes as well as women, and why shouldn't Frank? and may-be he wants to say something to her."

"He had better mind what he says to her, or he will have me on his 'weather bow;' he don't get up early enough in the morning for such a wife as our Susie would make," was the captain's reply.

Had Julia been anything but what she was, such expressions would have disturbed her. They did not, but on the contrary, were encouraging to her, as they lessened the chance of Susie's acceptance, and increased her own prospects at some day of receiving a proposal from Frank.

Julia could not divest herself of the idea that in the end Susie would accept, because she could not fully comprehend the possibility of such an offer being rejected.

The drive over to Saratoga Springs was a pleasant one; not by the road now traveled, as at that time there was no bridge at the Narrows of the Lake, only a scow-ferry, and most of the travel was by Stafford's bridge, across Fish creek.

There was much company at the Springs—many known both to Captain Waters and to Frank, so that a few hours were passed very agreeably in visiting the different watering spots, and enjoying the walks of the well-laid out grounds belonging to the different hotels.

It was when returning from the Springs that Frank Livingston, after deep thought, and under more embarrassment than he was accustomed to feel, made the attempt to convey to Susie Morton the feelings and wishes of his heart. Frank had a heart, and a good one; it was his head that was weak and always at fault. He was not deficient in knowledge, nor did he want language to convey his views and wishes. He thought his offer would be such a surprise, such an agreeable surprise, that there would be no hesitation on Susie's part in accepting it.

Frank said: "Miss Morton, are you aware that I have long been an admirer of you,—long loved and adored you?"

Susie looked him calmly and earnestly in the face, without being in the least excited, or disturbed, and replied:

"I am not. How could I be?"

"I know," continued Frank, "that I have not shown you how deeply I have loved you, because I wished to keep in reserve this great surprise of offering you my hand in marriage, which I now do, with all that I possess in this world, and leave it to you to name the day of our union."

"Susie was still calm, still undisturbed, and bestowing the same kind look that she gave him when he put the first question to her, answered in her softest and sweetest tones of voice;

"Mr. Livingston, I thank you for your kind offer; thank you for the honor you are willing to confer on me, and for the expression of your esteem; but without consulting my parents, or taking time for consideration, I most respectfully decline it."

Until the last sentence was uttered, Frank had no doubt but his offer would be accepted, subject to the approval of Susie's parents, nor could he for a moment comprehend that such was not the case, so certain was he that his offer would be favorably received. He carefully weighed in his own mind every word of the answer, and thought the last part of it was only to gain time and have the proposal repeated, and then said:

"Miss Morton, you do not certainly mean for me to understand that you positively decline my offer, and refuse to take it into consideration for future decision?"

"I can't see, sir, in what plainer or stronger language I could have put my answer, and leave no doubt on your mind of my meaning."

"How is it possible, Susie, that you can disregard such an opportunity of being settled in life, and of making me happy, and securing your own happiness?"

"Mr. Livingston, when two persons enter into a marriage engagement for mutual happiness, they must be congenial in all things, and love each other, or they don't attain the object of their union. In this case whatever love there is, certainly is all on one side, for I do not, cannot love you as a wife should, and therefore cannot marry you. I speak very plainly,—it is best in such a case, and is a trait in my character that I have inherited from my grandfather."

The more Frank listened to Susie, the more anxious he was to secure her for his wife, and he urged upon her his birth, fortune, position in society, and his sincere love for her, and what a brilliant career she would have in the world of fashion ; and then told her that he had made the proposal with the consent and sanction of her parents, who would bestow upon their union a father's and a mother's blessing.

Susie Morton remained firm in her decision, but still kind and calm in her manner, saying in reply :

"Frank, I wish you well from the bottom of my heart (one of her grandfather's expressions); would do anything consistent with my own happiness to secure yours; shall ever think the more of you for this offer of yourself and all you possess, but I cannot be your wife."

A new idea now flashed on Frank's mind. There must be an object in the form of a young man, that somehow stood between them, and he said :

"Pardon me, Miss Susie, if I trespass the bounds of prudence and propriety, and ask if a prior engagement prevents you from accepting my offer ?"

Susie's eyes flashed with an unusual brightness. The fire of the Captain's eyes was seen, though only for an instant, when the same calm, quiet face that she had maintained through the whole conversation was again before the man who had asked the question, and waited for an answer. Frank saw the rapid changes of Susie's countenance, and attributed them to any but the right cause.

After a moment Susie answered, saying :

" Frank Livingston, I will be as candid in answering your last question as I have been in answering all the others that you have asked, though you really have no right to put the last one, or to expect an answer ; but I will concede it in this case. Yours is the first offer of marriage that I have received, and if I knew it would be the last, my answer would be the same. So let us continue to be friends, and not again allude to marriage."

Frank was astonished at the firmness and candor of the woman he so wished to make his wife, and equally surprised that she should reject his offer, and by no means disposed to give up the contest.

"I can't promise that;" said Frank, "but here we are at home, and for the present our conversation must close."

As they drove through the gate into the yard, Susie whispered in Frank's ear: " Let it close forever."

CHAPTER XXI.

THE BO'SON UNDERTAKES TO NAVIGATE AN OX-CART, AND BREAKS AN AXLE-TREE.

THE Bo'son having learned from Susie Morton enough of what transpired between Mr. Livingston and herself during the ride from Saratoga Springs, to satisfy him that there was no immediate danger to be apprehended, turned his attention to other matters. Bill had a great desire to become master of the art of driving oxen, and he lost no opportunity of improving himself. The farmer and his assistant were both willing to instruct the Bo'son, because the Bo'son was always willing to help them in whatever they were doing.

The Bo'son had fixed up a small building, that was some distance from the dwelling-house, as a blacksmith's and carpenter's shop.   He had all the necessary tools to make the little establishment complete.   Any of the farming utensils that were out of repair could be put in order at the shop, and that made it very convenient for the farmer, saving him the time that would have been necessary to take them to the village.

Such had been the Bo'son's life and habits, that he must be busy about something, and as there was nothing more to be done at carpentering, blacksmithing or painting, he devoted his whole time to farming.

Bill concluded that he knew enough of the science of "ox-navigation" to take charge for a short voyage near the coast, and run without a pilot.   He yoked up the oxen, put them before a cart, and went to the meadow, where the farmer loaded him with hay, and Bill, to use his own language, "made sail for a home port."

The oxen, and with them the cart, hay and Bo'son, went along very well for a time, but in passing through a gate, the oxen suddenly sheered off, struck the gate-post, knocking it down and breaking the axle-tree of the cart. The cart fell on one side, and the oxen stopped.

Bill, as was his custom when in trouble, went for his captain, who was found on the piazza, reading the marine news from a late paper.   The Bo'son touched his hat, at the same time saying :

"Capt'n Waters, is the farm well insured ?"

"Yes, Bill; the buildings are all insured ; the land is safe without insurance.   But why do you ask ?"

"The ox-cart has been stranded on a reef, and may be a total loss.   I want you to go alongside, sir, and give orders how to save what can be saved from the wreck."

The captain went, and found matters as above stated, and asked Bill how it happened.

"I was running along," said Bill, "under easy sail, when I found that I was coming to a narrow part of the chan-nel, and I sung out, 'Steady, there, mind your lee wheel ;' then I remembered that I wasn't on board of a ship, and I sung out 'shee," when I ought to have sung out 'haw,' and she answered her helm, 'fell off,' and before I could bring her to the wind, was hard and fast on the lee-shore, and a wreck. Now, sir, what I want is orders how to save the cargo and float the wreck."

"In the first place, Bo'son, take the oxen from before the cart, and then go and call Mr. Harrowell, ask him to come here with the horses and hay-wagon, and we will lighten the wreck, and after that get her off."

Aye, aye, sir!" was Bill's reply.

When the farmer reached the place, the hay was un-loaded; a rail fixed and lashed under the cart, and it was then taken to the shop, Captain Waters saying, "there isn't time to send it to the village."

"Captain," said Bill, "you don't want to send that cart away to be repaired."

"You have no timber, Bo'son, fit for an axle-tree."

"Yes, sir, I have; some of that seven-inch Delaware oak, such as the staunchions between decks of the 'Neptune' were made of, will do for the axle-tree of an ox cart, as it is home seasoned."

"Have you any of that here on the farm, Bo'son?"

"Yes, sir, enough for a dozen axle-trees, and it can't be beat for that or any other purpose; as it has been seven years on the ship, it is well seasoned."

"That is so, Bo'son; but what made you think of bringing timber to the farm?"

"I thought, sir, it might be wanted, same as the tar; you haven't called for anything yet that your Bo'son hasn't on board, and there are many things stowed away that have not been wanted; when they are, the Bo'son will 'break them out' you may be sure."

Bill went to work with a will, and soon constructed a new axle-tree of the seven-inch Delaware oak, and when it was finished, he offered to bet his best go-ashore jacket that he could "knock down every gate-post on board the ship without breaking it."

After the ox-cart was ready for use, Bill found a saw-log that would square eighteen inches, and prepared it for a gate-post. With the assistance of the farm hands it was set in its place, and the gate again hung. When it was finished, the Bo'son said:

"There's a gate-post strong enough to break all the

axle-trees on board of the farm.   The next time that the
ox-cart gets ashore on this coast and breaks something, it
will not be a gate-post or axle-tree."

Captain Waters had his eye on the Bo'son, watching
him while he was mending the cart and fixing the gate.
It was not with any ill-feelings, but with pride and satisfaction, that an old ship-master was watching his Bo'son,
carpenter, blacksmith, his man of all work and all care,
repairing some damage done for want of proper knowledge
or proper care.   The Captain mused awhile, and then
went to the house, where he found Mrs. Waters in the
sitting-room, engaged with some light sewing work, and
he said:

"Mother, that Bill Thomas is worth his weight in
diamonds; he is just the same on the farm that he was on
the ship; if anything gives way, the Bo'son is on hand to
repair it, and has with him the materials to do it."

"Well, what do you think, 'Old Boy,' you would do
without him?—could you 'navigate' the farm without your
Bo'son and steward?"

"No, Nancy, not very well, though I have not ordered
the Bo'son 'to call all hands and ready about,' nor have I
'carried away a spar and wanted him to make another.'"

"If you have not parted a log-chain, you have come
very near wanting the tongue of an ox-cart fished," was
the lady's reply.

"That is so, old girl, and I perceive that you have not
forgotten the evening when you helped Bill with some
land phrases in the cabin of the 'Neptune.'"

"And for it was accused of mutiny," said Mrs. Waters.

The old captain put his arm around the neck of his wife,
and gave her an affectionate and hearty kiss, saying as he
did so :

"There, take that for your mutiny."

The lady must have been used to such treatment, for
she was neither vexed nor disturbed, but after returning
the kiss, continued her work, and said :

"Joe, my old bluster, there will always be a young and
warm place about your heart, that neither years nor climate can change."

"I hope so, for I don't wish to grow cold until the end of the voyage, when I stop breathing; and I am at present so agreeably situated, that I don't care how long the voyage lasts. All of the old crew, the Bo'son, steward and Lizzie, appear so well satisfied with the change, and so contented on the farm, that there is nothing now wanting to complete my happiness."

"Except a husband for Susie."

"He will come along, all in good time," said the Captain.

"He may be here now, Joseph, in the person of Mr. Livingston."

"Nancy Waters, would you be willing that our pet should be his wife?"

"No, never; I had rather follow her to the grave, or see her buried in the middle of the ocean, than see her the wife of Frank Livingston."

"She is an uncommon girl, Nancy, but I think she would not make up her mind to marry any-one without saying something to us about it."

"Such, Joseph, is my opinion; but we must watch over her, and if we find that her heart is warming towards him, we must tell her what his habits are."

"Never you fear, mother, Susie will not throw herself away on such a fellow, if he had twice his weight in diamonds to back his suit with."

CHAPTER XXII.

FRANK LIVINGSTON TALKS WITH THE FAMILY.

FRANK Livingston felt that he was placed in rather an unpleasant position, but did not doubt his final success, which he concluded would be accomplished with the assistance of Susie's parents, notwithstanding her decided denial. Little did he realize with whom he had to deal, little did he understand the strength of Susie Morton's character, or the combination of persons and influence that she could array against him.   It may, in such cases, be considered unfortunate for a young man, who has the richest gifts of nature, improved and polished by education and intercourse with the best society; one who has been born heir to a fortune ample enough to gratify every taste and every desire ; if he has not been taught that the world and people in it were not created especially for his benefit. Frank Livingston had been so much sought after, and so often given to understand, by young ladies and their parents, that an offer of marriage would be considered a very agreeable affair, and accepted; that in making such an offer for the first time, and having it declined, which was so unexpected to him, that the whole groundwork of his reasoning was swept away.   An earthquake, or the sun suddenly turned to darkness, would not have more surprised him, and yet he had firmness and command enough over himself to completely hide his feelings and disappointment from others.   He spent the night as he had the previous one, on the piazza, drinking, smoking and thinking ; and when he left the piazza for his bed, it was near morning, and he had fully determined how he would proceed to accomplish his object of securing the hand of Susie Morton in marriage.

Frank determined first to renew the proposal to Susie, and if she continued to decline the offer, he would secure the assistance of Julia on the inside, and of Bo'son, as a guard, on the outside; and then, by way of the Springs, visit New York, and seek the aid of William and Laura Morton, father and mother of Susie.

His first object was to obtain an interview with Susie, which he did about an hour before Julia made her appearance from her sleeping apartment.

Susie was alone in the sitting-room, engaged in looking over the papers and late publications of the day, when Frank entered, and in that easy and polished manner natural to him, said :

"Good morning, Miss Susie."

"Good morning, Mr. Livingston."

"I hope you are not suffering any ill effects from your ride yesterday."

"None whatever; the weather was so fine, and the roads so good, that the ride could not but be pleasant," was Susie's reply.

"The ride having been pleasant, Miss Morton, I hope that after a night's reflection you will be disposed to give my proposal a more favorable consideration."

"Mr. Livingston, if there had been the least chance of my giving at a future day any different answer than I gave you yesterday, I should have frankly told you so; but there has been and can be no change in my decision; the answer was final."

"I still think that you have not considered all the advantages of such a union, and therefore shall still hope and believe that your parents' wishes and influence, joined with my own pleadings, will change your mind."

There was a perceptible flush passed over the face of the young lady, but it instantly faded away, leaving her countenance as calm and as decided as before it appeared. Few could have seen Susie Morton, sitting as she was at the centre table, to which she had returned after leaving it to receive Mr. Livingston when he entered the room, combining as she did in her mind, mildness and firmness, and in her person, beauty and grace, and not have loved her. Frank Livingston knew not until this interview how much he really loved her. He had been pleased with her, and had concluded to marry her, and so sure of an acceptance was he, that he had wagered a large sum of money with a brother gambler that within a certain time Susie Morton would be his wife. Susie, after sitting a moment in silence, looked him mildly in the face and said:

"Mr. Livingston, the wishes of my father and mother in regard to myself will be gratified on my part, at the sacrifice of every desire and every personal consideration but that of my future happiness. Their influence cannot change my mind in regard to yourself. Now Frank, take the advice of one you consider and wish to call your friend. Go seek some young lady's hand in marriage, who can love you as a wife should love her husband, to make both happy; discard some of your young men acquaintances, get married, become a domestic, and you will become a happy man. Susie Morton will pray for such a result, and rejoice in seeing you realize it."

"By all that is lovely, if you will be my wife, such shall be my future life."

"It cannot be, Frank, you have my answer, and with me there can be no change. So let me say good morning to you," and she immediately left the room.

After Susie had left the room, Frank sat and thought for a time, and was there joined by Julia Fizzlebaugh, the very person he most wished to see.

Frank Livingston was in just that state of mind which qualifies a man for acts, and urges him on to do them. He had much at stake. He had set his heart on having Susie for a wife, he had wagered his money on the result, he had offered himself and been refused. . He hoped still to succeed, and knew that if he failed he must lose his money, and bear the jeers of his friends. Nothing must be left undone to accomplish his object, so he at once opened the subject by saying:

"Miss Fizzlebaugh, I want your assistance; I have offered myself to Susie, and have been refused; I must make her my wife if possible, and you must help me."

Here was a beautiful state of things, and none but a half or wholly madman would have sought such assistance, nor would Frank Livingston, had he known all the facts. It was a fine opportunity for Julia, knowing as she did so many of the circumstances; and whatever else she may have been, she was smart enough to perceive all the advantages of a pleader for Mr. Livingston in such a cause, and she at once said:

"Frank, I will do anything that will secure your happiness, and aid you as far as I can in persuading Susie to become your wife."

"I only wish," said Frank, "for you to talk to Susie at proper times and in a proper way, of the many advantages that she would enjoy by marrying me, of the high position in society that she would occupy, and the wealth that would be at her command; urge everything that you can think of in my favor, and write me if there is any young man calls often to see her. You can talk freely with the Bo'son, and have him take your letters to the office, for he will be in my interest."

Julia promised to do what she could, and they parted, each feeling for the other some considerable friendship. Julia now would have opportunities of writing to Mr. Livingston, and she intended improving them.

Frank, after leaving Julia, sought and found the Bo'son in his midship-house, where he was making a canvas covering for the farm wagon, that was to be used in taking the products of the farm to market.

"Bo'son," said Frank, "what do you think of Miss Susie Morton?"

"I think, sir, that black eyed Susan is just the best and handsomest girl in the world?"

"Would you do her a favor and a kindness?"

"When the time comes that Bill Thomas refuses to board black-eyed Susan when she is in distress, may he be struck with a squall, and lose all three masts," was the Bo'son's answer.

"I thought as much, Bo'son; now give me your hand."

The Bo'son gave his hand, because he seldom refused it, and was willing to shake hands with anybody on that subject.

"What I want of you, Bo'son, is that you will keep a sharp eye on Miss Morton, and not let her get married to any improper person."

"You can depend on my doing that," said the Bo'son.

"If you find any such chap around, will you tell Miss Julia?"

"Yes, sir; if I can't run him off with the dog,—and I am sure to do so if black-eyed Susan don't want him about."

That was not exactly what Frank wanted, but he was talking to a son of "Neptune," and felt that he must make every suitable allowance. Frank did not for a moment consider himself an improper person to be the husband of Susie Morton, so nothing that the Bo'son had said applied to him.

"You will have no objection to taking letters to the office for Miss Julia?"

"No, sir;" was the Bo'son's only answer.

"I can then surely count on your looking after Miss Susie?"

"If there is anything sure, that is."

Frank took out his pocket book, and taking some bills from it, handed them to the Bo'son. Bill declined them, saying:

"Put up your bills, sir; the Bo'son never takes money for doing his duty."

Frank put up his money and said : "I shall depend on you."

"You can do that with perfect safety," answered the Bo'son.

Frank then shook hands again with Bill, and left.

When Frank turned away, Bill shut his right eye, and drew down the right corner of his mouth, following him with the other eye,—he commenced talking to his dog.

"Yes, old dog; the Bo'son will look sharp after black-eyed Susan, and when such a craft as that 'cuts her out of the fleet,' Bill Thomas will throw his Bo'son's whistle overboard, and in the next engagement act as powder monkey."

———

CHAPTER XXIII.

FRANK LIVINGSTON LEAVES THE FARM.

FRANK Livingston left the farm-house of Captain Waters and went to Saratoga Springs, where he remained a few days, and then to New York, in order to confer with the parents of Susie Morton. He called on Mr. Morton at his store, and they had a lengthy conversation in the private office, and there arranged for a meeting that evening, at the house of the Mortons.

Frank called, and found Mr. and Mrs. Morton at home to receive him. He frankly and fully told them all that had taken place between their daughter and himself, detailed their whole conversation just as it occurred, and then declared his fixed intention of using every honorable means to become the husband of Susie Morton.

Mr. and Mrs. Morton had letters from their daughter, in which she mentioned that Frank and Julia were at the farm, spoke of their visit to the Springs, and in her last letter wrote that Mr. Livingston had left; but in none of her letters did she in any way allude to the offer of marriage from him. That very much surprised both her father and mother.

Mr. Morton and his wife were much grieved at the course taken by their daughter, and encouraged Mr. Livingston not to despair, assuring him that he should have their united influence, and also the influence of Captain and Mrs. Waters, who, they felt certain, would see all the advantages of such a marriage.

It was arranged that at the end of three weeks Mr. and Mrs. Morton should visit the farm together, and there, assisted by the Captain and his wife, bring such an influence to bear on Susie as would be irresistible. It was also arranged that during that time nothing should be said or written to Susie on the subject, nor should Mr. Livingston visit her, but at the appointed time he should be at the Springs, ready to go to the farm when sent for.

It was thought by all that a few weeks in the country, where Susie would have time to reflect, might change her views, and that after consideration she would look upon the offer in a more favorable light.

Julia and Susie freely conversed with each other, and fully understood how matters were, excepting the conversation and arrangement between Frank and Julia. That Julia kept to herself. She fulfilled her promise of showing Susie all the advantages of a marriage with Mr. Livingston, and as she was now fully satisfied that Susie would not marry him, her determination was strengthened to marry him herself if possible, and to accomplish that object she would have sacrificed the happiness of her cousin, or even the cousin herself.

Julia repeated to Susie her determination, and exacted from her a promise not to reveal it. Susie also repeated her irrevocable resolution not to marry Mr. Livingston, and then used her strongest arguments, and exhausted her childlike and truthful eloquence to lead Julia to the same conclusion. Never were such appeals before made by one so young. She told her cousin again that it was impossible for her to be long happy with such a man as Frank for a husband. Susie urged against the marriage of her cousin with Mr. Livingston: his habits of drinking and gambling, his constant association with men who were debasing him with their characters and acts, his being out late every night, and how entirely unfitted he was to make any woman long happy as his wife. That however large his fortune then was, the course that he was pursuing would soon lessen, and eventually exhaust it all; and then besought her, by every consideration, to forbear in time, and seek her happiness where it was more sure to be found.

Julia listened to her cousin as though she had been a grandmother, and was giving her the benefit of many years experience, and at the conclusion of Susie's very kind and strong appeal, Julia indulged herself with a loud laugh, and said :

"What a sensible, silly little creature you are, if the terms are not too contradictory. One would think that you had the advantage of many years experience, and still you really know nothing of the world, the fashionable world, in which I must live and flourish to be happy. I do not wish to receive without proper consideration, what you so earnestly and kindly mean, but you know not the joy and intoxicating pleasures of fashionable life, because you have not tasted them, and you have been so much at sea with your grandparents, that Aunt Nancy has filled your little head with strange notions about life and its duties.

"For which I shall ever be very grateful," said Susie.

"You talk of love, duty, contentment and life in a cottage on the bank of some river, and I talk of life in the gay world, at the fashionable summer resorts, with wealth enough to meet the expenses, and shine as brightly as the brightest. You talk of home duties and housekeeping; I have no taste for such things, and hope I never shall have, for if I marry Frank Livingston, or some other rich man, I shall have servants to attend to those matters."

" Has affection nothing to do with marriage in your opinion, Julia ? "

" Nothing whatever with me, my sentimental cousin; money, money, high life and easy times is what I want, and will have, if I can get them."

" I would press this subject more home to your consideration, Julia, but I see that it is useless. I greatly fear, entering life as you propose to do, that you will live to regret and suffer for your want of a proper understanding of its duties and responsibilities. In my former conversation with you on this subject, a few evenings since, I then had only faint hopes of changing your views, and those hopes have now faded entirely away."

" Yes, Susie ; it must, by you at least, be understood that I am not to be a bread and butter wife. I shall pretend to love Frank, and endeavor to make him and the world believe it, but such foolish feelings have nothing to do with my marriage." Here Julia excused herself, and going to her room wrote the following letter to Mr. Livingston :

" WATERS' SNUG HARBOR, *August 2d,* 185–.
" FRANK LIVINGSTON, ESQ.,

" DEAR SIR : In accordance with your wishes I have closely watched our mutual friend, and lost no opportunity to talk with her of the many and great advantages the young lady will enjoy who becomes your wife. I have spoken to her of your fortune, family, position and person in the highest possible terms; presented to her the brilliant career that the future Mrs. Livingston will have in the fashionable world, and that in refusing the generous offer you have made, she rejects one of the noblest and best of men, with a heart overflowing with warm and strong affection for her ; such an offer as she will never again receive, and one that few would refuse. The only answer I can draw from her is : ' I do not love him, and under no circumstances will I marry him.' Susie is a strange girl, who has been much with her grandmother, and from her received some strange ideas.   There has been no young gentleman visiting her, nor has she, to my knowledge, received letters, except from her family.   It is my firm opinion that her heart has been bestowed on another, or why should she refuse one who has few equals and no superior?   The only reason that can be assigned, is that her pure and childish heart has been bestowed on or exchanged with some one, and that she has some of the stubborn nature of her grandfather, and determines not to change it.   You have my warmest sympathy for your suffering in disappointment, and the assurance that I will do all in my power, to aid you in securing happiness.

"Yours to command,

"JULIA FIZZLEBAUGH.

"P. S. Please have some lady direct your letters to me, in case you write, or your hand may be recognized. J. F."

CHAPTER XXIV.

WELCOME GOODWIN VISITS THE BO'SON.

WELCOME Goodwin, having returned from the New York yearly meeting, and having a wish to be better acquainted with the the man who had so interested him, and that to him seemed such a strange creature, called on Captain Waters, and after spending an hour inspecting the house and furniture, and in conversation with the family, who appeared much pleased with him and he with them, asked:

"Where is William?"

The captain answered: "I don't know who you mean; we have no person of that name on the farm."

"I mean that man with such an unusual dress on, who was at meeting with you the first time you attended. Since then I have been away, and not seen him, and I am very desirous of knowing more about him."

"Oh! you mean Bill Thomas the Bo'son," said the captain.

"Surely that is what he said of himself, now thou bringest it to my mind ; but thou knowest peradventure that we Friends do not call people by nick-names, and that was my reason for asking after William."

"His name is no more William than mine is Jonathan, for I have seen it written many times."

"Well, well, friend Waters; tell me, if thou canst, why he comes to have such a name."

"Mr. Goodwin, you must ask the Bo'son that question."

"I shall do so, with thy permission, when I see him. Is he on the farm ?"

"Yes, sir. He is in his house 'strapping a block' for neighbor Hardengrip, and if you would like to see him, Mr. Goodwin, we will walk out there," said the captain.

"That is exactly to my mind, friend Waters, for I am credibly informed that in the house thou speakest of there are many, very many curious things not before seen in these parts, and that some of them have been brought from foreign countries."

"That is really so, Mr. Goodwin. The Bo'son has brought from the ship many articles, some that may be useful, and some that I can see no good cause for bringing; but Bill says 'they'll come handy some time before the voyage ends,' and he may be right."

Captain Waters and Welcome Goodwin left the dwelling, and went to the midship-house, where they found the Bo'son engaged as Captain Waters had stated. When they went in Captain Waters said :

"Bill, Mr. Goodwin has called to see you and your house."

The Bo'son left his seat, a small wooden stool, placed on a piece of old canvas spread on the floor, to keep any little drop of tar or grease that might fall, from spotting the floor. On the canvas, and near the stool, was a small bucket of tar and another of slush (grease), a "marlin-spike" and "serving-mallet," which the Bo'son had been using. He had just completed his job when the gentlemen entered. Bill advanced to meet Mr. Goodwin, saying :

"You are very welcome, sir; but excuse me, I can't

shake hands with you, for I have a little tar and slush on my fingers from that block-strap of Mr. Hardgripe. I hope you are very well, Mr. Goodwin ? "

" I am in usual health, Bo'son, and hope that thou art also well ? "

" Very well, thank you, sir ; and if you will wait a few minutes, I'll clear up the decks, wash my hands, and be ready to serve you."

The Bo'son rolled up the piece of canvass, after putting away the little buckets, and then swept the floor, afterwards offering chairs, and asking the callers to be seated. Captain Waters wished to visit the hay field where the men were, and saying that he would soon return, left Mr. Goodwin and the Bo'son by themselves. Mr. Goodwin looked carefully and earnestly around the room for some minutes, and then said :

" William, thou hast indeed many wonderful and strange things in this room."

" Mr. Goodwin, let me tell you again that my name is not William ; it is Bill Thomas, but I am mostly called Bo'son."

" It is not the custom of our society to call any one out of his name, and I am far from wishing to depart from that custom ; and thou hast again brought the subject forcibly to my mind, and will not, I trust, feel agrieved with me for asking why thou hast such a strange name, and who could have given it to thee ?"

Bill related to the friend all the circumstances of his early life, and how it happened that he was called Bill Thomas, a name that he had been known by for many years, and one that he did not wish to change.

" It is wonderful, strange, and indeed marvelous, that a boy should have been so circumstanced and so neglected in childhood and early youth, as not to know its parents, and not to have a name. Who superintended thy education ?"

" No one, sir ; I was never inside of a school-house until I came to the farm. I mean the one up the road, and near the meeting-house."

" Canst thou neither read nor write ?"

"Yes, sir; I can now do both tolerably well."

"Where, then, didst thou learn?"

"On the ship, since I have been sailing with Cap'n Waters."

"Who has been thy teacher?"

"The steward mostly; some little I learned from Lizzie."

"Has the steward sufficient learning to do more than teach the first simple lessons of an education?"

"Yes, sir; the steward has a superior education, speaking and writing the French, Spanish, and German languages. He has done all the cap'n's writing for many years."

"Has he many books here with him?"

"Yes, sir; enough to fill six full-sized sea-chests."

"Thou givest me but a vague idea of the number of books that the steward may have, as I have no notion in regard to the size of a sea-chest."

"A full-size sea-chest—that is for a whaleman—is three feet and a half long, by two feet square."

"The steward, then, must have very many books. Dost thou think that he would be willing for me to see them?"

"Certainly, sir; and we'll go to his room after you have looked over the things here."

"I shall be glad to do so; and now I will say to thee, that in future I can call thee Bill Thomas, or Bo'son, whichever first comes to my mind, and not feel that I am departing from the customs of our society. If thou wilt explain the use of these things that are unknown to me, and tell me their names, I will be obliged to thee."

The Bo'son called his attention to the signal-lanterns, and though of different colors, might be useful on the farm or anywhere else. There were a great many lanterns of different sizes, and the number only astonished Mr. Goodwin. The top-sail sheet couplings, the Bo'son said, would be handy on a farm in case a log-chain was broken. Mr. Goodwin was much pleased with the coupling, and wished to buy one. The Bo'son declined to sell, but asked him to accept of two of them, saying:

"I have enough on board to last many voyages, and you can have more if you need them."

" Thou art very kind, and I am much obliged to thee, but are these things thine to give; do they not belong to friend Waters?"

" It was Cap'n Waters' money that paid for them, but the Bo'son that took them from the ship and brought them to the farm, or they would have been left in the ship and not been paid for. Whatever is in the Bo'son's charge on board of this farm, the Bo'son is allowed to sell or give away. I have sailed with Cap'n Waters too long for him not to trust me, and he knows that everybody belonging to the ship will look after his interest. He would be offended if I asked permission to give you them couplings, or anything else that I saw fit to give away."

" My mind is perfectly clear on the subject, and I feel easy after what thou hast said, and free to accept thy gift."

Mr. Goodwin, after examining all that was worthy of notice in the Bo'son's house, asked to be taken to the steward's room; that was in the mansion house. When they passed into the house, the steward was in the kitchen, but Bill called him, and he went with them to his room. The room was a large one, over the kitchen portion of the house It was in perfect order, the ceiling of good height, the walls papered and the floor carpeted. The furniture consisted of a mahogany bedstead, with a bed made up and covered with a white counterpane, two large rocking-chairs, one arm-chair for sitting at a writing-table, writing-desk and book-cases, all of mahogany; there were also two wardrobes, a bureau and washstand, the last two with marble tops. The steward, as usual, was neatly dressed, and immediately on entering the room asked the visitor to be seated in one of the rocking-chairs, taking the other himself. Mr. Goodwin, after sitting a few minutes in silence, said:

" Steward, I am so amazed at what I have seen to-day, and am now seeing, that I am not prepared to learn what I wish to know. I am amazed; there must be something mysteriously attractive that binds you all so closely and harmoniously together. At some other time, if thou art willing, I shall be very glad to talk with thee and learn thy history."

The steward said: "I shall be pleased to see you in my room any day between one and four o'clock, listen to your instruction, or impart to you any information in my possession."

"I thank thee, steward; now farewell," and warmly shaking the steward's hand, left, as the steward said—

"Good-bye, sir."

CHAPTER XXV.

AMOS HARDENGRIP AND FAMILY

AMOS Hardengrip, the man that the Bo'son strapped a block for, was one of nature's strange productions, who seemed to have only one idea, one wish, one ruling passion; and that was to get and keep money; possessing not a single wish to purchase with it any comforts, nor even necessaries for himself or his family.

He owned a farm of one hundred acres, about seven miles from that of Captain Waters. The farm was so situated, that in the hands of any other man would have been a pleasant and productive one. The farm descended to him from his father, and though his for twenty-five years, during all of that time no repairs had been put on the buildings, no improvements made in them, nor had a pound of paint been used on the inside or outside of any of them. The house was small, inconvenient, much out of repair, and hardly fit to live in.

He had three children; a daughter married and living in one of the new States at the West; one son about twenty years old, that the father hired out to one of the neighboring farmers, with the understanding that the farmer wasn't to pay the boy one cent of his wages, as the father was in the habit of saying: "All the money the boy earns to the day that he is twenty-one years old, and on that day until twelve o'clock, is mine, and I mean to have it." The other son was eighteen years old, and was on the farm with his father. The mother of the children died when the youngest son was two years old, and within a year the father again married, and the second wife reared the children.

Amos Hardengrip, at the time of which we are writing, was fifty years old; a tall, spare, raw-boned man, who was six feet high when he held his head up, which was very seldom. He had a thin, lantern-jawed face, with not enough flesh on it to produce and sustain any considerable growth of. beard, as the sides of his face and peaked chin were only thinly covered with coarse reddish hair, and there did not appear to be intellectual, nor any other power or soil enough in his head, to produce a decent crop of hair. He was not bald, but never had much hair, for the reason that the head wasn't of sufficient strength and depth to grow it. He had small, dull gray eyes, a few long black isolated teeth, and a whole appearance and manner that made him disagreeable wherever he went. He had but little education, and knew nothing of the world beyond the small circle in which he moved.

The second wife was a Christian, and proved a mother to his children; made a slave of herself for them, and failed in doing as much and as well for them as she wished to, in consequence of her husband's ruling passion to make and save money. They would have gone without proper clothing but for her, when they were young. She asked for money to supply the children with clothing, and he refused it. She went to the store, purchased what was needed, and had it charged. He paid the bill after trying to make things unpleasant at home, but forbid the storekeeper from giving credit again. It made no difference; when more clothing was wanted, more was charged to Amos Hardengrip, and Amos, after a fuss, paid the bill, to avoid a suit at law.

When the children were young, he sent them to the district school, because his wife made him believe they were in her way, and would prevent her from doing the necessary work of the farm-house. When the daughter was nine years old, he "declared that she was old enough to spin, and could earn the bread that went in at her mouth." After that she never went to school At the same age the boys were taken from school for the same reason, and put to work on the farm.

The Bo'son in some way became acquainted with Mr. Hardengrip, and offered to re-strap a block used to raise water from the well. Such a man would not refuse such an offer.

It was about a week after the time spoken of in the last chapter, that Mrs. Hardengrip died. She had not been well for some time, but he refused to call a doctor, saying " It is nothing but a cold, with a little fever. Stir around and work it off; that is better than having to pay a doctor for nothing. Keep a stirring, I say."

Betsey Hardengrip had stirred too long and too much, when she was unable to do so, from illness, and at last passed away, without the neighbors knowing that she was sick.

When it was known that she was no longer living, neighbors, who had not been at the house for years, called to give consolation to the afflicted, and offer such assistance as the circumstances rendered necessary.

It is ever thus, when death unexpectedly invades the dwelling of a neighbor. All indifference, all unkind feelings and all dislikes, for the time, are forgotten, or have no influence to prevent a well or undeserved sympathy for the living, and a proper respect to the departed.

The people of that neighborhood, alive to duty and sympathy, were not deterred from either, by the life and character of Amos Hardengrip.

Welcome Goodwin, never backward when any unusual circumstance called for aid or sympathy, with others went to what all expected was indeed a house of mourning. Bill Thomas the Bo'son, actuated by the same feelings, in the absence of Captain and Mrs. Waters from their home, felt that it was his duty to call and offer all the assistance possible.

Mr. Goodwin and the Bo'son met at the gate of Hardengrip, and entered the house together. They found others of the friends and neighbors already there.

Welcome Goodwin, being a minister in the society of Friends, was expected by the others to speak in sympathy, as the sad occasion called for. After sitting in silence for a time, Mr. Goodwin said :

"Amos, thou hast met with a great and unexpected loss, and we have called to offer our sympathy, and what consolation we can give."

"Yes, Mr. Goodwin, it is a great loss, at this season of the year ; if it had been after killing-time, when the fall work was over, I shouldn't have minded it so much, but now it comes a little tough."

"Thou, Amos Hardengrip, hast lost such a wife as every man has not been blessed with; a woman esteemed by all who knew her."

"Betsey was a very profitable wife,—she was a small eater and a good worker, and it didn't cost much for her clothes."

"She has left a vacancy that can't be filled; and thy children, though she was not their own mother, loved her as such, and will deeply regret her death, for she always did well for them."

"At the cost of many dollars to me," said Amos.

"Hast thou no regrets, no feelings of sadness nor sorrow for the death of one thou hast so long lived with, and who has been so kind and good to thee and thine ?"

"I have already said that coming before killing-time and the fall work, I do feel bad. What more can I say? I have some things to comfort me for the loss. There will be one mouth the less to fill through the coming long winter, and Betsey has left much good clothing, that I have been looking over this morning, and calculating will bring considerable money, which, with the preserves and sweet-meats that she lately put up, when all sold for cash, will more than make me whole for her loss."

"Amos, is there nothing but dollars and cents to be considered and sought after? Is there no friendship, no regrets, no kind remembrance, no broken links in the chain of affection, that money is not an equivalent for?"

"Money is the most precious thing in the world, if one could only get enough of it; and now let us talk business," said the wretch of a Hardengrip, who had not during the conversation exhibited in his face a single mark of sorrow, and certainly had not shown by his language any sorrow of the heart. He addressed himself to Bill, and said :

" Bo'son, you are handy at all work ; can you make me a coffin to bury the woman in? You will find old boards enough around, and if not, you can knock some off the fence that'll do, and save buying ? "

The request of such a man made to a warm and noble hearted sailor, who could estimate the cold-hearted Hardengrip at his true value, received a proper answer. The Bo'son said :

" Mr. Hardgripe (Bill could never get his name right), I have made many things, but not a box of that kind. I don't want to make the first one of old stuff; but I'll tell you what I can do. I have an old hammock that I will give you, and I can sew misses up in that, put some stones at the feet, and you can then bury her in the river, and that will save the cost of digging the grave."

" That would be some saving, Bo'son; but the people would talk about it, and might think strange of me; but, now I think of it, there is a man over near the lake that owes me a trifle. He is a carpenter, and will pay in work, so I will ride over there this afternoon, and kill two birds with one stone—collect the debt and get a coffin, to bury the woman, and in that way save the boards that are on the fence. I dare say some of the neighbors will dig the grave. May-be you will help them ?"

" It is a kind of work I don't know anything about. I may learn by the time you die, and then I will dig your grave with a good deal of pleasure, and may-be the neighbors would like to help me," said Bo'son.

Friend Goodwin here observed: "We all came, Amos, to sympathize with and assist thee, but I cannot see that we are of any benefit to thee, as thou hast no tender feelings that we can reach and touch."

" If your women folks could come in at killing time, and give me a lift, it will be of some account, as I shall then miss Betsey."

All that were present had become so disgusted with the man that, without any ceremony, they left, and when out of the house, Friend Goodwin said to Bill :

"That man has no heart.   I am glad there are but few like him in the land."

"He is so mean, and so worthless, that if he should fall overboard, my dog Bose wouldn't jump over and save him from drowning," was the Bo'son's reply.

CHAPTER XXVI.

GEORGE WILSON VISITS THE WATERS FARM.

ONE fine afternoon, not long after the death of Mrs. Hardengrip, George Wilson very unexpectedly made his appearance at the farm.   It was known that the ship had arrived, but he was not looked for at the "Snug Harbor," as the farm was generally called.

Captain and Mrs. Waters were still from home, though expected that evening.   They were over in Washington county, visiting an old sea-captain and family settled there.   The two captains and their families had been long acquainted, and for some years separated, until this visit, which had been prolonged beyond the time set by Captain Waters to be at home.

The old dog was lying on the horse-block, his favorite place when not engaged on any special duty, when he suddenly arose and sat up for a moment, and then gave one bark, and started down the road at the highest possible speed.

The Bo'son knew, by the action of the dog, that some friend was coming, and he supposed it to be the captain. The old dog was so delighted that he was nearly frantic, and the Bo'son soon discovered who was coming, and went to the gate, which he opened, and standing beside it, hat in hand, waited for the buggy to pass.   The old Bo'son's face was lit up with an expression of joy and gladness that was spreading all over it.   As the carriage was passing through the gate, without having it stopped, Mr. Wilson jumped and stood at the side of the Bo'son. They shook hands, and then the Bo'son took him in his arms and started for the house; but George said: "Hold on, Bo'son, none of that; put me down, and put on your hat, old boy."

The Bo'son obeyed orders, for that was one of his standing rules, no matter what the consequences might be. After a moment the Bo'son said:

"George—Mr. Wilson, I mean—you don't know how glad I am to see you. Coming, too, without being expected, makes it all the more welcome."

While all this was taking place, the two were passing from the gate towards the house, where they were met by the steward and Lizzie, who gave George Wilson such a reception as might be expected from those who for years had sailed with him on the ocean. The dog, that recognized his shipmate when some distance from the gate, was repaid for his sagacity by the caresses he received. Susie and Julia were engaged in their room, and hearing an unusual stir, concluded the captain had returned, and when informed by Lizzie who had come, Julia saw a sudden change in the face of her cousin that told a tale, and one that Julia was delighted to be in the possession of. Those changes told Julia Fizzlebaugh that Frank Livingston had nothing to rest a hope on.

Deep down in the pure heart of Susie Morton were hidden feelings known only to herself, and that would not have betrayed themselves had Susie been on her guard; and she was not now aware that Julia was possessor of her secret.

The young ladies arranged their dresses, and then went to the sitting room, where George Wilson and the Bo'son were waiting to receive them.

The meeting was friendly and cordial between George and Susie, for they had been some years acquainted with each other, and made a number of voyages together. Julia, herself, had she not been an interested spectator, could not have discovered any traces of latent feelings existing with either of them. They were both on their guard, and Julia on the watch.

Julia had not before seen George Wilson, and when introduced by Susie felt that she was making the acquaint-

ance of no ordinary man, and that if she was in the line
and business of love, and he not otherwise engaged, she
could love him very dearly, and especially so if he only
had plenty of money; but knowing that Wilson was poor,
no matter how much better and nobler he might be, by
nature and practice, than Frank Livingston was, there
were weightier reasons than the nobility of nature and
the dignity of manhood, that must influence her in marriage.　　Julia did not fail to see that Wilson was. just
the kind of a man such a girl as Susie Morton would
be likely to love.

The young ladies, George Wilson and Bo'son, remained
in the sitting-room until the dinner-bell rung, and then
the Bo'son left, after arranging with Mr. Wilson to meet
him in the midship-house in the afternoon.　Bill said to
the dog when he was about leaving:

"You, Bose, can stay with Mr. Wilson, if you wish;"
and Bose did stay.

At the table there were only Susie, Julia and George
Wilson.　The conversation was general, and when the
meal was over, Wilson and Susie were left by themselves,
Julia going to her room.　They had nothing particular to
say to each other, except to inquire after friends, and
speak of the voyages they had made together.　They
were to each other as brother and sister, yet there was
deep down in the heart of each warm feelings of affection,
that neither dared to confess, and that each wished for
the present to hide from the other.　They could not but
find a pleasure in each others company,—could remain
together unembarrassed, and freely talk on any and every
subject but the one nearest their hearts.

Mr. Wilson, according to promise, met the Bo'son in
his house, and there learned how things had been managed
on the farm, and that all there were contented.　The
Bo'son told Mr. Wilson about his first "milking voyage,"
and how it ended,—also his first introduction to "butts,"
the ram with black legs, and how that account was settled.　It was very difficult to tell which of the two
laughed the loudest or heartiest over those affairs.　It
was very evident that both enjoyed themselves.　Each

continued to be interested in what the other was telling, until the arrival of Captain Waters, which was just before supper-time.

Captain and Mrs. Waters were pleased to see Mr. Wilson, and gave him such a reception as convinced him that he was a welcome visitor.

Captain Waters inquired about tne ship "Neptune," in which Wilson had made a voyage since the ship had been sold. Mr. Wilson informed his old captain that the new owner and new master were pleased with the "Neptune," and he had engaged to go on another voyage to Liverpool in the ship. He also stated that he had only a few days leave of absence, and must make but a short visit to the farm, and spend only a few days with those that he had sailed with from the first of his going to sea; but he felt under so many obligations to Captain Waters and his family, that he couldn't make another voyage without coming up and seeing them, and learning how they were situated.

"You did right, George, perfectly right," said the Captain, " and I should have blamed you if you hadn't have come, my boy. It shows that you don't forget your old friends. How did you leave your mother and sister, George? "

" I thank you, sir; they are both very well, and wished to be remembered in kindness to you and the whole family."

"I am pleased to hear from them, and learn that they are well. How, George, do you like the Bo'son's quarters, and his system of navigating a farm ? "

" Bill Thomas can't change much, sir, and he will be good at everything he undertakes to do. That house of his, on the inside, is an improvement on the ' Neptune's ' midship-house, though in many respects like it; on the outside, with the mast, bowsprit and figure of old ' Neptune,' it shows that whoever rigged it was a finished sailor; but what a lot of stuff he has with him ! "

" The Bo'son, George, says ' everything there will be needed before the voyage is up;' and I shouldn't know how to sail the farm without him. He can do now anything that the others can do, and a great many things that they can't do. He is Bo'son all the time, everywhere, and will be while he lives, and is the same favorite in this neighborhood that he was on the ship. How did you get along without him?"

"I missed him, sir, more than the captain and first mate did, because they never had him with them; but Bill Williams, who had been three years in the ship, was our bo'son, and did very well, and we had a carpenter and a blacksmith, and the three of them together, were not equal to the old Bo'son."

"George, I would just like to see any three men that were equal and as good as Bill Thomas is by himself. They cannot be found, I believe. If I should lose him I think I should sell the farm, for without him and the steward it would be more care than I want on me, but with them I have but very little care about anything. Now, George, as you were traveling a long way, we may as well say good night all around, and 'turn in.'"

CHAPTER XXVII.

A FAMILY SOCIABLE.

EARLY the next morning George Wilson was up and out in the yard where the men were milking, and he saw the Bo'son milk two cows. When they were all milked Bill took two large pails of milk and asked George to go with him to the milk-room. At the milk-room they found Mrs. Waters, Lizzie and Susie. Susie was in the same morning dress and apron that she wore when she took her first lesson in butter-making. She was skimming a pan of milk when they went in, and the visit of George being unexpected, Susie blushed a little at his seeing her in such a dress. The slight blush only increased her beauty, and George Wilson from that day, and for many years afterwards, positively declared and said: "I never before nor since saw such a heavenly looking and beautiful creature."

The compliments of the morning were hardly passed when Captain Waters put in an appearance, looking pleased and very happy. When he was around, and Susie with him, there was sure to be a lively time. Captain Waters and the old Bo'son were about on a par in their opinion of Susie Morton, and both of them thought her little less than an angel, and considered it next to impossible for her to do anything wrong; and it was very seldom that Susie made even a slight mistake in not saying or doing the right thing. After the Captain had wished them all good morning he said:

"George, you see that sly puss of a Susie, sailing around the cream jar,—cats, you know, like cream. What do you think of her for a dairy-maid?"

"I think, sir, that like the Bo'son, Susie will learn only what is worth knowing, and be useful when learned. She will excel in whatever she undertakes."

"You are about right, George; but I pity the man who gets her for a wife, unless he can exercise more control over her than I am able to, for she will have her way, and get up early in the morning."

"Joe Waters," said his wife, "you had better tack ship and stand off shore, or you will be wrecked on a churn, or lose your life by being drowned in a jar of cream."

"I am not much of a coward, Nancy, and if I meet with any disaster that disables me, Susie will scull me ashore in her skimming shell."

"Not if you talk naughty about me, and tell wrong stories, Commodore."

Susie was in the habit of calling her grandfather Commodore, when they were fighting their sham battles.

"Having the Bo'son under your lee, you think you can venture to carry more sail, do you?"

"I can't carry this large pan of sour milk to the leader. Bo'son, you please do it for me?"

The Bo'son would have carried the farm over the river if Susie had wished it, and the moving of the milk-pan was the work of only a moment. Mr. Wilson examined the Bo'son's butter-pump, and asked where Julia was.

"Thunder and marlin-spikes!" exclaimed the captain; "Julia will not 'break bulk' before 'six bells' in the forenoon watch. I don't know what time she 'turns in,' but I know that she never 'turns out' until near noon. She is not worth her weight in sour milk, and if sold at auction wouldn't bring enough to pay freight and charges."

"Commodore, you stop talking about my cousin, or I will smother you in cream."

"Or with kisses," was the captain's reply.

"Julia is not more to blame than her father and mother; and, grandfather, you are very severe on poor Julia."

While Susie was speaking, her black, bright eyes filled with tears, and the captain noticed that her feelings were touched, and he said:

"Pet, you are over-tender. I, too, pity Julia, believing that she will have to learn some severe lessons before she leaves this world. Now let us go to breakfast, and fix on the plans of the day while eating."

It was decided that George should dispose of his time at his own pleasure during the forepart of the day, and that in the afternoon they would have a ride on the bank of the North river to Schuylerville, and beyond, as the road was very fine.

George and the Bo'son spent most of the forenoon in rambling over the farm, every acre of which the Bo'son had made himself acquainted with, and could tell his young friend much about. From the old residents the Bo'son had learned much about the battle fought on the farm, when the freedom of the country depended, or appeared to have depended, on the fate of that battle. What Bill had learned he imparted to Wilson, and in doing so deeply interested him.

George Wilson had served under the Bo'son when only a boy on board of the ship, and by him been taught all that he knew of seamanship. He learned to respect the Bo'son first, and afterward to entertain for him the strongest friendship, and when little more than a boy, Wilson was made an officer over the Bo'son.

The Bo'son was proud of his boy pupil, respected and

obeyed him, as he would one who had been his superior in age and experience, as in position.

Bill Thomas loved George Wilson next to Susie Morton, and his love for them was as the love of a father for his children. Nothing could have taken place in this world, that would have so pleased the Bo'son, as to have seen his two adopted children (for such he considered them) united in marriage.

Bill was satisfied that they loved each other, but was in a position that he could ask neither the question. Susie had confided some secrets to his keeping, but that one was not among them. For safety, Susie could not have been more secure if the secrets had been locked in her own bosom. There was never a hurricane hard enough to have blown them out of the Bo'son's safe keeping. The Bo'son, however, told Wilson that Frank Livingston had been there on a visit, and what took place between Livingston and himself. He was under no obligations to keep that as a secret. The Bo'son did not lisp a syllable of his knowledge gained from Susie, nor what he knew of her feelings. He said, when speaking of Livingston : "He don't sail fast enough to overhaul such a trim clip-per as black-eyed Susan. He will lose ground on every tack, and be hull down to leeward."

Wilson fully understood that Frank Livingston was not in his way; but what had he to say, or what right had he to think of anybody's being in his way ? That he loved Susie, he knew very well; whether she loved him or not he had no means of finding out. He had nothing but himself to offer, and therefore could not ask the question.

He was young, with nothing but his profession to depend upon for a support. He was now second officer, and how long it would take to reach the command, was more than he could tell. He said : "Bo'son, let us return to the house."

In the afternoon the ride was taken, as it had been proposed. The party consisted of the Captain, Wilson, Susie and Julia ; the Captain driving.

If there is anything that a sea-captain loves, besides his family and ship, it is a good horse or a pair of good horses.   That love is not exceptional,—it is universal, unless the captain goes to sea until he is so old as to be incapable of loving anything.   Captain Waters loved his family, his friends, his ship, and his horses in a superlative degree.   He loved and used horses when a boy and a young man ; he understood them and was a good driver. For his own use, he would keep nothing but the best of stock, and on that occasion showed George Wilson that he could handle horses, as well as ships.

The party returned in time for tea, and after spending a social, pleasant evening, all retired to their rooms. George Wilson was to leave the farm the next afternoon for New York, and to make a voyage before he again visited the family.

The following day, and that on which Wilson was to leave, he and Susie took a pleasant walk up to Burgoyne Hill, after breakfast and before Julia left her bed.   They spent two hours in their rambles, and rested in the shade of the noble trees on the hill ; but nothing was said by either that .the other could construe into more than an expression of common friendship.   As they were walking home, George said :

"We have been so much together when young, that we are like brother and sister, and we shall not easily forget each other."

"I cannot see why we should wish to do so, George. You know that grandfather and grandmother look upon you almost in the light of a child, and expect to see you here at the end of each voyage, and all the family will welcome you home."

"I can assure you that I shall always find a pleasure in coming."

They returned to the house, took dinner, and in the early part of the afternoon George and the Bo'son had a long and earnest conversation in the Bo'son's house, but what it was all about none but themselves ever knew.

The parting of George Wilson with the family was tender and affectionate, but not marked by any exhibition of feeling on his part, or that of Susie, that would have led any but such a person as Julia to believe there was a deep fountain of pure love, if not between them, somewhere very near. All that Julia observed was an exchange of looks, accompanied by the slightest possible change in their faces.

The Captain drove George to the depot, and the Bo'son by request went with them, which was observed by the dog, and so he concluded to make one of the party, and made more noise about it than all the rest.

CHAPTER XXVIII.

JULIA WRITES TO FRANK.

JULIA Fizzlebaugh had become fully satisfied that George and Susie were deeply in love with each other, but whether there had been any declaration or admission of it between them, she did not know. She had received a letter from Mr. Livingston, penned in such language as would now warrant her in addressing him in warmer and more affectionate terms. So far all had been as she wished, and her only fears were that Captain and Mrs. Waters would unite with the father and mother of Susie and persuade her to accept the offer of Mr. Livingston, and marry him. Julia was the only one who knew of the contemplated visit and its object, having been informed of the whole arrangement by letters from Frank Livingston.

Julia felt that it would be for her interest to again write Mr. Livingston, and freely express her opinion in regard to one of the causes of his being refused by Susie Morton. She was determined to write such a letter as would first touch his pride, and then, for what she intended to make him believe she considered a slight and positive contempt, deserving only his indifference or his scorn, to express for him so much sympathy that he would be induced to make the offer to her, which Susie Morton had refused.

It is generally understood that the assistance of a mother or aunt is very necessary to the successful carrying out of a well laid scheme to entrap a rich husband, but in this case Julia attempted it single-handed. The prize was a high one, and Julia felt that it must be played for.

Julia well knew that if she failed in her object, none but herself would know it, and that she alone would have to bear the disappointment, though she was aware that such a union was desired by her parents ; but they knew nothing about what she was trying to accomplish. After duly considering the matter, Julia wrote the following letter, differing materially in style and in every respect from the first :

"Waters' Snug Harber, *August* 14*th*, 185–.
"My Dear Mr. Livingston :
"Your last esteemed favor was received yesterday, after Mr. George Wilson, a special friend of the family, had left the house for New York. Mr. Wilson is a gentleman of uncommonly fine appearance, of polished manners and fine attainments. He is an officer on board of the ship formerly owned and commanded by Captain Waters, who took Mr. Wilson to sea with him on a number of voyages, and when old enough and sufficiently educated, made an officer of him. Miss Morton having made several voyages in the ship, she and George are well acquainted with each other, and it would be difficult to tell which of the two is the greatest favorite in the family of the Waters'. Mr. Wilson having traveled extensively, and possessing great and pleasing powers of conversation, could not fail, in relating what he had seen abroad, to interest a young lady with such romantic ideas as have full sway in the head of my fair and foolish cousin. I mean foolish only in refusing your offer; and I am now fully confirmed in the opinion expressed in a former letter, that the only reason she had for refusing you was, that she had no heart to give, and without it she would not give her hand. I saw at a glance when the two met that they loved each other, and had from childhood. Mr. Wilson, being so great a favorite in the family as he is, you will find difficulties to contend with, and an opposition on the

part of the Waters' that the influence of Susie's parents cannot overcome.

" Why, then, my dear friend, do you seek after what you can never possess,—the heart of Susie Morton? Should you succeed, with the influence of her whole family, in forcing her against her will to marry you, you would have only her hand, not her heart. Would not your pride and self-respect revolt at such a union? And could you expect to be happy in it?

"You are alone in the world; no mother, no sister to sympathize with you in your suffering, and I freely confess that while I have been watching Susie, earnestly and constantly pleading with her to change her mind, write her parents, and accept your offer, my feelings have been so enlisted in your cause that I have enjoyed only broken slumbers, in which I have dreamed that you were very miserable.

"Susie will not acknowledge that she loves Mr. Wilson, nor will she admit that any engagement exists between them. That she loves him there is no question, for she repeats his name in her sleep. In regard to the engagement, I have no means of finding out.

"As a friend, deeply interested in your future, let me presume,—and it is with great delicacy that I do,—to advise you not to repeat the offer, but find another lady, who has a heart, and will bestow it on you, and fully return the affection that you would so freely give, and with her be happy; and that such may be your lot, you will have the prayers and wishes of one who is

"Affectionately and truly yours,

"JULIA FIZZLEBAUGH."

If such a letter had been written under better influences, and for nobler purposes, it would have been a lasting credit to the writer; but it was not truthful, nor did Julia feel what she expressed in the letter.

When Frank received the letter, he pondered long over the contents of it; in the evening he made a visit at the house of Mr. Morton. He there learned the history of George Wilson, and informed Mr. and Mrs. Morton that

Mr. Wilson had recently visited the farm, and inquired if they thought he was the cause of Susie's refusal.

"Certainly not," said Mr. Morton; "Susie would not dare receive the addresses of any man without my approbation, and certainly would not engage herself without my consent. I can assure you, Mr. Livingston, that Susie will not marry George Wilson with my consent, and I haven't the least fear that she will marry him without it. No, sir, you have nothing to apprehend; Susie only needs a little talking to, which she will have in a few days, and all will be as you wish. You are aware that next week is the time we set for going up to the farm, and I know enough of father and mother Waters, to know that they will approve of the union, and assist us to overcome any slight objections that Susie may have to marrying at so early an age. I think that must be her only objection. What other can she possibly have?"

"I know not, sir, unless Mr. Wilson may have engaged her affections,—in which case I should not wish to interfere, much as I desire your daughter for a wife."

"My daughter shall be your wife; we have set our hearts on it, and it must be. Captain Waters will highly approve of the match, and what he wishes in the family generally takes place, and I count on him with certainty."

"I wish, Mr. Morton, that all may come to pass as you and I had arranged, and as all of us now wish; but I have some doubts about it, and will not marry your daughter unless it is with her free and full consent."

"Of course not,—of course not, Mr. Livingston," and the little party separated.

It was evident from the manner and language of Frank Livingston that the letter of Julia Fizzlebaugh was having some influence with him. It has already been stated that his head was weak, but that his heart was originally good. His heart told him in this case that he should make no further effort to become the husband of Susie Morton, but his weak head urged him on, that he might win his wagers, and not be laughed at by some that he called his friends. He consoled himself with the reflection that he should not have to see Susie again, unless her parents and friends arranged for their marriage, and then sent to Saratoga Springs for him to visit the farm.

Under the pressure of his feelings, and excitement of the circumstances, Frank Livingston had indulged more freely in the use of wine than was his custom, and under its stimulating influence had risked and lost considerable money. His fortune, however, was so ample that such slight inroads did not materially interfere with his finances, so far as the world knew.

Could a proper influence at that time have been brought to bear upon him, and he have been checked in his mad and downward career, a noble and generous-hearted man would have been saved from ruin. He had entered fashionable society when only a young man, with a large fortune at his command, and no restraint upon his actions; been surrounded with all the allurements put forth to entice the young, who have means at their command, from the paths of virtue and rectitude; and at that time was gradually falling, without being aware of the fact.

His case was only that of thousands in our large cities, who fall to rise no more; and young ladies are, indeed fortunate who, like Susie Morton, are in time apprised of danger, and have the judgment and courage to shun it.

———

CHAPTER XXIX.

SUSIE MORTON TELLS THE CAPTAIN AND HIS WIFE.

AFTER the visit of George Wilson, Susie Morton at times appeared to be engaged in earnest thought, but not otherwise to be changed. She was still an early riser, and found something about the rooms to occupy her time till her grandmother was ready to go with her to the milk-room. Activity, order and neatness were ruling elements in her character. George Wilson was right when he said : "I think, sir, that like the Bo'son, Susie will learn only what is worth knowing, and will be useful when learned. She will excel in whatever she undertakes." The constant self command that she maintained over herself, her activity and cheerfulness, enabled her to hide from others whatever feelings she possessed, and did not wish to exhibit.

Before leaving for the city, Susie Morton had determined to learn from her grandmother all that would in the future be useful to her in housekeeping. She did learn much, not only from her grandmother, but also from Lizzie and the old steward. While her cousin Julia was sleeping away the morning and early part of the day, Susie was engaged in different parts of the house, learning and practicing housekeeping.

Captain Waters would sometimes say :

"Susie, why don't Julia Fizzlebaugh once in a while get up in the morning, or do something after she does get up? She appears to have no more life than a mussel."

"I don't know, grandpa ; it may be she is not fond of early rising, and has not been used to it; you know there is a difference in girls as well as in men ? "

"Yes, I do know that; if they were all alike, I should want them all like you."

"You are very partial, grandpa, and Julia's grandpa may be equally partial towards her."

"If he thinks her lying in bed till near noon is smart, and recommends other young ladies to follow her example, I wouldn't trust him to command a small sloop, as I should be sure he would run her ashore for want of good judgment."

"You mustn't be severe on my poor cousin, grandpa, because she has not been well trained, and has grown up with false notions of life and its duties."

"I would be severe, and I would train her if she was under my control,—yes, I would for certain. I would throw a bucketfull of cold water into her bed every morning, time enough for her to get up and dress before the breakfast hour. If she didn't get up with that, after one or two trials, I would throw a bucketfull of hot water into her bed, and that would fetch her."

"O! grandpa, dont talk so; you wouldn't have the heart

to do it, I am sure you wouldn't, because you are such a good dear grandpa."

·"Wouldn't I have the heart to do it ? Did you ever know me not to have the courage to do my duty, or know of my failing to do a good act when I had an opportunity? It would do Julia an amazing sight of good to teach her that she was not created to be waited on, and do nothing herself."

"She may out-grow or out-live her false ideas, perhaps, grandpa."

"She may outlive her notions and habits; and I hope she will. I never wish anything but good to people, and I don't to Julia, but I hope the time will come when she will have to get up in the morning, earn the money, go out and buy her breakfast, and then go home and cook it before she has anything to eat."

"O ! what a severe and naughty grandpa I have."

"No, my dear child, I am not naughty, and I am not severe. Julia, as she is, is worthless,—knows nothing that she should know ; could not cook a meal for a husband, if she had one ; could not even make him a cup of coffee, or do the least thing about the house ; never leaves her bed before noon or near it; has not for years taken break-fast with the family. Of what use would such a wife be to a man ? Your grandmother, a few days since, asked her to set the tea-table, just to see what she would do. She kept a book in one hand, and continued to read something that she was interested in ; didn't know what dishes to put on, or where to place them ; let some fall, and they were broken, and your grandmother then desired her to give it up, which she did. What her father and mother have been thinking about, is more than I can tell. They have nothing in the way of property in this world but Julia, and the more one has of such personal property, the worse off they are."

"Oh, grandpa ! Julia may marry and do well, after all; and now we have been talking a long while, and it is time to retire ; " so kissing both grandparents, and saying "good night," Susie left the sitting-room.

Susie Morton had her own deep, secret thoughts, her

own sorrows and burdens to bear, and did bear them, notwithstanding her constant apparent cheerfulness, and it was only when she was alone that she fully indulged in her own feelings. She loved her parents, and she loved George Wilson ; she believed George loved her, though he had never told her so. Susie learned from a young lady friend at Saratoga that Mr. Livingston had spent most of the time in New York since he left the farm, and she concluded that some arrangement had been entered into between Mr. Livingston and her parents in regard to herself, and expected that her father and mother might soon be at the farm, and then would come her final struggle.

With one like Susie Morton, who was always so unwilling to give pain to any one, the thought that she must soon act against the wishes of her father and mother was extremely painful to her, and gladly would she have made very great sacrifices to avoid it, but could not consent to sacrifice her future happiness, and marry Frank Livingston.

Since Frank was at the Farm, Julia had been very reserved, and there was not that close communion that was desired by Susie ; but with all her efforts to induce Julia to be free and communicative to her, she could not succeed, and at last gave it up.

Susie had talked freely with the Bo'son in regard to her feelings, always excepting her love for George Wilson ; and the Bo'son wisely advised her, saying:

" Tell the captain and Mrs. Waters all about the matter, and they will give you a course to steer by that will take you clear of all difficulties and dangers,—that is the Bo'son's advice, morning-glory."

After retiring to her room, Susie sat and thought a long time before she went to bed, and after being in bed it was long before she could sleep, but before closing her eyes in slumber, she had fully determined that in the morning she would acquaint her grandparents with her fears and wishes.

In the morning, after breakfast, when the three had retired to the sitting-room, Susie went and sat on her grandpa's knee (not an uncommon thing with her), and putting her arms around his neck, gave him a kiss, at the same time saying :

"Grandpa, do you really love the girl you call 'pet?'"

"Yes, if I ever loved anyone. Why do you, with such a serious face, ask?"

"Do you really love me, too, grandma?"

"Why, certainly, child. What in the world is the matter, that you look so sad?"

"Would you both help me, if I was in trouble and needed assistance?"

"Help you? yes; and have the Bo'son pipe all hands to help you," said Captain Waters. "What can trouble our Susie?"

Mrs. Waters had laid down her work, taken off her glasses, and appeared interested and alarmed. After watching Susie closely for a moment, to be sure that she was in earnest, she said :

"Susie, my darling, whatever trouble you anticipate, or has reached you, tell us freely and fully, and we will help and shield you."

"It is such trouble, and coming from such a source as you little expect; and I shall indeed need all the aid you can give me."

"Has none of it actually come upon you yet?" asked the captain.

"No, grandpa; not actually come yet, but very near."

"Then let it come, and we'll be ready for it, no matter which way it comes from ; but tell us all about it, pet."

"Frank Livingston wants to marry me, and my father and mother are determined to make me marry him, against my own wishes, if possible."

Here Susie broke completely down, and laid her head on her grandfather's shoulder.

"Thunder and jews-harps!" exclaimed the captain. "I would sooner see all three top-masts go by the board ; yes, lower-masts and all, every spar over the side of the ship, and have nothing but the hull left, than see you the wife of Frank Livingston, my little singing bird. I swear by every point in the compass, and by the north star, it shall not be."

"Joseph! Joseph Waters! be calm; don't get excited. I am surprised," said the good wife.

"Lightning greased! talk to me about being calm, when such a fellow as Livingston is after Susie, and her father and mother helping him. Where is the Bo'son and dog?"

"Joseph Waters, be calm, and be yourself again. This is not a time for raising a breeze; you want your judgment on this occasion. I have not heard you use such language, or similar expressions, in many years. As no danger has yet come, now we know all about it, we can take care of our Susie when it does come, and no harm shall befall her."

"Nancy, you have been a great help to me for many years, and when I get into these tornadoes, you could always bring me safely out of them. You are a dear, good old girl; and if you and I, the Bo'son, steward, Lizzie, and the dog can't protect our pet, then let the ship and farm go ashore, and be wrecked." So, have no more fears, Susie; you are safe with us."

"Yes, Joseph; she is perfectly safe with us, and while we live shall never marry Frank Livingston."

"Susie," said her grandfather, "if you can't get any better man than he is for a husband, live single; stay with us,—that is better. You will be taken care of while we live, and before I die I'll take care that you are provided for after that takes place."

Susie had become perfectly calm, and fully herself again, after finding that she would have the help and protection of her grand-parents, and felt that all would be well. Susie told them that she thought her father and mother would soon be at the farm, and wished them not to mention this conversation, but to act as though ignorant of the whole matter, saying:

"That will be best; and please don't tell Julia. I have now nothing to fear, and am perfectly happy, and ready for what may come. I love father and mother, and they love me; but they have some peculiar notions about old families. I was afraid you would side with them. I ought to have known better. I thank you, and love you more than ever."

"We know you love us, and you needn't thank us, dear," said the grandmother.

Bill's whistle was heard, a signal that he wanted his captain, and the captain left.

CHAPTER XXX.

CAPTAIN WATERS IS BETTER INFORMED, AND TALKS WITH THE BO'SON.

WHEN Captain Waters returned to the sitting-room, every shade of sadness had passed from the face of Susie Morton. She had related to her grandmother all that passed between herself and Mr. Livingston, also what she knew of his character and habits, and then said that it was impossible, under any circumstances, for her to become his wife.

Mrs. Waters, exercising her sound judgment and good common sense, combined with her mildness and love for Susie, had succeeded in fully restoring her to cheerfulness, so that when the Captain returned, had he not been present earlier in the morning, he would not have supposed from appearances that any unusual affair had disturbed or distressed his pet grandchild. His ruffled feelings and appearance had also been quieted down, and he was fully himself again.

Captain Waters, having been put in possession of some general knowledge, wanted all the particulars, and seeing that Susie was in a proper state of mind to impart them without distressing herself, asked for them, and Susie related them to him as she had to her grandmother. When she had spoken of his character and habits, the Captain said to her:

"Susie, how did you learn what you know about him?"

"Do you remember Maria, my governess and teacher, grandpa?"

"Certainly, what of her?"

"She has a brother, a very smart young man, and being

an American and well educated, he can assume and personate almost any character. Knowing long since the feelings and wishes of my parents in regard to marrying Frank Livingston, I was anxious to know what his habits were, and how he spent his time, so I furnished the money, and Maria's brother made his acquaintance, and kept his company occasionally for months. John is only a little over twenty, and was represented as a young man who would come into possession of a large fortune when of age, consequently he found no difficulty in being received at the places frequented by Frank. John was smart enough not to spend much money, as he thought his sister furnished it all herself, and will never know why she wanted the information. All this must be a secret from my father and mother,—and, indeed, from every-one else."

"You are a wonderful woman for one of your age; but why did you not tell some of the family, Susie?" asked her grandfather."

"I did; I told Bill Thomas, the Bo'son."

"And what did the Bo'son offer to do, and what advice did he give? I don't believe any other girl in the world but yourself would have gone to a ship's Bo'son for advice in a love affair. He is good at every other thing, and may be good at that."

"The Bo'son offered to do anything and everything, and among others, that if nothing better would do, he would have old Bose take Mr. Livingston into the middle of the river, and hold his head under water until he would never think about a wife again." Here Susie indulged in one of her old-fashioned joyous laughs, in which she was joined by the Captain and Mrs. Waters. Susie then continued.

"The Bo'son watched Mr. Livingston very closely all the time he was here, and always had the dog with him, to be used if necessary." At this stage of the narrative Susie again indulged in one of her laughs, and then went on;

"The Bo'son all the time advised me to do just what I at last did,—go and tell you all about it, and having done so, my mind is easy, and I am free from apprehension."

"You have done just right, and not at first wishing to

tell us, the Bo'son was the next best one to tell, for he has a heart as large as an ox, and as warm as the sunny side of a building in a summer day.   But isn't it funny,—the old Bo'son appealed to in a love affair?" and the Captain came near choking with laughter.

"Joseph, take care, or you will go off in one of those spells some day," said the wife.

"Let me alone, Nancy, I can't help it, I must have it out, because there is fun in it."

"Yes, Joseph ; but a man of your years should have discretion."   While, with assumed gravity, Mrs. Waters had to make a great effort to prevent herself from joining in the laugh.   Susie did join and heartily so.

"Discretion, mother; who ever heard of such a thing in a love matter?"

All of them having arisen from their seats, Captain Waters picked Susie up in his arms, and trotted around the room with her as though she was an infant, and then giving her a good kissing, sat her in an easy-chair and left, laughing loud enough to be heard all over the farm.

Captain Waters went directly to the Bo'son's house, where he found Bill, and seizing him with one hand laid the other heavily on his shoulder, making an attempt to shake him, and with equal success might have attempted to shake a church; at length the Captain said :

"You old sea-shell, you! I have a great mind to hang you at the yard-arm, or set old 'butts' at you again."

Bill knew his Captain too well not to perceive that he was in extra good spirits, and answered :

"What, sir, has the old Bo'son done that he should swing at the yard-arm, or have old 'butts' at him? You can hang me, sir, if you wish, but you can never persuade that ram to butt the Bo'son again.   I soaked all the butts out of him, and if I hadn't I would like the hanging best."

"What have you been doing that you should be hung or butted ? You have been interfering in a love affair between Susie and Mr. Livingston."

"Livingston be ——"

"Hold on, Bo'son; remember your promise when I brought you to the farm, not to swear."

"I remember it all the time, sir, and I don't swear; but Livingston be tarred and slushed,—he isn't worth salting, or being butted by a respectable ram; but wouldn't I like to see old 'butts' at him once, just for the fun of it. I'ould never soak him for it."

" Bo'son, Mr. Livingston shouldn't be injured for wanting Susie for a wife,—everybody wants her that knows her, and why shouldn't they? 'She is built of good timber and well modeled.' There are few like her."

There was a respect that the Bo'son felt was due his captain, that he never failed to pay. It may have been from long habit, but whatever it was, no familiarity on the part of Captain Waters could prevent Bill from paying it. The Bo'son stood before his captain, with his hat in his hand, as he would have done in the cabin of the ship " Neptune."

" After all, sir, Mr. Livingston is not to blame for loving black-eyed Susan, but he is to blame for insisting on marrying her after she had told him that she didn't love him, and wouldn't marry him."

" What did you do about it, Bo'son, when you found it out ? "

" When, sir, I saw black-eyed Susan with her colors half-mast, union down, I knew she was in distress; so I hoisted the big-jib, filled away, went alongside and aboard, and offered assistance."

" Well, Bo'son, how were you able to render assistance ?"

" By keeping a good look-out, and sailing most of the time between her and the enemy."

" Did you say anything to Mr. Livingston about it ? "

" No, sir ; not until he first spoke to me, and asked me what I thought of Miss Morton; and I soon told him what I thought of her, and I would just liked to have had the same chance to have given my opinion of him. He wanted to give me money, and that I declined ; then he wanted me to look out that no unsuitable person married and run off with her. That I promised, and if Bill Thomas ever breaks a promise, that will not be the one."

" Bo'son, these family affairs must be stowed snug away, and not be overhauled."

"I know that, sir; and the Bo'son don't blow his call without orders. I am off duty now,—you are on deck,—except to obey orders. I told the morning-glory that if she would only let you and Mrs. Waters look over her log-book, you would give her the correct course to steer."

"You did all right, Bo'son; and though you have had but little experience in such matters, you couldn't have done better. I don't expect much trouble with Susie's father and mother, but there will be nothing for you to do. There is good timber in Mr. Morton,—though a little sappy on the outside he is sound in the heart, and so is his wife; but their compass is a little out of order, and they are out of their true course. After overhauling their reckoning, they will see where the error is, and rectify their mistake. One thing is certain,—Susie will never marry Mr. Livingston."

"Hurrah! hurrah!" shouted the Bo'son.

"Bo'son, keep quiet."

"Aye, aye, sir, but it's hard work."

Captain Waters said, "You are a soft-hearted old fool, Bill Thomas," and left.

When he was gone, the Bo'son remarked to himself: "That is one of the best men that ever walked a ship's deck."

CHAPTER XXXI.

WELCOME GOODWIN AND THE STEWARD.

WELCOME Goodwin having expressed a desire to talk with the old steward, and by the steward having been invited to call at the farm and at his room, soon after his first visit and conversation with the Bo'son, found an opportunity of doing so.

When friend Goodwin called, the steward was in his room, engaged in writing up some accounts. The steward received the caller with an ease and grace that could not have been excelled by the most accomplished of gentlemen.   His politeness consisted not only in his language and expressions, but in every act and movement.

Welcome Goodwin, though a member and minister in the society of Friends, and a plain farmer in the country, had traveled extensively in the United States, both north and south, in the capacity of an individual and in that of a minister, often having felt that he was called to visit other lands than that in which he dwelt, to proclaim the glad tidings of great joy to all who would believe and obey the Lord and Master.   He had for many years mingled freely with the best and most refined society; was liberal in his own views, a good judge of real and assumed character, and possessed the secret and Heaven-given power of finding and unlocking the door of a heart, however securely it might be barred against the entrance of others.

After the usual salutations of meeting had been passed, friend Goodwin opened the conversation by saying:

"Steward, I have called because I have felt very desirous of doing so after my short visit to thy room, late in the afternoon of one day last week, after spending a couple of hours in the house of the Bo'son.   I then felt that thou wert one who hast seen much of the world, and filled places different from the one thou art now filling, and I have felt a secret desire to know more of thy life and wanderings about the world, than I am now possessed of; that is, if thou canst communicate freely with me, and not lacerate thy own feelings.   Let me say to thee, steward, that it is with feelings of friendship that I ask for what information thou mayest feel at liberty to give, because thou seemest to me to have been prepared by education and habit for a higher position in life than thou now occupiest."

"Perhaps, Mr. Goodwin, you do not fully comprehend the position that I occupy?"

"That is very likely, steward.   Finding thee in a room furnished as this is, not only with every comfort, but I may truly say with all the luxuries that a large room like this could possible hold, I must conclude that thou art indeed something more than a man hired to cook on a farm, though that is honorable if faithfully performed, and wouldn't lessen thee in my esteem."

The steward had been in the company of many of the society of which Mr. Goodwin was a member, besides he was a highly educated man. Consequently he fully understood the plain language of the Scriptures; and who that is educated and reads them does not?

"It is true, Mr. Goodwin, that I am something besides the cook in a farm kitchen, though I do cook some, yes, many of the dishes eaten at the table, and so does Mrs. Waters. There is nothing in my life, character or history that may not be told—nothing that I am unwilling to communicate, and yet nothing that I am anxious that the world should know, because the world has no special interest in me; but as you have expressed a wish to be informed, and appear to feel some interest in obtaining the knowledge, I will impart it."

"In doing so thou wilt very much oblige me, and thy best way will be to give it as though thou wert writing a history of thy life."

"That will be the easiest and best way," said the steward.

THE STEWARD'S ACCOUNT OF HIMSELF.

"I was born on the island of Cuba. My father was a French gentleman and a merchant. My mother a native of the island, and my grandmother on my mother's side was an imported African, said to have been a princess in her own country. My grandfather on my mother's side was also a Frenchman. So that I have far more French than African blood in my veins."

"I should judge so from thy complexion," observed Mr. Goodwin; "for thou art as light as some who claim to be all white; but continue, if thou pleases."

"I remained at home with my parents until I was twelve years old. Our residence was a few miles from the city of Havana, in which city my father was engaged in business. In the family was spoken the French and

Spanish languages. My mother was well educated, and perfectly understood both languages. At the age of twelve years I was sent to England, and there placed in school. Up to that time I had received all my instruction from private tutors, and in my father's house.

"It was my father's wish that I should receive a thorough English education, and be able to speak that language fluently and properly. I remained in England four years, and then returned to Cuba, where I spent one year; and at the end of that time I was sent to Germany, and there attended school for two years. From Germany I went to France, and completed my French education, occupying for that purpose two years. It was in France that I learned to cook, and I acquired the knowledge more for amusement, than for any other purpose. Four of us who were attending the University engaged a celebrated cook, and each of us, for amusement or some other senseless motive, learned the art of cooking, which when once learned thoroughly, can never be forgotten.

"After leaving the university, with such an education as few are fortunate enough to acquire, at my father's request I traveled for one year in Europe and in England, and then returned home, at the age of twenty-two years. My father, then a wealthy merchant, left it with me to choose an occupation. I decided to become a merchant, and went into my father's counting-house, where I studied commerce, and conducted the correspondence of the house in the four languages of which I was master. At the age of twenty-six I became a partner in the house, and married. Six years afterwards, I went to France, and it being found advantageous for me to remain there, I sent for my wife and three children."

Here the steward paused, appeared to be deeply exercised in feeling, and wiped a moisture from his forehead, and also from his eyes. Welcome Goodwin was far too familiar with the workings of the mind and the wellsprings of the heart, to urge the steward on with his history, knowing that after a little reflection, when the keenness of his feeling, that had been sharpened by calling to mind the past had subsided, that he would proceed of his own accord. After sitting in silence a little while, the steward went on by saying :

"Mr. Goodwin, I am now coming to the most painful period of my life, which had such an influence over my actions as to change my course and destiny in the world. By some unexpected reverses and convulsions in the commercial world, the house of which my father was the head, failed; the ship in which my family had sailed for France to join me was lost at sea, with all on board. A few months later my father died with a broken heart, and my mother soon followed him to the grave. I found myself in a foreign country, with only a small sum of money at my command, was taken immediately sick, and so remained for nearly a year. When I recovered, I found myself entirely destitute of money, and at that time Captain Waters arrived in Havre, where we met in one of the streets.

"Captain Waters had known and done business with our house at Havana, and often been at my father's home. The captain had also known me, for we were then both of us much younger than we are now, as that was over twenty-three years ago. Captain Waters offered me all the assistance I required, and being bound to China, invited me to make the voyage with him, and I accepted the invitation. At his request, I took charge of his books and accounts, and with my knowledge of languages, was able to render him what he considered valuable assistance. I made a second voyage with him as clerk, for even at that time he generally owned the cargo and the ship. On the second voyage, the steward died on the homeward passage, and I volunteered to fill his place, as no other person in the ship could.

"In the two voyages I had been restored to health, and somewhat risen above my misfortunes, but not fully, nor shall I ever. Since that time, I have sailed with Captain Waters as his head steward and book-keeper. My duties have been light and pleasant. A few years after my misfortunes, I visited Havana, and found some property belonging to me, which I converted into cash and invested in this country, and to that sum I have yearly made additions, until I have enough to take care of me in age, sick or well. For many years I have had charge of Captain Waters' books, and much of his personal property, received and paid out his money, and he seldom knows how much I have on hand. At times I have had in that iron safe, on board of the ship, fifty thousand dollars in gold at a time. I am the only person, except Mrs. Waters, who knows how much property the captain is worth, and where it is.

"What I do for the Captain is from choice and not necessity, and for the esteem I have for him and Mrs. Waters. I believe he bought this farm to keep the family together,—that is, the Bo'son, Lizzie and myself. This furniture and these books are my property, and are here to gratify my taste and pleasure. Since I have been sailing with the Captain, and certainly since Mrs. Waters has been making all the voyages with us, I have been happier than I ever expected to be, and have no desire to leave them; and now, sir, you have my whole history."

"I thank thee, steward, and assure thee that I have been very much interested. I thought it singular if friend Waters furnished a room like this for thee; but if the furniture is thine, that is another affair."

"Mr. Goodwin, Captain Waters wished me to select it, and pay for it with his money, but I preferred it otherwise."

"Well, well; you sea-faring people are a wonderful people, bound to each other by some strange and mysterious tie that landsmen will never comprehend. So let me again thank thee, and say farewell, for it is getting late in the afternoon."

"Good-bye, sir; call again when convenient," said the steward, as they shook hands and parted.

CHAPTER XXXII.

MR. AND MRS. MORTON VISIT THE FARM.

THREE weeks after Frank Livingston left the farm, Mr. and Mrs. Morton, without any previous notice that they contemplated making the visit, late one beautiful afternoon arrived at the country home of Captain Waters. They met with as warm a welcome as ever parents bestowed upon their much-loved children. Susie appeared, and really was, exceedingly glad to see her father and mother. She was aware that there would be a very strong effort made to change her mind and induce her to marry Frank, but knowing that her grandfather and grandmother Waters would oppose the views and wishes of her parents, and having decided not to marry him, she felt that soon all would be settled, and was determined that the coming storm should not lessen her pleasure at meeting with her father and mother.

It is not every one who can so school and discipline their mind and control their feelings, but Susie Morton had by nature a superior mind, and had so cultivated and exercised it that her will could always master her feelings, and at no period of her life, though short, had there been an occasion for a greater effort on her part. It had been determined by Mr. and Mrs. Morton not to allude to the object of their visit on the first day, hoping that if Captain or Mrs. Waters knew anything of the matter, that they would speak of it. However strong that hope was, they would have died with it in their hearts if they had waited until either of the parties possessing the secret had gratified them.

Captain Waters invited Mr. Morton to view the farm and improvements made on it; Mrs. Waters asked her daughter to examine the house and the furniture.

Susie was joined by her cousin Julia, it being late in the afternoon, and past the hour of Julia's getting up in the morning. The indolent creature had no other means of whiling away some tedious moments, and concluded to pass over the house and hear what her aunt might have to say about it.

Laura Morton found much in the house to admire, and all in and about the new home of her father and mother so pleasant and so beautiful, that she thought they could not be otherwise than satisfied and happy.

Mr. Morton went over the farm with Captain Waters, and closely inspected all that claimed his notice, and as usual, lastly taking the visitor to the Bo'son's house. The Bo'son was well acquainted with Mr. Morton, and entered freely into conversation with him, explaining, in his own way, the use of articles that were new to Mr. Morton.

The Bo'son watched the countenance of his visitor more closely than was his custom, but could discover nothing in it to indicate the feelings and purposes of the individual he was watching. There was nothing in the appearance or manner of William Morton but that of a well-bred and accomplished gentleman, who could command himself, and sometimes showed a slight disposition to command others.

When they left the house of the Bo'son, he looked long after them as they were walking towards the mansion, and talked to himself as was his custom.

"The barometer indicates a change in the weather, and there will be a hurricane, tornado, or water-spout within the next eight and forty hours, or the Bo'son is no judge of the weather. Let it come we are ready for it."

At the tea-table the conversation was lively and general, without in one instance betraying the wishes or feelings of any present, though each had a purpose to accomplish. Mr. and Mrs. Morton had seen too much of the world and of society to be at any time or place at a loss for subjects of conversation, and in their father's house they could not but feel at home, and would have been perfectly so under all circumstances but those that were weighing heavily at their hearts, and required some effort to conceal.

Mr. Morton addressed the Captain by saying:

"Father, how does Bill Thomas the Bo'son get along on the farm?"

"Very well, William; he can 'navigate' an ox team and 'discharge' a cargo of milk from a cow, though he was 'knocked overboard and went astern,' the first 'milking voyage' that he made."

" Joseph," said the wife, "why do you continue to use nautical phrases in answering William's question?" You ought to 'tack ship and make the land,' now you are on a farm."

" Ready about, call the Bo'son and tell him to 'pipe all hands to stations.' You can all see how completely mother has lost her knowledge of the ocean language. Never mind, mother, it comes natural and handy to us both, and we have learned it so thoroughly that neither of us can easily forget it. The Bo'son, William, has encountered some heavy squalls, but he proves equal to them all. He has not at any time entirely lost his good nature, though he came very near it when old 'butts' got in his wake."

The Captain related, with some embellishments, Bill's encounter with the ram, and how the account was settled.

They all joined in a hearty laugh at the Bo'son's expense, who would have joined in it had he been present.

Mr. Morton next addressed Julia Fizzlebaugh, and asked her how she liked the country, and how she passed her time?

" I don't like the country any how, uncle; it is too dull for me. Nothing to interest; nothing to excite; no piano in the house, and no way of amusing one's self. Readable books are out of the question. I have come very near dying for want of excitement."

" Why, I am surprised," said her uncle. "I thought father had a fine library, and so has the steward. How is that, Julia?"

" There are books enough to be sure, but they are not to my liking,—not new works just from the press; they are far too antiquated for the times. What does one want of history, and of the old authors and poets, I should like to know?"

" Why not ride and walk in the fields, and enjoy the benefits of the morning air?"

" Uncle Joseph mostly rides too early in the day to suit

my taste and convenience, and walking requires more effort than I am willing to make."

" I see, Julia, that the country has produced no change in you, and that you were born for a city life, and a lady," was the reply of Laura Morton.   " I wish that Susie may learn some valuable lessons from you, and be an accomplished lady."

"Laura," said Captain Waters, " Susie has been learning better lessons from her grandmother than Julia can teach her."

" I should like to hear from mother how Susie has behaved, and what valuable lessons she has learned."

" Laura, Susie is up every morning before the sun is; and by the time I am ready to go to the milk-room, this room and the sitting-room are in order ; and then she assists me with the milk and butter.   Sometimes she helps in the kitchen, and anywhere that light work is to be done.   She is becoming quite a cook."

" I thought, mother, that you had servants enough to do all your work, or I should not have consented for Susie to have remained so long.   Poor, delicate creature ! it will ruin her and all her future prospects I am afraid, though I know it is well meant."

" O, no, Laura," said her father ; " it will do her good, you may depend on it.   Mother knows what is right and best, because she has sailed for it."

" It may be so, father; but I am not a judge.   Going as I did from a boarding-school to the head of a house, I had to learn all that I know about house-keeping after I was married."

"Yes, yes, that is so; for your mother and myself were then at sea, or it would have been otherwise, I am certain."

The evening passed away with pleasant conversation, and at an early hour all retired to meditate on the past, scheme for and dream of the future.

CHAPTER XXXIII.

MR. AND MRS. MORTON OBTAIN SUSIE'S CONDITIONAL CONSENT TO MARRY FRANK LIVINGSTON.

THE following morning, after breakfast, Mrs. Morton asked Susie to go with her to the parlor, where they found Mr. Morton engaged in looking over the books on the center-table. Mr. Morton closed the book in his hand, laid it on the table, and received the wife and daughter in the kindest and most affectionate manner.

Mrs. Morton manifested, in her face and by her actions, a deep anxiety that all her efforts failed to disguise. It was not so with her husband; for whatever may have been his feelings, they were locked securely in his own bosom, and outwardly there was no evidence that any important matters were disturbing his mind.

Susie Morton was fully satisfied about the object of the meeting, and felt far more anxiety for her parents, than on her own account. Susie was desirous of doing nothing that it was possible to avoid, that would be in opposition to their wishes, or that would give them pain. She was calm in appearance, and lovely to look upon; if possible more so than usual, from the plainness and simplicity of her morning dress. The parents looked upon her with pride, and in their hearts dearly loved her. How could they help loving such a child? A beautiful daughter, having just reached the age of womanhood, one that had never manifested a disposition to be disobedient, or to give her parents pain. It was the love of the father and mother for their daughter that prompted them to do as they were about doing. If they could see their daughter married to Frank Livingston, and settled in her own home with such a husband, belonging to one of the oldest families in the State, who would move in the highest circles of society, they felt that the daughter must be happy, and the one great object of years' contemplation and struggle would be accomplished.

Mr. Morton, noticing the anxiety of his wife, and

knowing enough of the daughter's command over herself to control her feelings, and fully believing that Susie comprehended the object of their coming to the farm, and of that meeting, addressed himself directly to the subject, by saying :

"Susie, your mother and myself were greatly disappointed in your declining to accept the offer of Mr. Livingston without consulting us, and declining it in such mild though decided terms as to nearly close the door of hope against him; and we thought you might take a more favorable view of it, after talking the matter over with us, and your grandfather and grandmother."

During this opening address, in what may be considered a romance of real life, Susie Morton had sat on the opposite side of the table, and near her mother, with her beautiful dark eyes fixed earnestly on her father, and a countenance expressive of love and goodness, and also of firmness and decision. After a little reflection, she said :

"Father, dear, I could not do otherwise. I do not love him, and could not be his wife without loving him."

"My dear child, at your age you hardly know whether you love him or not. You could marry him, and learn to love him afterwards."

"That is an experiment, father, that would not be safe for a young girl to try."

"There are worldly circumstances and considerations in marriage that make it safer for a daughter to depend on the experience of her parents, than on her own judgment; and this is one of them."

"It may be so, my dear father; but worldly circumstances and considerations cannot foster or control the warm and tender feelings that must ever cluster around the heart of a wife for her husband, to make them both happy."

"Love, my child, must be something more than the workings of a romantic young lady's wild imagination ; it must have something to subsist on, something to feed and nourish it, or it dies young. It is, after all, only friendship purified; and in married life, in all cases, can be increased and strengthened by cultivation. In selecting a husband, and becoming settled in life, a young woman should take into consideration the family that she marries into, and the position she will occupy in society."

"Yes, sir, that is a subject for deep reflection ; but a young woman, before she consents to marry, should calculate the chances of her happiness or misery in so doing."

"That is very true, Susie, and for that reason your mother and myself offer the aid of our experience, and our assistance in selecting a husband for you. We know all about Mr. Livingston, and about his wealth and family, and with him for a husband, we feel assured you will be very happy, and occupy a distinguished place in the fashionable world."

"Father, you and my mother have the same object in wishing me to marry Mr. Livingston, that I have in declining his offer. You are desirous of seeing me happy. I wish to be so, and that is my only reason for refusing to become his wife; besides, I am too young to be the wife of any one. I require age and more knowledge of the duties of a wife before I become one."

"Susie," said her mother, "you are older and have more experience than I had when I married your father, and there is a great difference between the circumstances of Mr. Livingston and those of your father, at the time we were married. Your father had his fortune to make, Mr. Livingston has one in hand ; your father had no rich, no influential friends, Mr. Livingston has many. I had no good grandmother to assist me when beginning housekeeping, and my mother was at sea. You can have the advice of both mother and grandmother, and what you don't know, they will gladly teach you. You must remember, dear, that in being Mrs. Frank Livingston, you will have a housekeeper and plenty of servants to attend to your wishes; so be a good girl, and do as we wish you to, and accept the offer."

"Mother, it cannot be. I am sorry to have to decide against your wishes, but to marry Frank Livingston with me is impossible."

"Don't say that, Susie," interposed her father, "you

have not fully and fairly considered the subject, nor have you heard all that we shall urge in favor of it.   Mr. Livingston is a gentleman of family and wealth, possessing all the accomplishments that can make him attractive in fashionable society, which, added to his wealth and name, gives him a position that few occupy. We have no name, no family, to refer back to,—for I went to the City of New York a poor orphan boy,—your grandfather is unknown in the fashionable world; and now since I have accumulated some considerable property, I want a place higher than I occupy, and wish you and your brother to marry into the highest circles of society.   Such an offer as is now made to you, may never again be yours to accept, and you must not think of rejecting it.   I do not now command, I only entreat you to reconsider your answer, and write Frank that you accept his offer."

Susie Morton had listened with earnest attention to all that had been urged by her father and mother, without having changed her mind or for a moment wavered in her first and final decision.   The parents watched her closely, but her face was so calm and so sweet that they were unable to form any opinion of what impressions had been made, and though they had decided to command and threaten unless she yielded, the time had not yet come for that, as they both hoped, with the assistance of Captain Waters and his wife, to persuade their daughter to comply with their wishes.

After a short silence, looking first at her father, then at her mother, Susie said :

"Father, mother, would you sacrifice your daughter, wreck her happiness in this world, for all time, to gratify your desire for a position in the fashionable world ? You love me, and I know it full well ; you have both lavished upon me your love and affection from my earliest recollection to the present, denied me nothing that you thought would add to my happiness, and what you now wish is for the same object, but you are mistaken. The glitter of fashionable life has no charms for me, if to obtain it I must be the wife of Frank Livingston.   I could endure anything, with a husband that I loved.   I would not consent to share a throne, and wear a diadem, with one I did not love. Urge me no further to be the wife of the man you recommend as my life long companion. It cannot be, and I earnestly entreat you not to press the subject,—not to insist on my compliance. For the love I bear you, for the kindness and affection you have bestowed upon me, I will make every suitable return, any sacrifice, even life if necessary; but cannot, will not, marry Frank Livingston. By your affections, by the remembrance of my happy home and childhood, and your earnest hopes of seeing that happiness continued, yield in this to me, and claim in all things else the obedience of a daughter who loves and will obey you."

The father and mother were astonished at the calm, loving and decided manner of their daughter. Their love, if possible, was increased, and their tenderest feelings were touched. They, however, thought that Susie was not as capable as themselves of judging what was most for her interest and happiness, and were determined not to give up their wishes. Mr. Morton was the first to speak.

"Susie, we have lived longer, and can judge better than you can about these matters, and you mustn't place your young and unmatured judgment against that of older and wiser heads than yours. Now, if grandfather and grandmother Waters unite with us in urging your acceptance of Mr. Livingston's offer, will you seriously consider the matter, and try to love him enough to be his wife?"

Susie appeared to be earnestly engaged in deep thought, as though she was considering the matter; and knowing how perfectly safe she would be, said:

"It would not be right for me to oppose my wishes and judgment against the recommendation of all my best and loved friends; and if they agree with you and mother, then I will endeavor to comply."

"I know that father Waters will take the same view of it that we do; and, Susie, you have made me very happy in consenting under such circumstances. Laura, you please go and call your father and mother, and their consent will make us all very cheerful and happy. You mustn't tell them for what they are wanted, as we wish to treat them to an agreeable surprise, at the prospect of being grandparents to so distinguished a young gentleman as Frank Livingston."

Mr. Morton's face beamed with perfect delight, and he walked across the floor rubbing his hands; but as the Captain's consent was not readily given, it will require another chapter to relate what transpired after the old folks entered the parlor.

CHAPTER XXXIV.

CAPTAIN WATERS SHAKES MR. MORTON, AND HE BECOMES SENSIBLE.

CAPTAIN and Mrs. Waters entered the parlor with their daughter Laura, where Mr. Morton was still walking the floor, and rubbing his hands in the best possible spirits, and with the greatest delight, believing that his father and mother Waters would unite with himself and wife, and immediately settle the subject of Susie's marriage with Frank Livingston.

While her mother was absent from the room, Susie had remained quietly sitting in the place she had occupied from the first, and without speaking a single word, as her father was so overjoyed at obtaining a conditional promise from her, that he was unable or unwilling to continue the conversation.

"Sit down, father and mother," said the joyful Mr. Morton. "I have a great surprise for you,—something to tell that will make your hearts jump for joy. I have lived many years, but never seen such a happy day. Frank Livingston, Esq., has offered himself in marriage to our Susie! What do you think of that for good news?"

"Well, William, has Susie accepted the offer?" asked the Captain.

"No, father, not exactly; she pleads her youth and

inexperience, and seems a little disposed to hesitate in accepting the offer, but you are aware that young women often do so, when their minds are fully made up on the subject. Susie, however, says that if you and mother Waters approve and recommend her to do so, that she will accept the offer. Neither you nor mother can fail to see the great advantages of such a marriage, and I am certain that you will sanction it."

"Does Susie love him enough to marry him and be happy; how is it, pet?"

"No, grandpa, I do not love him, and cannot marry him."

"Then that ends the whole matter, William, and there is no use in talking any more about it," said Captain Waters.

William Morton was amazed; he was disappointed, and had met opposition where he had expected assistance. He walked a few times across the floor, and then stopping before Mrs. Waters, said:

"Mother, that is certainly not your opinion?"

"William, how is it possible for me to entertain any different opinion? I would never consent for Susie to marry a man she didn't love. The voyage of life is too long for that."

"You are all against me, but that don't end the matter. Laura and myself have both fully decided that Susie must and shall marry Frank Livingston."

"Must and shall, William, are positive expressions. You certainly wouldn't marry Susie against her will?" was Captain Waters reply.

"They are positive expressions, and convey my meaning. I would marry her against her wishes, knowing it to be for her interest and the interest of the family."

"You mustn't be rash, William; there is some of the Waters' blood in Susie's veins, and that is very hard to 'must and shall' against its better judgment; besides, Susie is of age."

"I don't care anything about her age; she is my daughter, and must do as I wish her to. Mr. Livingston is a gentleman without a blemish in his character; one of

wealth, of distinguished family connections and considerations, which make him a very desirable son-in-law. I
have promised him my daughter for a wife, and mean to
keep that promise at all hazards."

" Family fiddle-strings ! Talk of family connections,
family considerations, and promises to be kept at all
hazards,—how are you going to keep that promise if
Susie continues to say no? and having said it once, she
will not be likely to change her answer, and I, her grandfather, will commend her for it. Exercise your reason,
William, and give up your wish in this matter for the
happiness of all."

" I will not give it up. Susie shall marry him or cease
to be my daughter,—never again enter my house. I will
disinherit her, and give all my property to her brother."

Susie was greatly distressed in her heart to witness her
father's excitement, and went to where he had seated himself, and putting her arms around his neck kissed him.
Mr. Morton put his arm around the waist of his daughter
and said :

" Susie, will you marry Frank and make us all happy?"

" Dear father, anything else that you require I will
cheerfully do, but never be the wife of Frank Livingston."

William Morton pushed his daughter from him saying,
as he did so : "Go, ungrateful child."

It was the first unkind word received, the first unkind
act of her father, and her heart was nearly broken. She
burst into tears, and found herself in her grandfather's
arms. The old Captain,—for him,—had been very calm,
but there was a hurricane coming, and it was very near,
for Susie was one that no harm must approach, or her
grandfather would " call all hands."

" William Morton, you cou— "

" Stop, Joseph," said his wife.

" You don't deserve such a daughter. You will close
your doors against her, will you ? Well, her grandfather
has a house and heart large enough to hold her all the
time, and all that she wants of both of them are her's.
You will disinherit her, will you? Just do it if you like,

and I will disinherit your wife, and give one-third of my property to Susie, and that will be more than you will ever have to give any one. I sold the ' Neptune ' for one hundred and ten thousand dollars,—it has been at interest since the sale, and is not one quarter of my property. So pet will be well provided for."

The Captain had said more about property than he intended to, for he was never boastful, but he was greatly excited on that occasion.

Mrs. Morton had remained silent, leaving her husband to do all the talking, but when her father ceased speaking, she turned to Mrs. Waters, saying :

" Mother, help us with your good common sense and sound judgment, out of all these difficulties. You know how very anxious William is, that our children should marry into some distinguished old families that have honored names."

" Distinguished old cats that have kittens ! What are names worth without proper men to bear them ? We all want to see Susie happy, but I am satisfied she couldn't be so as the wife of Mr. Livingston," was Mrs. Waters' reply.

" Perhaps, mother," said Mr. Morton, " you have other arrangements of your own, in regard to a husband for Susie."

" Nothing of the kind, William, I do assure you; nor do I know of any."

" Hasn't George Wilson been here of late ? "

" Yes ; but not after Susie."

" Susie," asked her father, " are you engaged to George Wilson ? "

' No, father; he never intimated anything of the kind to me."

" I would sooner see you dead and buried, than the wife of such a nameless wretch."

Captain Waters jumped and took his son-in-law by the collar and gave him a shake, shouting:

" What do you mean by calling my boy a nameless wretch ? I'll shake you out of your boots and stockings, if you are one of the family."

"Joseph, Joseph," cried the wife, "I do believe you have lost your senses."

"Don't talk to me, Nancy; I can't allow any one to speak ill of George."

"I beg your pardon, sir; I am over excited," said Mr. Morton. "I know nothing bad about him personally. He has no rich or powerful friends, and his mother took in sewing to educate him and his sister."

"Suppose she did,—that is a thundering sight better than for them to have gone without an education, or not been able to pay the bills for their instruction."

"Joseph Waters, do stop using such expressions," said his wife.

"It isn't much worse than 'distinguished old cat,' is it, mother?"

"No matter how the boy was educated, without friends and a name, he could never marry my daughter."

"William," replied the Captain, "Mrs. Wilson didn't take in sewing to educate her children, after I found it out. I went there and asked it as a favor that she would allow me to educate them as my own, for their father sailed 'long with me. Mrs. Wilson was so over-joyed that she took my hand and was about to kiss it, but I stopped that, and offered her something more acceptable to kiss, which she accepted; and I gave her another to pay. I don't care if mother and Laura do know it. I dare say I told mother all about it at the time, but don't remember."

"Yes, yes, you did, Joseph; and I told you at the time that you did just right, kissing and all; and we have none of us been sorry for it yet. George is a good boy, and his sister is a sweet girl."

"Now, William Morton," continued Captain Waters, "you talk of George Wilson being 'a nameless wretch, and having no rich friends.' Let me tell you that he is of a distinguished family, and his name has been honored since ships sailed from American ports. Should he marry your daughter (and I hope he will, for he is just the kind of a man to be the husband of such a woman, though I never thought about the matter till since we have been

talking), he will have one powerful friend and a rich relative, for he will have Joseph Waters for a grandfather."

" Joseph, this is the first time in my hearing, that you
have boasted of being rich."

" I know it, mother ; but it is the first time that I have
fully realized the power of money,—not for myself, but to
make others happy. If George should marry our Susie,
—and she will not have him unless she loves him,—then
some of the money that I have made and saved will go
to buy him a good ship, when he feels competent to command one ; and I shall be very happy in seeing others
happy whom I love."

A tear of heart-felt joy, from each of the Captain's eyes,
were rolling down his benevolent face, at the thought of
making others happy.

Mr. Morton had calmed down entirely. Whether it
was the shaking that the captain gave him, or the knowledge that his father-in-law possessed over half a million
of dollars, none but himself knew. He at length said :

" Father and mother, we will leave this unpleasant subject for the present, and you, Susie, will forgive a father's
first unkindness, and come to him with a kiss."

Susie did forgive him, and kissed him until there was
no unkindness or harsh feelings left in his heart.

" I will tell you things this afternoon, William, about
Frank, that will cure you of every wish to have him a
member of your family. Now for dinner," said the
captain.

CHAPTER XXXV.

CAPTAIN AND MRS. WATERS' OPINION ON HAPPINESS.

NOTHING was said during the time occupied at the
dinner-table on the subject that had been discussed
in the forepart of the day. Captain and Mrs. Waters,
by a judicious exercise of their practical good sense and
good nature, had succeeded in restoring Mr. and Mrs.

Morton and Susie, if not to perfect cheerfulness, to a state of mind bordering closely upon it, long before the meal ended. When they were about leaving the dining-room, Captain Waters, in a tone of great kindness, said :

"Now, mother and children, let us return to the parlor, that I may tell William and Laura what I know of Frank Livingston, and learn from them if they still wish him to be the husband of Susie. We are all of us in a mind at the present moment to speak and listen calmly to the truth."

When they were again in the parlor, and seated near each other, the Captain, after a little thinking, first addressed himself to Mr. Morton by saying :

"William, we were stormy this morning, but that is now passed, and has been followed by a calm. If on this your first visit to our country home, and last anchoring place in this world, you should leave with unpleasant feelings towards any under this roof, one of the great objects of settling here would be defeated. I want this to be not only a 'Snug Harbor,' but a home of happiness, where the children and grandchildren can come and enjoy themselves; and also to be a comfortable home for those that have sailed many times around the world with us. The ties that bind sailors together are next in strength to those that bind parents and children to each other."

Captain Waters had with a design spoken longer than was his custom, in order to draw the mind of his son-in-law, and that of his daughter, away from the subject that he well knew was nearest their hearts. Mrs. Waters fully understood his purpose, and was as usual prepared to act as his powerful auxiliary. When he ceased speaking, she took up the subject, and continued it by saying :

" Before selling the ship and coming here, we had seen enough of the storms and excitements of life to sincerely, wish for rest and quiet. We wanted such a home as we have succeeded in obtaining. Our children never had a permanent home. There is no spot on earth that is hallowed in their memory, as the home of their childhood,

—no place place that they can visit and say : 'Here our father and mother reared us from infancy ; under that tree in the heat of summer our father smoked his pipe ; in that warm corner of this room, in a winter evening, our mother knit and read her bible.' For that want we are now endeavoring to provide. This place we wish our children and grandchildren to remember, when our voyage of life is ended. We wish them to remember it without the sweetness of their recollections being lessened by a single sad occurrence."

All listened with affectionate interest to what the good and kind-hearted woman was saying, and the Captain nodded his head a number of times in approval ; when she ceased speaking, he immediately asked :

"William, do you love your daughter Susie as we love her ?"

"If a father ever loved a child with his whole heart, then I love Susie."

"I knew it all the time ; and so does Laura. Would you not make any sacrifice for her happiness ? "

"I certainly would sacrifice all that I have, to secure her happiness."

"It is for her happiness that you have wished to marry her to Frank Livingston ? "

"For that, and for that alone, father, have I urged and would have forced it, because I believed my judgment to be better in this case than her own."

"My children, I have not been mistaken in my conclusions. You wish to see Susie very happy. Know then that Frank Livingston is a gambler, and a free drinker of wine,—I may safely say an occasional drunkard ; and when in the city seldom reaches his home until near morning, and often requires assistance to get home. However large his fortune, it will in time be wasted at the gaming table, and no drunkard can make a woman happy."

"Father, do you know such things to be true of Mr. Livingston ?"

"I do, or I shouldn't state them ; but do not ask how I obtained the information. I will pledge my word for its truth."

"Susie, my daughter, did you know of his failings when you declined his offer?"

"Yes, father, I did; but without such faults I could not love him, for he has no heart."

Mr. and Mrs. Morton were greatly astonished at such revelations, and Mrs. Morton, always accustomed to depend on some one for counsel and advice, was pleased that her father and mother were near to give it. She wished in all cases to do right, and especially in all that related to Susie. It was her head and not her heart which was at fault, and in that she differed but little from her husband.

Captain Waters had watched the effect of his information, and saw that the father and mother of Susie would not be likely to urge the acceptance of that offer of marriage, and then asked:

"William, are you willing to risk the happiness of your only daughter in the hands of such a man?"

"No sir; not if he was worth his weight in diamonds, and was full brother to a king. You, father, have cured me of a great and life-long folly, and I thank you for it."

"Give me your hand, my noble boy, and say you own a large interest in the heart of Joe Waters, who always talks what he means."

They did shake hands, and there was a hearty meaning in it. Mrs. Waters, Laura and Susie got mixed up with them, some way, while they were shaking hands, and there was such a hand-shaking all around, and such a hugging and kissing as did them all good, and Captain Waters in speaking of it afterwards said

"Everybody's eyes 'sprung aleak,' my own included."

When they were all again seated, Mrs. Waters offered her opinion on married life and happiness.

"In every part of the world where I have been and staid long enough to become acquainted, I have found rich and fast young men, always finding and occupying high places in fashionable society, always sought after; and those having daughters, over-willing to bestow them as wives on such husbands. Where I have had opportunities to observe, but very few such marriages have been productive of lasting happiness. Parents make great mistakes when they think the richer and higher in society their daughters can marry, the more sure of happiness they will be. It is indeed a sad mistake to look for happiness which can be obtained only with money."

"I fully believe you, mother, and am wiser, and I think better, than I was when I came to the farm; and now, Susie, my dear child, what have you to say to your father?"

"I have much to say, and much to thank you for, and also my dear mother; but I have this day, with you, been deeply exercised in mind, and we all need rest. My future life will prove how grateful I am."

"And my future life shall show you, dear, that your happiness shall be one of the great objects of my future actions."

"Now, father, I have a request to make,—a favor to ask."

"Name it, my child, and if consistent, and in my power, it shall be granted."

"It is that you and mother will use your influence at the proper time, to prevent Mr. Livingston from becoming the husband of cousin Julia."

"Who ever heard the like? Susie, you are the strangest creature for one of your age that ever lived; but your request is granted, though I don't see the motive."

"I do not wish to see Julia marry him, for the same reason that I could not accept his offer myself. The offer will be made, and I fear accepted; but we have not now time to talk about it, as I see grandfather is impatient to break up this assembly."

"You little rose-bud, I will try and break you from being saucy to your old grandfather; but you all know I have been more indoors to-day than usual, and I must go and set the Bo'son at something that will lead him to do funny things for our amusement, without injury to himself. The people hereabouts will never have the blues while the Bo'son lives."

CHAPTER XXXVI.

THE BO'SON TOWS A STEER OUT OF THE PASTURE.

CAPTAIN Waters was as great a lover of fun as the Bo'son was, and often set Bill Thomas at something that he thought would furnish amusement. Much of the day having been spent in discussing unpleasant subjects, and in reconciling conflicting opinions, and all having ended to the satisfaction of the family, the Captain wished that something amusing might occur that would waft away the last little cloud of the morning's discontent. To accomplish his wish, he concluded that the Bo'son must play a conspicuous part, feeling assured that if Bill only had an opportunity, he would play his part well. There were no cows to milk, and if there had been, Bill was master of that art; there were no sheep to salt, and if there had been, "old butts" was cured of a bad propensity, and wished no further acquaintance with the Bo'son.

When the family left the parlor, they went on the front piazza, where they were soon joined by Julia Fizzlebaugh. The Captain, casting his eyes over that portion of the farm in front of the house, and on the opposite side of the road, discovered a young steer, not belonging to the farm, that had broken into a mowing lot. He called the Bo'son, and requested him to drive the animal out, and put up the fence.

"Aye, aye, sir," answered Bill, touching his hat, and moving towards the pasture.

The Bo'son saw at a glance that all family difficulties had been satisfactorily arranged, and a telegraphic dispatch, received from Susie's eyes, told all that he cared then to learn, and put him in the very best of spirits.

Captain Waters, when he saw the Bo'son moving on the steer, said to the family:

"If the Bo'son don't get into a scrape before that steer leaves the pasture, I shall be mistaken, and it will be the first new thing that he has done, without encountering difficulties.

The steer had broken the two upper rails in a length of fence, and then jumped the others into the pasture. The Bo'son reasoned that if the animal could jump into the pasture, he could jump out, and Bill attempted to make him do so ; but though the steer was chased a number of times around the enclosure, he showed no disposition to leave such good feeding ground. At length the Bo'son got the animal by the tail, and they both went around together ; the Bo'son, as was his custom, talking to himself.

"Run now, do your best, the Bo'son has you by the tail ; I have been fast to bigger things than you are, when I was a whaling. I never cut my line, and you must go out of this before I let go of your tail, old calf."

These expressions seemed to come from Bill's lips in a jerking kind of way, but the steer and Bo'son were both on a smart run. After running a number of times around the pasture, which was not large, the steer made an extra jump in crossing a small, dry ditch, and the Bo'son's tarpaulin hat went off, going a number of feet above his head. The old dog, from some comfortable place where he had been sleeping, made his way to the piazza just as the Bo'son's hat went into the air, and seeing it, knew that his master must be there, though he couldn't see him, being too low in stature for that. One encouraging word from the Captain, and Bose went to the assistance of his master.

When the dog reached the pasture, his master and the steer were still making their rounds, and the Bo'son still having the animal by the tail. The dog appeared to think that it was rare sport, and readily joined in it, by running at the side of the steer, shaking his tail and barking cheerfully. When the dog came to his master's hat, he considered it his duty to take care of it ; so picking it up, he ran again to the steer, and to his head, shaking the hat and long ribbon on it in the face of the animal. He would drop the hat, have a few barks, then run back, pick up the hat and again shake it in the face of the steer, which he continued repeating, in the apparent belief that it was the finest sport he had enjoyed in a long time.

The Bo'son was so out of breath, that he couldn't direct the dog, for the more the dog barked and shook the hat in his face, the faster the steer run. At last the Bo'son found that his patience was leaving him with his breath, though at first he liked the fun of running around, fast to the steer's tail; but he was growing a little tired of it, and tried to talk to the dog, out of breath as he was.

" Yo yoo-you con-tempt-i-ble cu-cu," and the steer again jumped the dry ditch, when Bill finished the word " cuss."

Bill afterwards said that he intended calling the dog a contemptible cur, but only succeeded with great difficulty in saying " contemptible cu," when the " 'tarnal critter " jumped the ditch and jerked the double " s " out before he could shut his mouth, making cuss for cur. A moment after Bill had called his dog a hard name, the steer, in turning short in a corner of the pasture, threw the Bo'son, and they parted company.

Bose was at his master's side the instant he was on the ground, and ready to help him up. When the Bo'son got on his feet, he said :

" You good for nothing dog; what do you mean ? I am ashamed of you. You are not half a sailor. Go bring that hat here."

Poor Bose was greatly disappointed. He expected praise, and had been more severely censured than ever before, and couldn't understand it. He had done his best to keep up the sport, and been scolded for it. With his head and tail drooping, he took the hat to his master, and then at a little distance sat down, and looked upon the ground as though engaged in thought, and expecting trouble   The Bo'son soon recovered his breath and good nature, and feeling that he had done the dog in-justice, called him kindly, patting him on the head, and saying :

" It wasn't your fault after all, was it, Bose ? I couldn't tell you what to do, and how should you know ? You are a good old dog any how."

The dog appeared to understand and appreciate what was being said to him, and became reconciled.

"Now, old dog, lend the Bo'son a hand to chase or tow that craft out of the harbor?"

The dog gave one short bark, which the Bo'son understood. Bill went and opened the gate, which he should have done in the first place, and then said to the dog:

"You go and make fast to him forward, and I will make fast again aft, and if he don't tow easy, we will anchor him," which meant to throw him down.

The dog obeyed, and soon had the steer fast by the nose, and then the Bo'son found no difficulty in again getting him by the tail. The steer under such circumstances couldn't run, and the Bo'son with his dog had a good time, both working hard, and both enjoying the sport. They had succeeded in getting him near the gate, when the animal stopped, and Bo'son said:

"Bose, we are hard and fast aground. Hang to him, old dog; rouse his head up stream."

The dog pulled the animals's head towards the gate, when Bill sang out:

"There, hold on all you have got, while I bouse his stern to windward."

Then the Bo'son hauled his end of the steer a little nearer the gate. Under the same order, the dog worked the head of the beast again towards the gate, and held it there while Bill worked the other end of the animal that way; and so, little by little, they got the steer into the road, when the Bo'son sung out, as though he had been on shipboard:

"Let go forward, Bose!" At the same time letting go himself aft, and giving the steer a good kick. The animal started down the road on the run, and Bill shouted:

"There she goes down stream under full sail; studdensails on both sides."

The Bo'son soon convinced the dog that his master entertained no unkind feelings towards him for not understanding and doing his duty at the beginning, repaired the fence, and went to the house.

The family on the piazza enjoyed the sport; and the Captain laughed until the big tears rolled down his face, and when he could speak, said:

"William, if it wasn't for the Bo'son, I should sometimes be at a loss for amusement."

"I have enjoyed this last exploit as much as you have, father."

"Wait a little, William, till the Bo'son comes here to report, and hear what he says."

Bill, with the dog at his side, walked up to the piazza; touching his hat, said:

"Orders obeyed, sir. The steer has gone to sea, and by this time is out of sight of land."

"You had a rough time of it, Bo'son," said the captain.

"Yes, sir ; when I first went on board, I was 'short handed, and he out-towed me;' but after the dog got along side, and I could give him orders, we managed to haul him square to windward against the tide till we worked him into the middle of the stream, and then sent him a-flying to sea."

"You have done well, Bo'son, as you generally do."

"Thank you, sir. When the Bo'son and dog undertake a job, they always manage to do it, in some way."

"That is so, Bill ; and now I hear the supper bell," said the Captain.

The Bo'son again touched his hat, and left with his dog for the midship-house.

CHAPTER XXXVII.

SUSIE AND JULIA TALK, AND MR. MORTON AND JULIA
WRITE.

THAT night, after retiring from the sitting-room, Susie and her cousin Julia had a very long conversation together.   Julia had asked no questions, but felt assured that her uncle and aunt had failed in persuading Susie to accept the offer made her by Mr. Livingston.

After conversing on other subjects for some time, with more freedom on the part of Julia than she had manifested towards her cousin since Frank left the farm, she said :

"Cousin, have you at last concluded to be the wife of Mr. Livingston ? "

"No ; my father and mother, after hearing all my reasons for not accepting his offer, have both ceased to wish him to become my husband, and commend me for declining to be his wife."

"That appears very strange to me, Susie, when they have been so anxious and so earnest about it. What could have so changed their views and wishes ?"

"I will freely and frankly tell you, cousin Julia. When they wished him to become a member of the family, they knew nothing of his character and habits. Now they know all about him, and my father would not consent to the union if Mr. Livingston 'was worth his weight in diamonds, and was full brother of a king.' If I now wished it myself, the consent of my father and mother could not be obtained. You must know that there are some strong objections to our union, some good and powerful reasons, or my parents would not have relinquished such long cherished desires ; and I still entertain some hopes that the same reasons which have so changed the wishes of my parents, will change yours. Do not, Julia, throw away every chance of future happiness, which you will do if you become the wife of Frank Livingston. You may, for a very brief time, move in fashionable society, but you will know nothing of real happiness."

"I believe you are sincere, Susie, but how little you know of real life, and the charming and thrilling delights of fashionable society. It is you who have thrown away one of the best chances a young woman ever had of being happy. When such a chance comes to me, if I am fool enough to reject it, then may I be wretched all the remainder of my life. All that I hope for is, that I may have an opportunity of displaying my wisdom and good judgment, in accepting an offer of marriage from Frank Livingston."

"I have told you enough, Julia, of his habits, to sufficiently warn you of the danger to your happiness in such a union. Don't deceive yourself, and sacrifice the future for the present. Remember that there is a near, as well as a far future, and for both we should be prepared and provided."

"Once for all again I tell you, that if I receive, I shall accept his offer. I am bound to have a rich husband if I can get one. I have been educated for such a condition in life, have been brought up a lady, and my mother has been my servant when I had no other, and now she is getting old and feeble, and I want money to hire servants, —a want my father can't supply. I do not mean to work myself, I don't like it, and I don't think it would agree with me. The idea of my getting up in the morning and preparing breakfast for a toiling husband! No matter what else he might be, if he was poor, he wouldn't be loved by Julia Fizzlebaugh. You know that I never get up in time to eat breakfast with people who are unfashionable and vulgar enough to rise early in the morning; and how can it be expected for me to do things that I have not been educated to, and have no taste for."

"Julia, you have, I think, very erroneous ideas of life, its duties and pleasures. Future years of disappointment, sorrow and suffering, will teach you wisdom, when too late for you to profit by it. It is not all your fault. It is the fault of your parents in educating you with no higher aspirations, no nobler aims, than a rich husband and the enjoyments of fashionable society. It is growing late and we should retire; but think, dear cousin, these things over seriously, and endeavor to arrive at wiser conclusions than you have yet reached."

Julia did think seriously of all the matters that had been spoken of, and concluded that her cousin was a beautiful, kind-hearted, well-meaning simpleton, eminently fitted by nature and education to adorn some sea-side or country cottage, and share it with a frugal and ever-toiling husband; and that she, herself, was fitted and destined to reign a queen in the fashionable world.

Susie pitied her cousin, and hoped that what had been told her of Frank Livingston and his habits would have

been a sufficient warning,—but with his money and character (both having been inherited, and both in a fair
way of being sacrificed on the alter of his folly), no
matter what might be his faults or his habits, they would
not weigh against his wealth and position in society,
and he would be an acceptable offering to her.

It was long after Susie left her cousin, and retired
to her bed, before she closed her eyes in slumber. The
one great disturbing subject, which had in some form prevented her from enjoying all the pleasures of country
life, was now finally disposed of, and with less difficulty
than she had anticipated. Her father and mother were
satisfied, and there was nothing but love and harmony in
the family. It was true that Susie Morton felt sorry and
anxious for her cousin, but felt that she had done all in
her power to save Julia from future wretchedness.

There was with Susie another cause of anxiety, known
only to herself. George Wilson at sea ; she dearly loved
him, but knew not whether he loved her in return. They
had been much together, and were like brother and sister,
but that was not sufficient to satisfy such a warm and
loving heart as dwelt in the bosom of Susie Morton.

All that had been said and acted in the parlor during
the day, passed in review before her mind, and all the
feelings which she had entertained at different periods of
that long interview, were again her companions ; and at
last she came to the closing scene of the Bo'son and the
steer, and then in spite of her previous reflections, she
was induced to laugh, though only slightly and to herself,
which put her in a frame of mind to sleep. With the
Bo'son, dog, and the amusement they furnished in their
contest with the steer, last on her mind, Susie slept, was
refreshed, and during the night enjoyed pleasant dreams.

Early the next morning, William Morton addressed the
following business-like letter to Mr. Livingston :

WATERS' SNUG HARBOR, September 10th, 185—.
FRANK LIVINGSTON, Esq., Saratoga Springs :—
Dear Sir—The contemplated visit here has been made,
and the conversation with my daughter taken place.

Susie takes the same view of your offer now, which she did
when it was made, and the answer she then gave you
must be considered final. After listening to all the reasons given by my daughter for declining your offer, neither
Mrs. Morton nor myself could urge upon her the acceptance of it ; nor would Susie's grandparents recommend
such a course. However long you may have cherished
the wish and the hope of having my daughter for a wife,
and however much I may have encouraged you, I have
now to inform you, that circumstances over which I have
no control, forbid such a union, and prevent me from
recommending it to my daughter. Wishing you health,
happiness, and prosperity, I remain

Your obedient servant,

WILLIAM MORTON.

Julia Fizzlebaugh also wrote and mailed a letter to
Mr. Livingston.

"WATERS' SNUG HARBOR, *September 10th*, 185-.
"*My Dear Friend:*—Yesterday was an important day
here, and until late in the afternoon I hoped that you
were not doomed to disappointment. The father and
mother of my cousin were not able to persuade her to
accept your noble and generous offer. Susie is a very
headstrong girl, and when excited, ungovernable. I presume that you will learn the final decision from my uncle.
Nothing has been said on the subject, except among themselves. What I know about it has been communicated to
me by my cousin, who has constantly said to me : ' Julia, your pleading for Mr. Livingston is all in vain. I
shall never be his wife.' My anxiety to see you happy
has in this case urged me to greater efforts than it would
have been possible for any other cause to have done, and
the long and close intimacy existing between my cousin
and myself has given me opportunities that no other person could have enjoyed. Susie has been very free with
me on all subjects but her reasons for not accepting your
offer. On that subject she is silent. Notwithstanding
that my heart aches for you in your disappointment, I am

full in the belief that, after a little reflection, you will conclude that it was more for your happiness to be rejected than to have been accepted. When you marry, you want a wife with a large and noble heart, capable of receiving, appreciating, and returning such love as you would bestow. Susie Morton is sadly deficient in all the requisite qualifications, to be the wife of such a noble-hearted man. That you may find one worthy of you, and with her long enjoy the happiness you so richly deserve, is, and ever will be, the wish of

Yours, very truly,
Julia Fizzlebaugh

To Frank Livingston, Esq., Saratoga Springs.

CHAPTER XXXVIII.

JULIA FIZZLEBAUGH RECEIVES AN OFFER.

FRANK Livingston received the letters from Mr. Morton and Julia at the same time. He was disappointed when he offered himself to Susie and was refused, but far more disappointed after reading the letter from Mr. Morton. He was in the full belief that Susie would listen to her parents, and comply with their wishes. The parents had assured him that such would be the result of their visit to the farm. Mr. Livingston was satisfied that it was now useless for him to entertain any hopes of a change in his favor. He was disappointed in love, and must lose all the foolish wagers he had made, that within a stated time Susie Morton would be Mrs. Livingston. The wagers were large, but his fortune was so ample that they would not materially inconvenience him, as he could raise the money by a mortgage on some of his real estate. It was the jeers of his friends among sporting men that he most dreaded.

When not under the influence of strong drink, Frank Livingston had too nice and delicate a sense of what belonged to the proprieties of life, to have made any wager to be decided by the action of a young lady whom he would gladly accept as a wife. Of late he had been so constantly under the effects of stimulants, that he was hardly capable of forming a correct opinion on any difficult subject. He had not lost his pride, and was determined to maintain it, notwithstanding his disappointment, and felt that he must do something brilliant, which would eclipse the past, and create for the present a new subject for gossip.

Frank walked the floor for some time in deep thought; stung to madness by his disappointments and loss of money, and acting under the influence of over-excited feelings, he arrived at conclusions that he would never have reached in his calmer moments. He read Julia's letter a second time, and in his own mind concluded that she must be a perfect angel,—one of the most lovely and disinterested beings who had ever inhabited this earth. Julia had labored so earnestly in his cause, and used such noble efforts to aid him in accomplishing his object, and after failing in it, had expressed so much sympathy for him in his disappointment, and also expressed such solicitude for his future happiness, that she must, indeed, be a noble-hearted woman. He would write her immediately and ask her to meet him in New York, and would there offer himself in marriage to her, feeling certain that she would accept the offer, and when married he would, with a woman worthy of his love and companionship, make such a display of his wealth and power in the fashionable world, as would teach the Waters' and Mortons' what they had lost in rejecting a rich young gentleman, belonging to one of the old families. Mr. Livingston also decided in his wrathy and vengeful mood that should he ever meet with George Wilson in this world, that he would pull his nose,—an act which would have been very hazardous to the health of Mr. Frank Livingston.

Frank had worked himself into such a state of mind that he would gladly have annihilated time, space, and many other things besides the nose of George Wilson, so he did one of the foolishest things that he could have done under the circumstances. He wrote a letter to Julia Fizzlebaugh, to which he wanted an immediate answer, and wouldn't wait for the mails. By one of his servants, dressed in his livery, and driving one of his horses, he sent to Julia this letter:

"SARATOGA SPRINGS, September 12th, 185—.
"MISS JULIA FIZZLEBAUGH :—

"*My dearest friend*—Your esteemed favor of the 10th instant reached me only this morning. I freely confess to you that it gave me great pleasure. The knowledge that I am no longer bound by my offer to Miss Morton is indeed a great relief to me. I am now satisfied that united in marriage, we could not have been happy together, and that we were not designed for each other. Our tastes, desires and habits are not in harmony. Miss Morton, to be happy, must have a husband with a different disposition than I possess, and with different associations than I am surrounded with. I, to be happy, must have a wife who with me can enter into all the gayeties of fashionable life, and with me enjoy them. Your interest in my behalf, your sympathy for what you supposed was a great disappointment to me, and the kind advice you were pleased to offer, have placed me under such great obligations to you, that a lifetime only, can cancel them. It will be my greatest pleasure, in the future, to show by every act of mine, how much you have become endeared to me. Please inform me, by the return of the bearer, when you propose leaving the farm of your uncle, and when I can have the pleasure of meeting you in the city. I have much that I wish to communicate to you, that will be interesting to us both, and hope the day is not distant when we shall understand and more fully appreciate each other. I have been living on fancies and dreams, existing in fairy lands ; in future I must enjoy the realities of life, and depend on you, to lead and guide me to true happiness ; that is, if you will kindly accept such a mission. Hoping to receive a few lines from you by the return messenger, I remain, with great esteem,   "Affectionately yours,
                    "FRANK LIVINGSTON."

The messenger from the Springs appeared at the farm, and inquired for Miss Julia Fizzlebaugh, saying that he had a letter for her from Mr. Livingston, and was directed to wait for an answer. Neither master nor the servant showed wisdom or judgment in what they had done; the master must have been drunk, and the servant a fool. Julia made her appearance, received the letter, and retired to her room to read and answer it.

The circumstances under which she received the letter, in the presence of the whole family, embarrassed Julia; but the contents of the letter were really astonishing to her. All that Julia had hoped for came so suddenly and unexpectedly, that she was not in the least prepared for it. She read the letter over a number of times, weighing in her mind the full meaning of each expression, and concluded that the letter was, if not an offer of marriage, something very near it. After thinking it over as long as it was prudent to keep the servant waiting, she wrote as follows:

"WATERS' SNUG HARBOR, September 12th, 185—.

"*Dear Friend*—Your kindly expressed note of this date has just been placed in my hands by your servant. Its contents are of such a character, and you express so much confidence in my being able to aid you in your pursuit after happiness, that I am alarmed at my own weakness, fearing that my efforts may not be equal to my wishes, or your expectations. Be assured, however, my dearest friend, that I have earnestly hoped for your happiness, without ever dreaming that I should be the means of contributing to it. All that I can do, all the heart and soul of affection that I have to give, shall be yours. Previous to receiving your letter, I had arranged to return to the city with my uncle and aunt, reaching there on the morning of the 18th instant. Your letter has made me more anxious for the time to arrive, than I was before receiving it. When in the city, and at my father's house, I shall be pleased to see you, and learn how I can make you very, very happy.

                    "Yours in true affection,
"FRANK LIVINGSTON.   "JULIA."

Julia, with her utmost efforts, was unable to hide within herself, her joy. Under any other circumstances but those occurring in the family so recently, she would have told all that was in the letter just received. Appearances justified the family in believing that Julia had all the time been a spy on their actions, and corresponding with Frank Livingston. Under such embarrassments, nothing could be explained without telling the whole, and the time had not come for that, so Julia concluded to wait and let matters explain themselves.

Susie Morton was the only one in the family who suspected the truth, and the whole truth didn't suggest itself to her mind, not thinking that Mr. Livingston would, so soon after being refused by one, offer himself to another.

How little the pure-hearted Susie Morton knew of the motives and feelings that would prompt such a man to action? Little did Susie think that madness and revénge would induce Frank to marry her cousin. Could Susie have penetrated all the secrets of his faithless and impure heart, she would have shrunk from him with greater horror than she felt when her father urged her acceptance of his offer. Believing that the letter Julia had received related in part to herself, and in part to Julia's future, Susie felt some anxiety to learn the contents of that letter, if they could be revealed without a betrayal of confidence on the part of her cousin. When the cousins retired to their room, Julia, though still manifesting strong symptons of great delight, appeared a little disturbed and flustered in her mind, when Susie asked :

"Cousin Julia, did the letter you received from Mr. Livingston relate to you or me?"

"Both," was the answer.

"Are the contents a secret?"

"Not to you, Susie, under a promise that you keep, them until I leave the farm."

"Let it be so, then, as I can have no object in making known the contents of the letter."

Julia handed the letter to her cousin, and Susie carefully read it, and when returning it Julia saw that her cousin's eyes were filled with tears, and said :

"I thought, Susie, that you would repent when too late."

"I am not weeping for myself, but for you.   Could I by any possible means dissuade you from being the wife of Frank Livingston, I should feel very happy.   I have told you of his habits, and know that all your fond hopes will soon be blighted, and that for your folly you will be miserable."

"With plenty of money, and a high position in the fashionable world, I am not afraid that misery will overtake me.   I will show you, cousin, between now and next spring, what real life means and is.   I did not expect so soon to be gratified in my wishes, but fortune has favored me, and I am her pet child."

Susie had so frequently and so earnestly pleaded with her cousin, without effect, that she concluded it would be useless to offer any additional advice, and so wished Julia good night.

CHAPTER XXXIX.

THE BO'SON PLOWS, AND THE OXEN TURN THEIR YOKE.

SUSIE Morton had a long talk with the Bo'son the day after the meeting of the family in the parlor, and told him all that was proper for him to know, and enough to put his mind at perfect ease about herself.   The Bo'son was greatly relieved of his anxiety after he was satisfied that Captain Waters was opposed to the marriage of Mr. Livingston and "black-eyed Susan."   Bill Thomas had so long been accustomed to regard Captain and Mrs. Waters as superior beings, able to accomplish whatever they desired, that he really felt that Susie was safe, when they promised their aid and protection.   The Bo'son, however, concluded that he and the dog might yet be needed to guard and protect his "morning-glory." From the time that Mr. Livingston first appeared at the farm, the Bo'son had slept with his clothes on, and the dog at the side of his bed, that he might be ready at a moment's call to place himself between Susie Morton and any danger of her being run away with by Mr. Livingston. He could sleep well, because the dog was ordered to watch, and Bill could depend on him to give the alarm if any thing moved around, near the house.

When the letter was brought to Julia by a servant of Mr. Livingston, the Bo'son concluded that there was a conspiracy, and would be a mutiny. His captain being "on board," the Bo'son knew he must wait for orders, and having such confidence in his commander, he was sure that they could suppress the mutiny. After the servant had left with Julia's answer, the Bo'son from Lizzie learned all that could then be known; also the suspicions of Lizzie, that Julia Fizzlebaugh would, at some day not far distant, be the wife of Frank Livingston.

It is wonderful to notice the faculty of a naturally smart woman, who has long been domesticated in a family, of finding out, or suspecting events, long before they occur. That faculty is always displayed in an eminent degree in all matters relating to love, courtship and marriage. The Bo'son had some suspicions, but they were so vague as to amount to nothing, that he could satisfy his own mind about. The first opportunity he had of seeing Susie, he asked:

"Sunshine, is the flying-sky-sail going to be the wife of Mr. Livingston?"

"Bo'son, what makes you call my cousin such unheard-of names? I am most a mind not to answer you, or tell you what I think."

"I call her 'flying-sky-sail' because she is furled most of the time, and only used in light winds."

"Bo'son, how can you expect me to understand your sea language? In answer to your question, all I can say is I don't know, but fear Julia will be Mrs. Livingston."

"I hope," said the Bo'son, "she will, for she is good for nothing else, but to be the wife of such a worthless fellow, and hardly fit for that."

"Bo'son, how can you use such language about Julia? You mustn't do it, or I shall run away and leave you."

"You know, rose-bud, as well as I do, that Miss 'Fizzlebob' never 'stands a watch,' day or night; never 'goes aloft;' never 'steers a trick;' don't help 'take in' nor 'discharge cargo,' and that she lets her poor, feeble mother do double duty, while she 'sogers' about, doing nothing. Now, I say such a girl isn't worth ship-room, and isn't fit to lay things to."

"Bo'son, I am ashamed of you, and am going into the house. So be a good boy, and don't get into difficulty with any of the animals belonging to the farm."

The Bo'son put on his hat, which he had held in his hand while talking to Susie, as was his custom when talking or listening to ladies, made a funny face, and had a good laugh.

While Susie and the Bo'son were conversing outside, the Captain and Mr. Morton were talking in the house.

"I don't like the look of things, William," said the Captain. "There is something in the wind, and that letter means either mischief or marriage; and Susie may be right in her suspicions about Frank and Julia; and as you leave here the day after to-morrow, on your arrival in the city, I would recommend that you at once see your sister and brother-in-law, and tell them what you know of Livingston."

"I shall not fail in doing so, and if any offer of marriage is then made, I will prevent its being accepted."

"It may not be such an easy matter as you imagine."

"I think, father, that I can manage it, as my sister will listen to me; so we will dismiss the subject, without at present giving ourselves any further trouble. Now, let me ask if the Bo'son has encountered any new difficulties, or been engaged in any new adventures?"

"Nothing," said the Captain, "worthy of notice, since he and the dog worked the steer out of the meadow. He has become very fond of driving the oxen, and believes he is an excellent yeoman. He is now plowing for a winter crop, and manages the plow better than he does the oxen. I can't see how he will get into any difficulty to-day, though he may; and if he does, we shall hear from him."

The Bo'son had yoked up the oxen, and was, as stated by the Captain, plowing one of the fields. He appeared very happy; singing, whistling, and urging his team, by singing out "haw, shee, step along, stiff-legs," and sometimes using nautical language to them,—such as "port, starboard, gather ahead, boys." The Bo'son made "bout after bout" with the oxen and plow, watching the furrow as it constantly turned, when, to his surprise, the oxen stopped. Bill shouted and helped them with his gad, and there was a manœuvre that the Bo'son couldn't understand. The oxen had changed places; the off ox was on the near side, and the yoke was under instead of over their necks. If a ship had been taken aback in a squall, the Bo'son would have known exactly what to do, but in having the oxen in such a fix, he thought it best to call the Captain.

While the Captain and Mr. Morton were conversing, and very soon after Mr. Morton had made enquiry about Bill, the Captain saw his Bo'son coming, and said :

"Here comes the Bo'son, and I know by his manner that there is something amiss. How now, Bill; what has been carried away?"

Touching his hat, Bill said : "Struck with a squall, sir, and knocked on her beam-ends."

"What is on her beam-ends, Bo'son; let me know what the trouble is."

"I was plowing along, under easy sail, when she brought up all standing. I sung out 'haw, shee, get along, you stiff-legged lubbers,' and I stirred them up with my flag-staff. I can't say they didn't obey orders, for one hawed, and at the same time the other sheed, and burst the scuttle-butt, sir. Quicker than you ever saw a close-reefed top-sail blown out of the bolt-rope, in a hurricane, the starboard ox was on the port side, and the port ox on the starboard side; and the fife-rail that belongs athawt their necks, was under their windpipes. I want you to come alongside, sir, and help me clear the wreck."

"I'll be there directly," said the captain.

The Bo'son started back on the run, and when he

reached the place again, saw Friend Goodwin at a short distance. Bill tied his handkerchief on the gad, a third of the distance from one end, placed his hat on the end of the gad, then raised it high above his head, shouting at the same time:

"A ship in distress!"

Mr. Goodwin saw the signal, and was soon at Bill's side.

"Did you ever see such a wreck as this, Mr. Goodwin?"

"This is nothing, Bo'son, they have only turned their yoke,—not an uncommon thing with oxen, when they are unable to draw what they are hitched to," was Mr. Goodwin's answer.

"One more such a turn," said the Bo'son, "and I should expect to see Davy Jones' locker inside out, and upside down."

"I know not what thou meanest, Bo'son, by Davy Jones' locker, but this yoke turning I understand full well, and can show thee how to turn it back."

"I mean, sir, that place where ice is in great demand, with no supply."

"I think I now understand thee; thou speakest of the abode of darkness and despair, where the wicked are supposed to dwell when beyond the grave. I fain wouldn't have that place turned inside out, fearing some might return again to earth to trouble us."

Mr. Goodwin then placed a thumb and finger in the nostrils of each ox, and twisted them back to their places; an operation well understood by regular teamsters, but a perfect marvel to the Bo'son.

"Mr. Goodwin, if you had turned both of them oxen inside out, I shouldn't have been more astonished,—but you understand it and the Bo'son don't."

"Thou wilt learn after a while, Bo'son, only have patience and perseverance. Never abuse cattle, nor expect them to plow rocks. The plow has struck a rock, and the oxen couldn't draw it through, and so turned the yoke."

Friend Goodwin backed the oxen, drew back the plow, raised the point above the rock and started the cattle.

Bill thanked him for his kindness, and so did Captain Waters, who reached the field just as the oxen, plow and Bo'son again moved on.

CHAPTER XL.

FRANK LIVINGSTON AND JULIA COMPLETE THEIR ENGAGEMENT.

BEFORE Mr. and Mrs. Morton left the country, it was arranged that Susie should remain at the farm, and learn from Mrs. Waters, Lizzie and the old steward, whatever could be learned about cooking and housekeeping.

Susie made one more desperate effort to prevent Julia from being the wife of Frank Livingston. Susie asked her cousin:

"Can you love such a man? Can you ever respect a man of such habits? Can you marry one whom I have refused for such causes? Have you no respect for yourself, no regard for the opinion of the world, no wish to be happy here on earth, and respected in the community where you live? O! give it up, Julia, and seek happiness in the companionship of one that you can love."

Julia answered:

"If I cannot love such a man, I can love his money; if I cannot respect a man of such habits, I can respect the position he holds in fashionable society; I can and will marry a man that your folly refused, and have so much respect for my own wishes, that I am regardless of the opinion of the world; and mean to be happy amid the gayeties of high and fashionable life, and compel others to respect me for my position in the world. What is the love you talk about compared to the love of admiration and love of ease? I believe in the last, but not in the first."

"Poor Julia, time will answer your question to me, about such love as I talk of, and the time may come when you will understand and wish for it. Do you pretend to Mr. Livingston that you love him?"

"Certainly I do ; or how could I expect him to marry me. I will make him believe that he is the dearest creature in the world, though I care nothing about him, or whether he loves me or not, if he will only marry me, and then give me plenty of money to spend,—and you may be sure that I will spend it."

"What will you do if he has no money to give ? and that time will come."

"I don't believe that time will ever come; he is too rich for that, and should it come, it will be after I have had a glorious good time in the fashionable world, and then I will do the next best. To-morrow evening I shall see Frank, and all will be arranged."

"Julia, I can urge no more; you will follow your own wishes, and must suffer all the consequences. In the future there is hid and waiting for you sorrows wnich will break your heart; and now, I will say good night, and before I sleep, pray my Heavenly Father to spare and shield you!"

The next morning Mr. and Mrs. Morton left the farm for New York, and Julia went with them. They reached the city that evening, and Mr. Morton drove to the house of Julia's father before going to his own. He met his sister at the door, as he handed Julia from the carriage, and said to her that he would call and see her the next day.

That evening, as Julia expected, Frank Livingston called, and the two spent some hours together. They engaged themselves, and fixed the day for their marriage, and then called in the father and mother, as a matter of form, to ask their consent.

Mr. and Mrs. Fizzlebaugh were really taken by surprise, though very much gratified. The parents were as much embarrassed in this case, as children generally are in such cases, but managed in some way to give their consent, after stating how very much they should miss their only daughter, and how very lonely they should feel without her.

After Frank had left, Julia was nearly wild with delight at the prospect of being married in three weeks, to just such a man as she had long been hoping to find. The father and mother were as delighted as the daughter, but exercised greater control over their feelings and actions. With them there was one subject that weighed heavily on their minds, and that was the ways and means of meeting the extra expenses of such a wedding as they wished to give their daughter. The father said to his wife, that in some way, he would provide the means to meet such an occasion.

Neither Julia's father nor her mother knew that Mr. Livingston had offered himself to Susie Morton, and been refused, but had they known it, that would have made no more difference with them than it did with Julia.

The next day Mr. Morton called on his sister, and was spared from having to speak first on what was to him an unpleasant business. He had been but a few minutes in the house when his sister said:

"Oh, William! I have such good news to tell you! our Julia is to be married in three weeks to Mr. Livingston! Isn't that good news, brother?"

"No, sister, it isn't good news; it is the worst that I have heard in a long time. It is only a few days since I wrote him a letter, conveying to him Susie's positive refusal of his offer to marry her, and my approval of her answer."

"You surprise me, William; what objection could you have to Mr. Livingston as a son-in-law?"

- "His habits, principles and general character," said Mr. Morton; and then told his sister all that he knew of Frank Livingston, which at first appeared to make some little impression on the mind of his sister, but she soon rallied, and said:

"William, I believe you are greatly mistaken, or else for some cause are endeavoring to deceive me. Frank is not the fallen man you represent him, that is certain."

"Sister, I am not mistaken, and have no wish to deceive you."

"Why then are you so earnest to prevent Julia from becoming the wife of Mr. Livingston?"

"Because I know that if she does, her future will be miserable."

"You don't know any such thing, brother, but you do know that all your life you have talked to my husband and myself about your own children and our Julia marrying into the highest circles, and it became a passion with us, as it was with you; and now, when there is a certainty that Julia is about to do so, you come here to discourage it."

"I have changed my views and opinions on that subject, and believe that worth, character and manhood should be sought in a husband, in preference to wealth and position in fashionable society; and that with worth, character, and true manhood only, can happiness in married life be found."

"You talk very differently now, my brother, than you formerly did."

"Yes, sister, and it is because I believe and feel differently."

"Brother, you know that we have brought Julia up as a lady; never allowed her to do anything, not even to wash out a pocket handkerchief; but you know not how hard we have struggled to do it. You know not how hard I have worked, and often when I was not able ; many days and weeks, when I should have been in bed, I have been in the kitchen, cooking and washing, because we couldn't hire help, and have the means to clothe and educate Julia. It has cost over two thousand dollars for her music lessons, and since she has been grown and in company, her ball and party dresses have been very expensive. It has taken all, and more than all, that Thomas has earned to educate, dress, and prepare Julia for the place she is now to fill, but we shall be more than repaid when she is really there."

"Have you calculated her chances of happiness after marriage ?"

"Yes—no; I can hardly tell if we have considered or calculated anything about it, for the offer was so unexpected to us, and so very acceptable, that we gave our immediate consent, and shall have but little time to prepare for so great an occasion."

At this stage of the conversation Thomas Fizzlebaugh

came in, and after giving Mr. Morton a very cordial welcome home from the country and to his house, asked what he thought of Julia's expected marriage.

Mr. Morton again related all that had taken place in regard to Mr. Livingston's offer to Susie, and what he knew of the habits and character of Frank.

"Mr. Fizzlebaugh was at first staggered with the information, but, after a little reflection, said:

"These wild young men often change after marriage, and make the very best of husbands, and girls must take some ventures to win a rich prize."

"Do you know, Thomas, of any individual cases of such reformation, among your personal acquaintance? Do you think it safe to trust an only daughter to such a chance?"

"I have read of such cases, and it is an old saying; but I don't know of any individual cases," was the answer of Mr. Fizzlebaugh.

"Yes, Thomas, you have read them in novels, but they don't often take place; and you mustn't depend on old sayings for the happiness of your daughter."

"It is too late to change, as all is now arranged, and Julia will soon be Mrs. Livingston."

"And Julia will soon be miserable," was her uncle's reply, as he was about to leave.

The evening that Mr. Livingston engaged himself to Julia, after leaving the house of Mr. Fizzlebaugh, Frank went to one of the fashionable gambling houses, where he had an unusual run of good luck, winning a very large sum of money, and going home at daylight less under the influence of stimulants than usual. He slept until after mid-day, and when he awoke was more the Frank Livingston of earlier days than he had been for a long time. He dressed himself with great care, partook of a hearty breakfast, and at two o'clock, in accordance with a previous arrangement, was driven to the house of Julia's father. He had a long talk with Julia, arranging their plans for the future, and then he was driven to the place of Mr. Fizzlebaugh's occupation, he being secretary of an insurance company.

They had a long consultation in a private office, in which Frank informed his future father-in-law that Julia and himself had arranged to be married in church, and have their reception at a house he would have furnished, and where they would reside after their marriage tour. Frank stated that the house was large, and would much better accommodate their mutual friends than the one occupied by Mr. Fizzlebaugh.

Such an arrangement was very satisfactory, as it relieved the father of Julia from an expense he was not well prepared to meet, and he fully united with it.

When Frank was about to leave the office, he handed Mr. Fizzlebaugh a package, with a request that it should not be opened while he was present.

Immediately after Frank left, Julia's father opened the package, and found that it contained two thousand dollars, and a very kind note, asking him to accept it as a token of friendship, and tell no one of it. It was a small part of Mr. Livingston's previous night's winnings, and being perfectly himself, he made a good use of it.

CHAPTER XLI.

FRANK AND JULIA ARE MARRIED.

PREPARATIONS for the marriage of Frank Livingston and Julia Fizzlebaugh were made on a magnificent scale. Mr. Livingston had his house furnished in the richest and most tasteful style. Nothing that convenience and fancy could suggest, or money purchase, was wanting.

Julia's father, being unexpectedly supplied with what appeared to him a large sum of money, determined that the whole amount should be expended in preparing his daughter to dignify and adorn an exalted position in the fashionable world. An accomplished waiting-maid was engaged to fill the place of first maid of honor, and another to act as her assistant; a cook and chambermaid engaged for his own family, that his house might have the appearance of one occupied by a man of distinction. Dressmakers were employed to prepare Julia's wardrobe, and such a general stir, excitement and talking about a wedding could not be remembered by the oldest single sister in New York's fashionable society.

Mr. Livingston, from some cause unknown to his best friends, had ceased drinking wine, and apparently become a changed man. His best friends believed the change had been produced by his contemplated marriage; and the influence over him of that angel-like being so soon to become his wife. They were both often congratulated on their approaching union, and prospect of long continued happiness. Julia's father and mother were particularly pleased, and in talking the subject over between themselves, concluded that Mr. Morton had been deceived, or for some unexplained cause wished to deceive them. Julia would also have been pleased if she could have found time to think of such trifles, when she was preparing for her own wedding, but what to her was the condition of Frank? Drunk or sober, he was rich, and she was to be his wife.

The real cause of Frank Livingston's being sober, was to win back the money lost by not succeeding in obtaining Susie Morton for a wife. When paying off those bets, he feigned to be much under the influence of stimulants, though perfectly sober, and succeeded in making bets that he would not drink, nor again be drunk, until after he was a married man.

Professed gamblers will bet any reasonable amount on an even chance. That class of men with whom Frank had long associated, believed that they knew him too well, not to understand the chances in their favor. Mr. Livingston obtained odds in every bet, and staked large sums on the result. His resolution was equal to the occasion, showing that, had he profited by it at all times, he might have been a better man.

The subject of sending cards to the Waters and Morton families was freely discussed by Frank and Julia. Julia was very anxious that her uncle, aunt and cousin, should receive cards, and not sending them, would cause a breach in the family which could never be closed up. Captain and Mrs. Waters were not related to Julia, but she had been so much in the family, with Susie, that she had become accustomed to regard them as such. Julia was anxious to have them all see her new house, and the display of wealth and fashion, that would assemble at their reception. Frank also wished Susie's family and friends to be convinced of what they had lost, in not admitting him into the family. Cards were sent to them all. When Mr. and Mrs. Morton received their cards, and were informed that cards had been sent to Susie, also to Captain Waters and wife, they decided to accept, and wrote to the farm, expressing a hope that those there receiving cards would accept, and be present at the marriage and reception. Mr. Morton thought it would be the easiest way of showing that there was nothing but kindly feelings existing in the family, towards Mr. Livingston, and that his offering himself to Susie did not destroy those feelings. None of them wished him otherwise than well and happy, and they desired to show it.

When Captain Waters received the cards by letter, he called Mrs. Waters and Susie into the sitting-room, and said :

"Frank and Julia are to be ' spliced ' in ten days, and we are all invited to go on board and see it done. Here, Sue, here is your ticket, tied up with ribbons ; and here are ours, Nancy. Now, what have you all to say about it ?"

"I am sorry," said Mrs. Waters ; "but there is no help for it. I fear that Julia will see her mistake when too late to profit by it."

"Grandma, Julia knows all, and did before she left here; I kept nothing from her; I was very free in telling all, and earnest in my entreaty that, under no circumstances, she would consent to marry him. Julia was candid, and informed me that she should marry him. The letter Julia received here, though not a direct offer, amounted to that."

"Susie," said the Captain, did you tell her that you had refused him ?"

"Yes, grandpa."

"Well, then, let her have him, and learn her fate as she sails along. Julia has been educated for just such a voyage, and is fit for no other. If she can lie in bed half of the day, do nothing the other half, and be at a ball or party all night, she will be satisfied. She will find some head winds and head currents before the end of the voyage, or Joe Waters is no sailor."

"Shall we attend the wedding?" asked Mrs. Waters.

"Yes; it is best, and I can see no objection," answered Susie.

"I also think it best; but who would have believed that Frank would have been mad enough, or drunk enough, to have offered himself so soon to Julia, after Susie refused him? Men are greater fools than women, on such occasions," said the Captain.

It being generally agreed, at the farm, that all invited should attend, Captain Waters concluded to go in great style, and have the Bo'son for a body-guard; and Mrs. Waters decided to have Lizzie as lady's-maid. The Captain would have taken the steward also, but some of the family must remain at the farm and look after things.

The great day came, and all were glad to see it. The servants of Mr. Livingston all had a new suit of livery, and appeared to the best advantage. The housekeeper had superintended everything, and everything about the house was in perfect order.

A large number of cards had been sent out, both for the church and the reception. The daily papers had announced the time and church where the marriage was to be, and commented freely on the great wedding about to take place. Julia Fizzlebaugh had all the notoriety her heart could desire, and her parents were as elated and gratified as was their daughter.

The arrangements were that the marriage should take place at Trinity Church, at seven in the evening; reception at the house, from eight to ten o'clock, and at midnight the married couple should leave by railroad for Washington and a bridal tour.

The church was filled, and all went well there. The

reception was satisfactory, as all appeared to pass off smoothly, each congratulating the new made pair, and receiving their thanks, and the favored ones a kiss from the bride. At ten o'clock all were invited to the dining-room for refreshments, of which all partook freely. When all were satisfied with the good things from the table, Frank waited on Julia to her room, that she might change her wedding, for a traveling dress, saying, as he left her at the door of the room, that he would call for her in time to meet the midnight train.

Frank had kept his pledge of total abstinence for three weeks, and won all his wagers, amounting to more than he lost when he failed to secure Susie for a wife. He was gratified at his success, and on the occasion of his marriage, felt that he could indulge again, and drink to his own happiness and that of his bride. Those who had lost money, but styled themselves his friends, determined to see him drunk, on an occasion when, if ever, he should have been sober. They succeeded in inducing him to drink freely, and long before the time when Frank should have called for his wife, he showed signs of becoming intoxicated. Each of the pretended friends urged him on, when he needed urging, until he was mad, crazy, drunk. It took a number of persons to hold him, and soon they became alarmed, when fortunately Captain Waters entered the room, with Mrs. Waters and Susie. The Captain at once comprehended the situation, and told Susie to go to the kitchen and call the Bo'son. The Bo'son was soon with his captain,—and both of them had been accustomed to handle drunken sailors, and knew how to take hold of them. Bill Thomas took Mr. Livingston in his arms, and sitting on a chair, held him so firmly that he could injure no one. Frank had drank so much, that when held perfectly quiet, he soon went to sleep. When the Bo'son discovered that he was sleeping, he said:

"Show me his state-room, and I will put him where he'll not move till eight bells in the morning watch."

The Bo'son carried him up stairs as easily as though he had been a child, took off his coat, vest, cravat and boots, and laid him on a bed, saying as he did so:

" He isn't the first lubber I have bunked that couldn't bunk himself. Black-eyed Susan didn't sign the article fo: this voyage; all right; set the flying-sky-sail. "

What the Bo'son said was understood only by the Captain, who had followed him up stairs.

What had taken place was known to all but Julia and the bridesmaids, who were with her in the room. Julia thought that Frank was long in coming for her, and when her mother with Susie rapped at the door, she supposed it was he.   Julia's mother told her all, and saw the daughter fall from her giddy height into a deep abyss of woe. All night long Susie staid with her cousin, soothed her sorrow, held her hands, bathed her temples, and mingled her own tears with those of Mrs. Livingston. Julia had in her own heart triumphed over others, believing that Susie must regret her refusal after seeing so much splendor, and while glorying in her victory, was herself subdued. Julia saw not her husband again until noon the next day, and then he was unfit to travel. " The evening and the morning were the first day " of Julia Fizzlebaugh's glory and despair.

CHAPTER XLIL

THE BO'SON'S OPINION OF DUTIES.

THE evening after Julia's marriage, Captain and Mrs. Waters, Mr. and Mrs. Morton and Susie were together, and the wedding of Frank and Julia was the most natural subject to converse about. Had it ended without an exhibition of Frank Livingston's weakness, it would have furnished a theme for the fashionables of New York to talk about for at least a month, or until another great display had taken place; but with the winding up of the marriage feast, added to the other novelties, it was expected that the sensation would outlive all its kindred. In referring to the condition of Mr. Livingston, before the guests left the house, and the disappointment of Julia in being prevented from leaving the city on her bridal t ar, and her subsequent sufferings through the night and early part of the next day, Captain Waters asked Mr. Morton:

"What do you think now, William, of Livingston, as a suitable husband for your daughter?"

"When I so wished, I did not know him. I thank God, you and Susie, that he is not a member of our family. You will remember that I did not urge, or wish it, after I was acquainted with his character and habits."

"That is true," replied the Captain, "nor did I expect that you would. I knew that you loved Susie too well to hazard her happiness on a doubtful chance, and that it was only necessary to convince you of the truth, and Susie would be the last earthly treasure offered by you as a sacrifice on the altar of ambition."

"You judged me rightly, father; that I was greatly mistaken in my general views, I am very free to admit; but I had only looked at the surface of things, without taking thought, or time, to fathom their depths, and in that matter allowed myself to reach a conclusion, because it corresponded with my wishes. I was ignorant enough to believe a rich husband was a very desirable article."

"I am glad, William," said Mrs. Waters, "that we were all united in our opinion, after we had all properly considered the subject of Susie's marriage with Mr. Livingston. It is always the best way in family matters of importance to just talk them over freely, having the opinion and judgment of all interested in the matter, and then determine what is best. Much misery, and many unpleasant feelings, would be saved by such a course. Now that Julia has a husband, do you think she is happy?"

"Let me answer that question," said the Captain, "and I'll say that, in my opinion, Julia is just about as happy as she would be if very sea-sick, on board of a ship, in a heavy gale of wind, and not half the chance of ever getting over it."

"Joseph Waters, what makes you put your oar in when I asked William a question?"

"You know, Nancy, that I like to take a pull once in a while, and speak my mind on great occasions; but if you will excuse me this time, I will try and not do so again."

"Yes, yes, Joseph; I know a considerable about your disposition to speak your mind, and when you think things are going wrong, you are apt to be very decided in your expressions; but I am still waiting for William's answer."

"No, mother, that can't possibly be, nor can she see the least glimmer of happiness in the future."

"I think," continued Mrs. Waters, "that you are right, and that Julia's future will be dark and dreary. You, Susie, spent the night with her, and can tell us how Julia regards her present and future prospects."

"Grandma, there is nothing but duty, or necessity, that could induce me to pass through such suffering of mind, such a disappointment, as Julia endured last night. I sometimes thought that she would lose her reason; and she was insensible at short periods, when in convulsions; and after all, it was not her love for Frank; she does not love him any more than I do. It was her disappointment in not being able to leave, as had been arranged, on the bridal tour. Julia said to me when she was at the farm, and after I had informed her what habits Frank had contracted: 'I had rather put a husband to bed drunk every night, than be the wife of a poor man.' Poor Julia! how little she knew what she was talking about, or what it was to be a drunkard's wife. She received her first lesson last night, and the sadness it caused will long abide in her heart."

"It was fortunate that I brought the Bo'son along with me, for no other man at the reception could have handled Livingston as Bill Thomas did," remarked the Captain.

"Has any one talked with the Bo'son about it since?" asked Mr. Morton.

"I think not," replied the Captain.

"Then let us call him, and see what he will have to say about the wedding, and all that he saw and did last night."

"Wait a moment, William, and let some of us tell you what the Bo'son knows about this whole matter, and then you can judge better what the Bo'son means from what he says. Susie, you tell your father all about it."

Susie did tell her father that the Bo'son had not only a large, but a warm and tender heart, and that Bill had been her friend and adviser from the first, and would have stowed her away in one of his private "lockers," if it had been necessary, to keep her from being the wife of Frank Livingston.   Captain Waters and all the others were amused at the idea of putting Susie in the "Bo'-son's locker," to keep her from Frank.   At the request of her father, Susie went for the Bo'son, who was in the dining-room with Lizzie, and some acquaintances, who had called to see them.

Susie had spent full an hour with the Bo'son, after returning from her attendance on Julia, and having a short sleep, so the Bo son knew all that had taken place after he left Mr. Livingston in one of the upper rooms of the house of reception.

· After Susie left the room, for the purpose of calling Bill Thomas, Mrs. Waters said to her daughter:

" Laura, we have all been blessed in saving Susie from being the wife of such a man,—one who has been fortune's favorite, and will be her discarded child."

The Bo'son entered the room with Susie, and by Mr. Morton was invited to a seat.   Bill Thomas had sailed so long with Captain Waters, and spent so many evenings in the cabin of the ship with the family, when in port, that he felt perfectly at home and at ease when in the family circle.   Under the instruction of the steward, Bill Thomas had learned enough to read, and fully understand the English language.   He often used nautical terms, and so will every sailor, but with the Bo'son it was not for want of other words, to express his meaning.   After the Bo'son had paid his compliments to all present, and taken a seat, Mr. Morton addressed him by saying:

" Well, Bo'son, I believe you and my daughter have had a private and a perfect understanding with each other about some love affairs.   How is it, Bill ? "

The Bo'son looked at his Captain, the speaker and the ladies, in doubt how to answer, which the Captain understood, and said :

" Speak freely, Bo'son; we are all friends, and all

understand each other, and will understand you." The Bo'son so encouraged, answered:

"The morning-glory was for a time under my lee. Old Bose and myself kept a good watch to prevent her being cut out of the fleet, and run off by an enemy."

"I don't know that I fully understand you, Bo'son,—explain yourself."

"Well, sir, after Mr. Livingston brought the flying-sky-sail on board of the farm, and I found out that Mr. Livingston wanted black-eyed Susan for his first mate, and that Susan didn't like the voyage, and wouldn't sign the articles, I mistrusted that the sky-sail was left on board as a spy, and one of a press-gang to seize Susan, and put her on board of Livingston's ship. Captain Waters was absent from the fleet, and I had to act without orders, with no one to talk to but old Bose, and we arranged it between us. I watched in the day time, and slept with my clothes on nights, with old Bose on the look-out, until you took the flying-sky-sail away with you; and it would have been after a hard fight, before the pride of the fleet could have been taken from under our guns."

"I fully understand all that you say and mean, excepting the 'flying-sky-sail.' What is that, Bo'son?"

"Miss Julia Fizzlebob, sir; Mrs. Livingston that now is."

"What do you think, Bo'son, of city life, and city weddings?"

"I can't say, sir, that I think much of either. I was glad that we had kept the pride under our guns, and that black-eyed Susan was not Mr. Livingston's mate, for a long voyage. Hoping that when she does ship, her captain will be able to sail on the day appointed, whether on a voyage or a pleasure cruise. A mate has a double duty to perform, and no pleasure to enjoy, when the captain is drunk in his berth at the beginning of his first voyage as master. Miss Fizzlebob left the wharf with everything set, but had to drop her anchor before she got outside of the Hook. The captain drunk, the mate sick, the crew disorderly, and but little chance of getting to sea for some time, and when they do sail, they are sure to have an unpleasant voyage."

All fully understood the Bo'son, and all had learned how dear to him was Susie, and how much he was willing to do to protect her, or to secure her happiness.   Mr. Morton now fully appreciated the Bo'son's character, and understood his motives, for Mrs. Waters had informed him of the strong attachment and fatherly love that Bill Thomas felt for Susie Morton.

Mr. Morton took the Bo'son warmly by the hand at the close of the evening, when they were about separating, and said:

"Bill, you have my hearty thanks for the interest you have taken in my daughter, and I shall feel that she is always safe when you are near her."

"The Bo'son will fire his last shot, and the old dog make his last bite, before any harm can reach her," was Bill's reply.

They all shook hands with the Bo'son, and as Susie did so, she gave him a kiss, and received one in return.

CHAPTER XLIII.

RETURN TO THE FARM.

THE Waters family returned to the farm, taking Susie Morton with them.   It was Susie's wish to go, and remain in the country until late in the fall, when she would return to the city, and spend a part of the winter with her parents, who were now disposed to let the daughter be governed by her own wishes in what she should do, or where she should reside.   Mr. and Mrs. Morton felt that they could trust to the judgment of Susie, in all things appertaining to her present residence and future settlement.

Bill Thomas, while in New York, had been on board of such ships as were in port, and whose officers he was acquainted with, and had met many an old shipmate; been at the Sailors' Snug Harbor, on Staten Island, where he found many an old, worn-out seaman, well cared for, by the ample provision made for such seamen by the will of Captain Richard Robert Randall, leaving a property, the income of which is now nearly one hundred thousand dollars annually; all of which is applied in supporting disabled and worn-out seamen. A nobler or more worthy bequest was never made, nor so large a yearly sum more faithfully administered.

Captain and Mrs. Waters also had opportunities of meeting and exchanging, with old friends, the warm greetings of those who had been acquainted, in other lands. All the family were ready and anxious to return to the farm, and attend to the gathering in of the fall crops.

Susie Morton, before leaving the city, requested her father and mother to write occasionally how it fared with Julia, saying:

"I know that she has a bitter cup to drink, and is not prepared by habit or education for such a draught. She has new lessons to learn, and new duties to perform, and they will both be hard to accomplish. In learning them, she may also learn wisdom, and profit by the lesson."

Captain Waters found all at the farm as it should be, and the whole family were welcomed back with such an earnest and hearty manner, as to satisfy them that their return was pleasing.

The Bo'son, as usual, was ready for duty, and ready to do the first thing that needed doing, and he did many things the first afternoon that he was again on the farm.

During the ten days that he had been absent, many little things had got out of place in the different departments, which the Bo'son considered under his special care. A hay-rake was broken, a wagon injured, and a horse had cast a shoe; but Bill managed to mend the rake, repair the wagon, and shoe the horse, before milking time. Being naturally industrious, and handy at many things, the Bo'son accomplished, in a given time, more than many persons would have supposed was possible. In the evening, Bill gave, in his own peculiar way, the old steward a full account of the great wedding, and of all that he had seen in New York. The steward had formed so just an estimate of the two contracting parties, that he was not surprised that the Bo'son had to look after the groom. These old seafaring men, who have been in every part of the world, and mingled in the society of many nations and peoples, can judge with tolerable correctness of the character of individuals they meet with.

The next morning, Susie was up before it was fairly light, causing her sweet, clear voice to ring through the farm-house, as she sung, "I am over young to marry yet," followed by "I am a merry mountain maid;" and while singing, she saw the Bo'son coming from his house; meeting him at the door, and putting her arms around his neck, she kissed him as she would have done her father, saying:

"Ain't you glad, Bo'son, that I am not Mrs. Livingston?"

"Yes, beauty, I am."

"So am I; but I am sorry for Julia."

"Never mind her; it is just what she wanted, and she got it, so don't let us worry about it," said the Bo'son.

Susie knew that her singing early did not disturb the family, and Mrs. Waters appearing while she was talking with the Bo'son, did not disturb either of them.

Bill Thomas found enough to occupy all his time, and for a number of days after his return met with no adventures, as he was most of the time in one of the fields assisting the farmer, Mr. Harrowell, in gathering the crops.

A few days after his return from New York, and while Captain Waters was absent from the farm, Welcome Goodwin stopped at the gate with a pair of horses harnessed, but no carriage. The Bo'son met him at the gate, and inquired if anything was the matter.

"Yes, Bo'son, I have broken an axle-tree of my wagon, just below here. I have a load of grain on, and am going to Waterford with it, and if I return for another wagon, it will make me late home this evening. I have called to see if I can borrow a wagon of friend Waters. Is he at home?"

"No, sir, the Captain is not on board, but you can have a wagon, and the Bo'son to help change your cargo; so just make fast to that barge lying on the starboard side of the barn, and we will soon have you running your course again."

"Bo'son, I am now too well acquainted with friend Waters and thyself, to ask if thou art at liberty to lend the wagon, and will hitch to it, and be obliged to thee for helping me unload one and load the other wagon."

Welcome Goodwin soon had his horses before the wagon, and a short distance down the road went alongside of the broken vehicle. The Bo'son wouldn't allow Mr. Goodwin to touch a sack of grain, and in a very short time transferred the load to the other wagon, showing such strength and activity as astonished the good farmer, saying, as one sack followed another: "You haven't the right suit on, Mr. Goodwin, to handle sacks of grain."

"I know it, Bo'son; but I did not wish to give thee so much trouble."

"It is no trouble to me to handle such a cargo as can be stowed in one of these crafts."

"I should think so, from the way thou hast handled this, and I thank thee for thy assistance. This afternoon I will return the wagon, and take mine to be repaired."

"You are very welcome to what little assistance the Bo'son could give you, and I wish you a pleasant voyage and a safe return."

"Thank thee, Bo'son, thank thee," and Mr. Goodwin drove on.

When he was out of sight, the Bo'son went to his house, got some small rope, returned to the wagon, and lashed a rail under it in such a manner that it could be moved. He then yoked up the oxen, and took the wagon to his workshop. The Bo'son got out a piece of his Delaware oak, and went to work making a new axle-tree, and long before farmer Goodwin returned, it was finished, and painted. When Captain Waters returned, having met Mr. Goodwin on the road, and learned from him what had taken place, he concluded that Bill would be very likely to repair the damage, and went immediately to the shop where the Bo'son was working, and said to him:

" Another wreck, Bo'son?"

" Yes, sir, but only a partial loss,—not an underwriter's case."

" I see you are repairing without calling a survey."

" Not necessary, sir, in this case; we will have all finished by the time the tide turns flood."

" I am glad, Bo'son, that you are fixing that wagon, because Mr. Goodwin is one of our kindest neighbors, and refused any pay for helping team our things from the canal-boat to the farm."

" I remember it, sir; and I remember, too, that he turned them stiff-legged oxen into their places for me, which it took a better land sailor than the Bo'son to do, and I have been wanting a chance to do him a good turn ever since."

" You are right, Bo'son; never forget a favor, though you may forgive an injury."

" There are but few men in the world I wouldn't gladly do a favor,—and none about here except old Hardgripe, on the Ruckatucks, who is not worthy of one."

When Welcome Goodwin returned in the afternoon, he was surprised to find his wagon ready for use, and offered to pay the Bo'son for the work.

" No, no; " said the Bo'son, " there is no pay for that job, and that axle will not break while the wagon lasts, for it is made of the best seasoned Delaware oak, that I have had on hand over seven years. You did us a favor when our goods were landed, and would take no pay for it, and you did me a great favor when I was struck with a squall plowing with the oxen, and got them in irons; and I have been wanting an opportunity to make some proper return for it."

" What I did was nothing compared to what thou hast done. That axle would have cost three dollars, and not been as good, and I wish to pay thee."

" It cost me less time than you used in helping us, and I can receive no pay for it."

While they were talking the Captain made his appear- ance, and justified his Bo'son in his declining any compensation for what had been done; and invited farmer Goodwin to take tea with the family, which was accepted, as he had been on the road all day, with only a light dinner.

While they were at tea, the Bo'son discovered that one of Mr. Goodwin's horses had lost a shoe, and he set another in the place of it.

When farmer Goodwin was about leaving, he remarked that he would have to drive slow, as one of his horses was without a shoe. Bill asked which horse and which foot, which at once explained what had been done. The good man was again anxious to pay, but was again respectfully refused. He left, after obtaining a promise from Bill to pay him a visit, and again thanking him for what he had done.

After Mr. Goodwin had gone, the Bo'son said to his Captain:

"If any of the kind people about here get on the weather-bow of the Bo'son in doing a good turn, they will have to sail fast."

CHAPTER XLIV.

THE BO'SON AND DOG SAVE A YOUNG LADY FROM DROWNING.

AFTER the return of the family from New York, everything at the Waters farm appeared to glide along smoothly. Captain Waters walked over his land occasionally, visited the men in the fields, conversed freely with them, and gave such directions to his farmer, as when followed, would carry out his wishes. When the weather was fine the Captain drove some of his horses every day on the road, and was accompanied by Mrs. Waters or Susie,—sometimes by them both, and often by Lizzie.

The Captain's two sons and their families visited the farm, and taking them to ride days, and entertaining them evenings, afforded the Captain and his wife much pleasure.

Captain Waters was much attached to his two sons and

their families, and so was Mrs. Waters. It was one of the objects of buying a farm, to have a comfortable home for the children and grandchildren to visit, and remember with pleasure, after the old folks shall pass away.   The Captain, when at sea, would often say :

"Nancy, how well I remember the old farm where I spent my youth, and also the looks and words of my grandfather and grandmother.   The impressions then made on my young mind will never fade from my memory, nor can I ever forget the kindness of those grandparents.   After their death, and while I was still a youth, that farm was my father's, and there I remained until I became a sailor.   Every hill and vale, every tree and stump, all the houses and buildings in the neighborhood, the old church and school-house, and the faces of all the masters who taught and whipped the boys, are now as fresh in memory as when I left to be baptized with the ocean's spray.   The faces of my schoolmates are still familiar to me, but many of them are no longer animated with delight, nor their eyes sparkling with pleasure, but are dimmed with age, or forever closed upon the world. They are still dear to my memory, and I am pleased to have a home, that our grandchildren may also remember, when we are no more."

Such a place the Captain now had, and in the full enjoyment of it, with his family, was realizing all the happiness he had anticipated.

The Captain was right, and his reflections in his midnight watches at sea had taught him the value and pleasures of a happy childhood home.   Those who have no such sweets to remember, lose half the charms of life, and often pass to the grave in the belief that there was nothing refreshing in youth, no green spots along the road of manhood, and nothing to cheer and console in the twilight of age.

Captain Waters' sons and their families do not belong to our narrative, and are only mentioned as being members of the family for whose happiness the country home had been provided.

Mrs. Waters, after her return from the city, assisted by

Susie and Lizzie, arranged the house for winter, though winter had not yet appeared. Mrs. Waters did not feel that because they possessed enough to hire all done that needed doing, that her hands must always be idle. She taught and practiced, that in the active duties of housekeeping, consisted most of its pleasures; and her daughter, Laura Morton, after visiting the farm, was willing to admit that her mother was right. Mrs. Waters now had a double motive in view. She wished to teach Susie many things about housekeeping, which could only be taught by practice. Susie was as anxious to learn as her grandmother was to teach. So they had a pleasant time together.

The duties performed by Mrs. Waters and Susie were not laborious, or fatiguing. Others were employed at that; but in a large and well kept house, with the changing of the seasons, there is always enough of light work for willing hands to do.

Susie worked and sung, cheering all that were in the house, including her grandfather, who was never wearied with her songs. Captain Waters was an inveterate hater of pianos, and loved Susie all the more because she liked them no better than he did himself.

Susie Morton was a child of nature, and one of nature's best children. She had a sweet, clear voice, and it seemed so natural for her to sing, and there was so much melody in her songs, that all who heard her listened with delight. She had taken lessons on the piano while at school, though much against her own wishes. She took the lessons in compliance with the wishes of her parents, but never used the piano for her own gratification. She disliked the tones of the instrument, believing that they drowned the sweetest tones of the voice.

The Bo'son, after returning from what he called his "last voyage,"—his trip to New York,—often spent an evening at the different neighboring farm-houses, where he was always a welcome guest, and interested the farmers and their families with tales of other lands, and of storms at sea. If there was a raising of a house, or a barn, the Bo'son was among the first invited. He would

take with him tackles and ropes, of which he had a large
supply, and well knew the use of, and on such occasions
could always do double duty. When the first piece was
raised and secured, the Bo'son would go " aloft," and with
a rope haul up others ; and when the highest piece was
in place, he would call for a flag, which he always took with
him, and raise it high above the building, where it would
float until sundown of that day. In moving buildings he
was equally useful, and always ready to go, and take with
him his dog. When on the ground, he would have the
dog fetch and carry articles that he could take in his
mouth ; and in moving a building, the dog was sure to
have hold of the fall of the tackle, and do as much pulling as the best man.

The dog was as well known, and as much of a favorite,
as his master. The story of his saving the life of little Nellie Williams was known to all the farmers for miles around.
The dog on great occasions, when he went visiting with his
master, wore on his neck a silver collar, the gift of Nellie,
with a full account of that act engraved on it ; and the
Bo'son wore a silver chronometer watch, the gift of Nellie's father.

Captain Williams, with his wife and little girl, often
stopped at the Basin, and visited the farm. The dog
was generally the first to see and welcome them. On
their first visit, Captain Williams presented the Bo'son
with the watch, and little Nellie clasped the collar
around the neck of the dog. The Bo'son refused money for
aiding to save the child from drowning, but did not
decline accepting the watch, as a keepsake and token
of regard.

Little Nellie was a favorite of the whole family, after
learning of her rescue from drowning, by the Bo'son and
his dog.

It was only a short time after returning from New
York, that the Bo'son, with his dog, was crossing the
Hudson River, on the old rope ferry-boat, when the dog
again distinguished himself by saving the life of a much
larger girl than Nellie Williams.

Mary Arnold, a beautiful young girl of twelve years,

was crossing from school, on the same boat, to meet her father, who was waiting with a carriage to take her home, a distance of about two miles. When the boat was two thirds the way over, a pair of horses attached to a wagon, became frightened from some cause, started suddenly, alarming Mary, who incautiously stepped backwards, and over the side of the boat. The Bo'son was on the opposite side of the boat, but the dog saw the young girl fall, and giving the alarm, followed her. The Bo'son comprehended the dog's alarm, and was soon in the water after the dog. The current was very strong, and swept them rapidly from the boat. Mary was greatly alarmed, and when the dog reached her, she clasped her arms around his neck in such a way as not to be able to raise her own head above the water, but to keep the nose of the dog under it. The Bo'son was not a half-minute later than the dog, or Mary Arnold and the Bo'son's dog might both have been drowned. The Bo'son took Mary in his arms, and she immediately let go of the dog and placed her arms around his neck, naturally supposing that he was the greatest safeguard. The result would have been the same as with the dog, had not the Bo'son's strength and experience as a swimmer, taught him how and enabled him to act. He placed himself on his back, and said encouragingly, "Don't be alarmed, miss, you can't be drowned where the Bo'son and his dog are."

Mary had heard of the Bo'son and his dog, and was no longer alarmed. Bill said:

"Now, miss, just place one arm over the dog's shoulder, and take hold of the loose skin on the other side ; and then take hold of my collar with the other hand, and we will soon be safe ashore."

Mary did as directed; the Bo'son swam quartering towards the shore, heading partly up stream, so as not to be swept too much down the river, and soon landed safely.

When the ferry-boat landed, and Mr. Arnold learned that his daughter had fallen into the river, he was greatly alarmed; but dismissed his fears when told who were with his child, saying:

" She will never drown where the Bo'son and his dog are."

Mr. Arnold drove down on the bank of the river, and was on the spot to receive his daughter, when the Bo'son landed. Great was his joy, and greater was that of his daughter, when they met. Old Bose was as joyful as any of them, and persisted in trying to lick all the dampness from Mary's hands and clothes.

Mr. Arnold thanked the Bo'son, and so did Mary, while she was petting the dog ; and the father and daughter both insisted on Bill's going home with them, after Mary had supplied herself with dry clothing, from an aunt near by ; but Bill said :

" I am on duty, sir, at the present time, and only fail in doing it, when life is in danger. I thank you for the invitation, and will call with the dog the first opportunity that I have. The dog will always be a friend to your daughter, and not forget her while he lives. If you have no objection, I will bring black-eyed Susan with me when I come."

" I don't know who you mean by black-eyed Susan, but assure you, that you and all your friends, will be always welcome at my house."

" I mean, sir, Miss Susie Morton, granddaughter of Captain Waters, and the pride and glory of the fleet."

" Miss Morton will be a very acceptable visitor. Please present my compliments to Captain Waters, and ask him to call with his lady."

They had all walked to the house of Mr. Arnold's sister, and while Mr. Arnold and the Bo'son were talking outside, Mary, in the house, had changed her clothing, and came to the door ready to ride home.

After again thanking the Bo'son, and petting the dog, Mr. Arnold and his daughter left for home.

·CHAPTER XLV.

FRIENDS VISIT THE FARM.

BILL Thomas the Bo'son, and his dog, had in **Saratoga** been objects for general remark and approbation ; and a second instance of their saving life,—that of Mary Arnold, who would have been drowned but for their assistance,—gave them, in Washington County, the same reputation they had in Saratoga.

As the story of Mary Arnold's falling into the river, and her rescue, was told from one to another, so was the history of the Bo'son and his dog, and their many successful efforts in saving life related. The story, as it was handed from one to another, so increased and magnified, that one credulous individual asserted that the Bo'son and his dog, after having saved at different times over one hundred lives, were shipwrecked, and succeeded only in saving themselves ; and that they landed on an uninhabited island, and there remained together twenty years. Not one word of which was true.

A few days after the time that Mary Arnold fell into the river, her father, mother and herself, called at the farm, on a visit to the family. The Captain and Mr. Arnold were previously acquainted. The ladies, old and young, soon became so, and were mutually pleased with each other.

The visitors had not alighted from the carriage, before the dog recognized those whom he had previously met. Great was the joy of the dog at the meeting. His particular attention was paid to Mary, and the two met as old friends.

The visit was made at the request of Mrs. Arnold, who wished to see the Bo'son and his noble dog, who had saved the life of her only child. Warm and earnest were her thanks, and great her admiration of the dog. Mrs. Arnold asked the Bo'son if he would sell the dog, that they might always have him with them, and treat him with kindness for saving their daughter. The Bo'son answered :

"I couldn't part with him, marm; we have been so long together that we should both be uncomfortable if separated. I have frequently been offered what some would consider large sums of money for him, but he is not for sale." Then turning to the dog he said : "Bose, do you hear ; the lady wants to buy you, because you are a good old dog. You go and bring me the collar that Nellie Williams gave you, and be sure you shut the door when you come out of the house."

The dog answered with one bark and left. Mrs. Arnold asked if the dog really understood all that was said to him.

"Yes, lady, every word ; and the door of my house is so arranged, that he can both open and shut it. He will soon return with the collar."

The dog did return, bringing with great care, in his mouth, the silver collar presented by Nellie Williams. The Bo's directed the dog to give it to Mrs. Arnold, which he did. The lady read the inscription, after having examined the collar, and then handed it to her daughter. Mary also examined it, and observed that it was very pretty.

The Bo'son said : "Mrs. Arnold, you have noticed by what is on the ring, that I refused one hundred dollars for the dog at that time."

"Yes, I do, Bo'son, and that is not strange. Now, Bo'son, as Mrs. Waters has suggested, will you let us see your house ? "

Bill answered in the affirmative, and led the way to his house. He sent the dog ahead, with directions to open the door, that the visitors might be convinced how well the dog understood the directions given him. When they reached the house, the Bo'son showed them the arrangements of the door, and how the dog could open and shut it.

Bill Thomas took as much pleasure in giving the names and explaining the uses of articles which were strange and new to visitors, as he did in keeping everything in and about the place in perfect order.

There were very many things in the Bo'son's house that

interested visitors. It was to many like a museum, because the articles were curiosities, and arranged with a taste which was specially characteristic of the owner. No visitor ever left the Bo'son's house without being gratified with the visit.

Mr. Arnold asked the Captain, when Bill was not in hearing, if the Bo'son would accept a sum of money for having, with his dog, saved Mary, and was informed that he would not.

Mr Arnold and family left, after a pleasant visit, and a promise from Captain Waters that it should be returned, with the Bo'son and dog in the party.

After the visitors had left, Susie said:

"I have never seen a more lady-like woman than Mrs. Arnold, nor a sweeter, prettier child than her daughter."

Captain Waters remarked: "I fully agree with you, Susie, and think that Mr. Arnold, and his pretty wife and daughter have captured us all."

"If there is a pretty woman about, you, Joseph, are always sure to notice and admire her," said the wife.

"I was always so—it is my nature, and that is why I went after you, Nancy, when you were young, for then you were the prettiest girl in the whole country, and you have been growing handsomer ever since."

"Hold your tongue, you silly old man; what nonsense for one of your years."

"I hope, mother, not to live to be too old to love a pretty woman, for then I shall cease to love you."

"There, there; stop where you are, Joseph Waters," said his wife, and left the room laughing.

"Susie, your grandmother likes a good joke, if she is getting in years."

"And you, grandpa, like to give one, if you are an elderly man."

"That is so, my dear; and your grandmother and myself have had many a one between us; but in the long years that we have lived and sailed together we have never had an unpleasant word with each other, never disputed, one with the other, about large or small matters. Your grandmother has been of great assistance to me, and often calmed my feelings, when they were ruffled by others.   We have lived together as man and wife should, each year increasing our love and esteem."

"I know it; and you are a warm-hearted, jolly old couple, commodore."

"Now, Susie, I am greatly pleased that you are here with us, for you may learn from your grandmother lessons that will be valuable to you through life."

"I am equally pleased to be here, and to learn and profit by her wisdom and her experience.   Father and mother, you are aware, are now not only reconciled to my learning all the duties of housekeeping, but anxious that I should do so.   They fully realize the difference between a useful and a superficial education for a young woman."

"Yes, my little humming-bird; and they fully realize how near they came in wrecking your happiness, which they would have done, could they have had their own way;   and done it to secure a happiness they would have destroyed. What have you learned about Frank and Julia?"

"Nothing that is encouraging for their future.   They have not made their bridal tour.   Before Frank had sufficiently recovered to travel, Julia had cried herself sick with disappointment, and is still in splendid wretchedness, confined to her sick-room, not having realized a single hour of happiness since she was married.   Frank continues to spend his evenings from home, returning late, and often so intoxicated that his servants have to help him to his room.   Mother has been much with Julia, both day and night, since we left, as my aunt broke down after the first few days, having shared in a measure the disappointment of my cousin."

"I am sorry," said the Captain, "for Julia, after all; though she entered into the arrangement in the full knowledge of facts, which should have restrained her."

"That is so, grandpa, but for all that I pity her; and the worst has not yet come.   What she now suffers is only the beginning of her sorrows."

"Yes, Susie, I think you are right; and the future to her will be dreary."

"Grandpa, I cannot tell why it was; but from my first acquaintance with Mr. Livingston, and before he became dissipated, whenever he approached me there was with me a feeling of chilliness, that I could never account for. He was a gentleman, and always courteous and polite to ladies. His person was pleasing, and his manner kind, but still there came the chilly dread of something unseen and unknown."

"It must have been electricity, my child; I have often felt it at sea, when a storm was approaching, and there was no visible signs of it; but why you should have felt it, at the approach of Mr. Livingston, is more than I can explain. Thank God you are not his wife," said Captain Waters, devoutly, taking off his hat before uttering his thanks.

"Yes, Grandpa, all my life will I thank my Heavenly Father, that he and you, and others, with my own resolution, saved me from such a fate, and I wish that Julia might also have been saved. Grandma is calling, and I must leave you."

Susie gave her grandfather a kiss, and left the room.

CHAPTER XLVI.

THE BO'SON REVEALS A SECRET, AND LOSES A CARGO OF TURNIPS.

DURING the fall months, and while the harvest was being gathered in, all at the Waters farm went smoothly, indoors and outside. If ever an old sea captain and his wife were happy and contented, Joseph and Nancy Waters were. Bill Thomas the Bo'son, the old steward, and Lizzie Jarvis, shared with their captain and his wife the happiness realized at the country home.

Susie Morton was full, and running over with happiness; not a difficulty now crossed her path, for the Bo'son had whispered something in her ear about George Wilson which gave a new and pleasing tone to the tenderest feelings of a pure and loving heart. It was nothing that George had authorized the Bo'son to say, but a full belief of his own, communicated in such a form as satisfied Susie that all would come to pass as she wished. Susie found something to occupy every moment, and in what she was doing, found amusement. With her grandfather Susie had many a severe test of wit, that kept him in good spirits, and amused Mrs. Waters. The Captain rallied her on every subject but the one nearest her heart, and failed not on that, because it never occurred to him but from his love for Susie, and a tender regard for the secret feelings of her heart. He never mentioned the name of George Wilson as being the lover of Susie, or likely to be her future companion, because his eyes were fixed on her, when her father asked the question, "Are you engaged to George Wilson?' Though Susie, with her accustomed command over every feeling and action, answered with apparent calmness and unconcern, that she was not, and that George had never intimated anything of the kind to her, Captain Waters saw, though only for an instant, a slight flush pass across the placid features of Susie Morton. The rose-tint that came and went so instantaneously, conveyed to the keen perceptions and penetrating eyes of the old Captain a secret of Susie's heart, which remained undiscovered by her father or any-one else in the room. That secret the Captain determined to keep until time and others' acts should reveal it.

Down deep in the heart of every pure-minded maiden, there is a fountain of love, that may long remain untasted by the one for whom it would freely flow, and in many instances is never drawn to the surface, remaining unknown to all, but its possessor. If the one for whom it would freely flow is so blessed as to discover and drink from it, happiness will surely be his reward.

Captain Joseph Waters found such a well, and for more than forty years had been drinking freely from it ; and sailor though he was, appearing at times, to some, as rough in his manners, yet none knew better than he the sweets of such a fountain. He had enjoyed a pure stream of love himself, and could fathom the depths of such a fountain in the heart of another. He accidentally discovered the spring in Susie's heart, and determined to let it flow undisturbed, until George Wilson should come and drink from it.

Susie, naturally happy in her disposition, at the house of her grandfather, in the country, found new sources of enjoyment, and new pleasures for every moment. In the fore-part of the day, she was with her grandmother in the house, perfecting herself in domestic duties, which she performed with the same pleasure, that too many appear to enjoy, in doing nothing. Susie was so cheerful and handy, that she was welcomed in every part of the house. Lizzie was pleased to see her up stairs, the steward in the kitchen, Mrs. Waters in the milk-room, the Bo'son in the midship-house, and Captain Waters everywhere. In every part of the house, during the forenoon of each day, Susie could find something for her little hands to do, while she told a pleasing tale, or sung a lively song. In the afternoon, if any one in the neighborhood was sick, Susie, with her grandmother and grandfather,—when he was at liberty,—and otherwise, with the Bo'son as driver, would visit the sick, always carrying with them comfort, and such delicacies as are acceptable to invalids. Susie, like the dog, possessed the secret of opening the door of the Bo'son's house, and in his absence, often visited it ; but always found it so clean and neat, that she could do very little to improve its appearance, though she always left some token of her regard for the occupant, to remind him of her esteem. Her tokens were such as a handkerchief, hemmed and marked ; a necktie, such as Bill wore ; a pair of socks, or mittens, of her own knitting, and sometimes a large bouquet would be left in a jar on his table. When the Bo'son returned, and found in his house such tokens of regard, he would say :

"The morning-glory has been here again. God bless her, all the time and everywhere."

Lizzie and Susie managed a little surprise for the Bo'son. They made a set of curtains for the windows and berths of his house, of the same kind of material used on board of ships, and put them up in the same manner ; and also two bed-spreads, one white for the spare berth, and one blue for the berth used by the Bo'son. When all was arranged, in the absence of the Bo'son, Susie placed herself in a large closet, opening from the room, leaving the door a little open, so that she could see the Bo'son when he entered, and hear what he would say, knowing his habit of talking to himself. Bill Thomas entered, and looking about the house a little surprised, but more delighted, said :

"Fayal and Pico, Floras, Ticera, and all the Azoras ! if that morning-glory hasn't been here again, and Lizzie with her ; for black-eyed Susan isn't sailor enough yet to fix things in such seaman-like manner. Well, Heaven bless them both, for they are worthy of it ; may Susie have George for a husband, and Lizzie the only man fit to be her mate, and that one is Bill Thomas the Bo'son."

The Bo'son had taken off his hat, in respect to what he saw and admired, and as he finished speaking to himself, the closet door opened, Susie sprang out, and throwing her arms around the Bo'son's neck, and kissing him, said :

"You dear, good old Bo'son ; so you love Lizzie, and mean to marry her some day. I am pleased to know it, for you both deserve to be happy."

"Yes, rosebud ; you have learned a secret, from my habit of talking to myself, and I know that you will keep it for us. Lizzie and I have known each other for more than twenty years, and together, have been many times around the world. Since we came here, we have had more time to think and talk, than we had at sea, for then we had other duties to perform. Our arrangement is only known to ourselves, and depends on what Captain and Mrs. Waters may say about it."

"They will think well of it, I am sure ; but you musn't be married till I am grown up, and get married myself."

"You needn't fear about that, little charmer, as it may be years before we are married ; and after that we shall remain with our Captain and his wife."

"That is all right, Bo'son ; now what do you think of these fixings ? "

"They are very fine, and make the house look all the better for their being here.   Wasn't I right in saying that Lizzie helped you ?"

"Yes ; and so did grandmother Waters."

"I didn't suspect her, but Mrs. Waters always has a hand in good works."

In a pleasant way the Bo'son and Susie passed an hour in talking about the past and future.   At the end of that time the Captain was heard shouting, "Bo'son! Bo'son !"

"Aye ! aye ! sir; coming."

"There is a strange hog in the potato field,—go drive him out, Bill."

"Aye ! aye! sir ;" answered Bill, touching his hat, and starting for the field in which the hog was.   The Bo'son opened the gate, and expected no trouble in driving out the hog, but found it was not so easy a matter.   The hog would pass the gate every time, with some snorting peculiar to the animal, and after many unsuccessful attemps to get the hog out, Bill caught him by the hind legs, saying: "I'll make a wheel-barrow of you, and wheel you out." It was a brilliant idea of the Bo'son's, and his first attempt at converting a four hundred pound hog into a wheel-barrow.   Bill was very strong in his hands and arms, or the hog might have converted him into some agricultural implement, or a dredging machine.   As it was, the hog kicked and squealed without being wheeled a foot, and Bill thought his arms might be unjointed at the shoulders; but as was his custom, talked or tried to talk, and succeeded only in a half way kind of saying something that sounded like :

"Ki-ke-kic, squeal all you ca-can, bu-but ge-get on out o-of th-this."

After a severe struggle, the Bo'son and hog both fell to the ground.   Bill was the first up, and holding the hog by one hind leg, placed the call in his mouth and blew some broken notes,—for the hog continued to kick.   The dog heard the whistle, and though he didn't understand the notes, he went to his master's assistance.   Bill was satisfied that he could manage any animal on the farm, with the help of the dog.   Bill was pleased when he saw the dog, and said :

"Now, Bose, take him by the ear and tow him out, and I'll push what I can aft, and the two of us will clear the coast of him."

The dog obeyed, and the field was soon free of the strange hog; the Bo'son saying either to the dog or himself, and it was difficult to determine which:

"We have had a tussle with all the different animals about here, and beat them all. They didn't understand us at first, nor we didn't understand them, but we are getting acquainted."

A few months on the farm had in no way changed the Bo'son, with the exception of the knowledge of farming and of cattle that he had gained. He was as active and industrious on the farm, as he had been on the ship; looking after and taking care of everything,—ever ready, with a strong helping hand, where he was most needed, and could be most useful. The Bo'son was as willing to help or oblige a neighbor, as to be engaged in duty at home. His good nature and good temper never departed from him, and it was generally remarked by the farmers in the neighborhood, that the Bo'son learned how to do farm work very fast, which must be accounted for by his desire to learn.

The Bo'son met with only one other mishap (shipwreck, as he would term it,) during the gathering of the crops. On that part of the farm most distant from the house, had been a field of turnips, which had been pulled and topped, ready for the cellar. Bill considered himself fully competent to hauling them with the oxen, and a two-wheeled cart. He yoked up the cattle, put them before the cart, went to the field, and loaded for home. All went well until he was ascending a steep hill near the house,—the Bo'son walking beside the oxen, with that peculiar wide movement of the legs belonging to sailors in general, and to the Bo'son in particular, the goad on his shoulder, and tarpaulin hat well back on his head, and he singing:

> "All in the Downs the fleet lay moored,
> The streamers waving in the wind,
> When black-eyed Susan came on board;
> O, where shall I "—

The dog gave a peculiar bark. Bill looked around, jumped before the oxen, and shouted:

"Whoa! stiff-legs!"

The back-board of the cart had fallen out, and the load of turnips had left the cart, and were rolling, one over another, down the hill, while the dog was making desperate efforts to stop them with his mouth and legs. Bill, in a half standing and half sitting posture, with a hand on each hip, watched them, laughing all over his face, and shouting:

"There's a mess of turnips for you! Go it, big ones! Go it, little ones! Now is your time, before you are biled! Let 'em go, Bose! it is their get this time."

After the Bo'son had enjoyed a long and hearty laugh at the accident and the result of it, he blew his whistle for assistance. Captain Waters was the first to hear and answer the signal of distress. The Captain saw at a glance what had happened, and, with his Bo'son, enjoyed it, saying:

"Another shipwreck, Bo'son?"

"Not of the ship, sir. She is sound, excepting the stern-frame; that has given away, and the whole cargo is overboard,—but it isn't perishable, or liable to damage from sea-water."

"What do you call this, Bo'son, a shifting of the cargo?"

"Yes, sir; from in-board to out-board."

"What are you going to do about it? Call a survey, or take it aboard again?"

"If you have no orders to give, sir, I will 'haul everything hard aback, and make a stern-board' down to the cargo, and take it in again."

"You have the deck, Bo'son, and can handle the ship to suit yourself," said the Captain, and left the ground.

Bill backed the oxen down the hill, and with assistance of one of the farm hands, soon loaded, and went safely to the barn cellar.

CHAPTER XLVII.

GEORGE WILSON ARRIVES, AND MATTERS ARE ARRANGED.

THE fall work was finished, and all prepared for winter at the Waters' farm, and the time was fast approaching when Susie Morton would leave for a visit to her father and mother in New York.

The name of George Wilson was often spoken in the family, but only as it had always been spoken, since Captain Waters first undertook to educate and prepare him to fight his way in the world, and seek his bread and honor on the ocean. The family regarded George as belonging to it, each and all of them feeling an interest in his welfare and success.

The ship that George was first officer of was expected soon to arrive, and all at the farm hoped that he would make them a visit, before sailing on another voyage. Could the family, or any member of it, have analyzed or understood George Wilson's feelings, they would have no doubt about a visit. Under ordinary circumstances he would have called on his Captain and Mrs. Waters; but Susie being with them, was an additional inducement for him to visit the farm.

When George was last at the farm, and when he sailed on his voyage, the question of Susie's marrying Frank Livingston was settled only in her own mind, and George had not felt at liberty, depending on his wages for support, to make any declaration of the interest he felt in Susie, or any opposition to her union with Livingston. The only hope he had was resting on an unguarded expression of the Bo'son,—"Susie will never be called Mrs. Livingston."

How the Bo'son knew was more than George could tell, for Bill Thomas, much as he loved Wilson, would not reveal to him any secret received from Susie Morton, though he hoped and trusted that he might live to see them united as husband and wife. It would have been hard for the Bo'son to tell which of the two he loved best, but they were both objects of his special care and esteem; one as a noble-hearted sailor-boy, the other as a tender-hearted, loving and confiding girl.

One forenoon, late in the fall, Captain Waters drove up to Quaker Springs on some business, and when returning discovered that the Bo'son had set the ship "Neptune's" private signal, and the American flag, at his masthead. The Captain knew that some of the family, or some old friend had arrived, and meeting Bill at the gate, said:

"Well, Bo'son, what saint's day is it now, that you display the colors?"

"Mr. Wilson has arrived, sir, and come on board."

"So you thought you would show the bunting. Why didn't you fire a salute?"

"I did think of it, sir, but concluded that it would make too much noise in the harbor, and the people would ask questions. I'll fire one now, if you will give the order."

"Never mind about it, Bo'son; but where is George?"

"In the house, sir, with the women folks."

"Very well, I'll go and see him."

In the short absence of Captain Waters, George Wilson had arrived at the farm, and been warmly welcomed by every member of the family. Susie met him as she would have met a dearly loved brother, and George met her as a few days before he had met his only sister, whom he loved better than he loved himself.

When Captain Waters entered the sitting-room, he found the whole family there, including Lizzie and the steward; the Bo'son following his Captain into the room. George left his seat and crossed the room to greet his Captain, who had been a father to him. Captain Waters was not satisfied with shaking him by the hand, but took him in his arms, and called him a brave sailor-boy, handling him as though he was only a young lad. At length he said:

"George, I am glad to see you, my boy; you are welcome to the harbor."

"Thank you, sir; I feel more at home in your family than anywhere, excepting when I am with mother and sister."

" We have always considered you one of our family,"
said Mrs. Waters, " and hope that you will always feel at
home with us."

" I am so much indebted to your kindness, and that of
Captain Waters, that I should be wanting in every good
feeling, if I was unmindful of my obligations, or ungrateful for your goodness.   I thank you, Mrs. Waters,
for your generous invitation, and assure you that your
home will always be like one to me."

The Bo'son had remained standing, unnoticed by the
Captain, who, when he perceived it, said :

" Sit down, Bo'son.   What are you standing there for,
with your hat in your hand ? "

" Waiting for orders, sir."

" You need no orders when you are in with the family ;
then you are off duty."

" Long service and habit have taught me not to act
without orders, sir."

" Well, don't be foolish because George is on board."

" Joseph," said the wife, " you are hauling your sea-
tacks aboard, because we have a young sailor with us."

" Yes, Nancy ; that is all natural ; and some of your
expressions are well salted.   We don't use tacks, nor sheets
on a farm."

What Mrs. Waters said about considering George as
one of the family, had no reference to any arrangements
which might be entered into between him and Susie ; nor
was it intended to open and pave the way for him to go
forward ; but all proceeded from her love for the youth,
and the innate goodness of her heart.

In the early part of the afternoon, George and Susie
spent an hour together, and were engaged to be companions through life.   They had known each other from
early childhood, had nothing to inquire about, nor anything to communicate, more than that they loved each
other, and desired to be happy.   The offer was made in
love and faith, accepted in candor and confidence.   They
were both in earnest, and both confiding.

Later in the afternoon, they asked an interview with
Captain and Mrs. Waters, when George fully and frankly

stated what had been done, and asked their approval and blessing.

"George, my boy, you have done the best thing you ever did in your life, and you have my full approbation, and best wishes for your happiness. And you, darling," (catching Susie in his arms and kissing her) "will have just the kind of a man you ought to marry. May Heaven bless you both."

Mrs. Waters remained silent, with a serious, but satisfied expression of her mild and sweet face. Susie, when released from her grandfather's arms, went and sat at the side of her grandmother, resting her head on grandmother's shoulder. The kind, good woman put one arm around Susie, and then calmly said:

"George, you will take our greatest treasure from us, but I had rather trust her with you than any other man that I know; take her, love her always, and be always happy. She is worthy of you, and you are worthy of her. May Heaven's richest and choicest blessings be scattered all around you."

After they had been sitting a little while together, George asked:

"Captain Waters, do you think that Mr. Morton will approve of our union?"

The Captain's warm feelings were all in favor of George, and his hot blood was stirred at the bare thought that any opposition on the part of Mr. Morton should interfere with his own wishes, and the happiness of those whom he loved; and without sufficient consideration, said:

"By thunder! he shall consent, or I'll break his——"

"Stop, stop, Joseph," said his wife.

"George, continued the Captain, very calmly, "Susie shall be your wife, with the full approbation of her father and mother."

"Now, Joseph, you talk like yourself again. I thought you were going to be struck with a heavy squall."

"I was very near being struck; but, mother, you got to windward of me, and broke its force, as you often do. I can't help getting off my course sometimes, in these variable winds, but you always set me right, Nancy. Now, having the present arranged, let us talk of the future."

"Grandfather, you will please remember that my dear father and mother are greatly changed in their views and wishes in regard to my settlement in life, and will chee-fully sanction my engagement with George, saving you' thunder and breakage."

"Yes, Susie, I am fully aware of it, and also that you enjoy a good joke as well as your grandmother."

"Or the Commodore," said Susie.

"George," continued the Captain, "you are now fairly started on the voyage of life, with brighter prospects than many start with, and so far you have acted wisely and justly. Knowing your great anxiety about your mother and sister, and your efforts to provide for their comfort and support, I conclude that you do not propose to be married immediately, nor would I recommend it."

"Capt'n, I am still young, and so is Susie. The world is before us, and we can well afford to wait our time. Had our family been situated as it now is, when I was last here, I should have then offered myself to Susie, but I was not in a situation to provide for mother and sister, and also support a wife, nor could I tell how long it would take me, to reach such a position. Favorable circumstances have changed our condition, and relieved me from responsibility and anxiety."

"What do you mean, George? I have heard nothing."

"You are aware, sir, that when my father was lost at sea, he was largely interested in the ship and cargo, and that the insurance companies, on some technical grounds, refused to pay their losses ; and that all these long past years, since my father's death, the owner of the ship has been fighting the insurance companies in the courts of law ?"

"I know it, George ! I know it !" said the Captain, a little excited.

"Well, sir," continued George, "the test suit has been decided in favor of the ship and owners, and all the offices have paid up,—my good mother receiving enough to amply supply her and sister with every comfort which money can purchase."

Captain Waters jumped from his chair, and shouted:

"Glory! glory to Gideon!"

"Joseph Waters, what in the world do you mean? Do stop using such words."

"I mean, Nancy, glory to Gideon Howland, for his pluck and success."

"If that is all you mean, what you said is not out of the way."

"George," said the Captain, "I congratulate your mother, sister, and yourself, on your receiving at last your just dues; and can trust one with Susie, who has been so mindful of his mother and sister. What say you to that, Nancy?"

"I say, Joseph, that young men, who are good to their mothers and sisters, always make good husbands, especially when they use no intoxicating drinks."

"That is so, my good woman; and now, George, you just go on as you have begun, and when you feel equal to the command of a ship, there will be no difficulty in procuring one for you."

"I understand, and thank you, Captain Waters," was George's reply, and the party separated.

CHAPTER XLVIII.

MR. AND MRS. MORTON CHANGE THEIR VIEWS.

GEORGE Wilson could spend only a few days at the farm, with his friends, as the ship was engaged to freight a cargo of flour and grain to Liverpool, at extra rates; being a fast ship and insuring low.

It was arranged that Susie should return to New York in company with George, as they both wished to see Mr. and Mrs. Morton before George sailed on another voyage, and it was recommended by Captain Waters, that all the parties interested should meet at the same time.

While at the farm, George and Susie spent together some very pleasant hours. Susie had much to tell, and George much to learn. Between them there was no foolish, sickening sentimentalism,—they loved each other, they both knew and both confessed it. Susie's love for George was as pure as the snow on the mountains ; his for Susie was as deep as the ocean, and as true as the needle to the pole. They spent the hours as they had always done when together, in social, unrestrained conversation. The presence of Captain and Mrs. Waters did not disturb them, nor interfere with their conversation ; and that delighted the Captain and his wife.

Susie gave George a full account of her long struggle to overcome her father's wish, that she should be the wife of Frank Livingston ; told him how much she had been assisted by her grandparents ; softening in her own gentle manner, all the hard points in the last conversation of the family on that subject. When Susie had related all that was proper of the interview with her father, mother and grandparents, and spoken affectionately of the happy change in her father's opinion and wishes ; she laid one of her little hands in George's, and the other on his shoulder, and looking him earnestly and lovingly in the face, said :

"George, you have sailed long with Bill Thomas the Bo'son; you think you know him, you think you esteem him, but you do not know him, nor do you esteem him, as he should be known and esteemed. The Bo'son has a heart as large as an elephant, and it is full of tender feelings and of warm blood. All his tender feelings and warm sympathies he would lavish on your little affianced bride, and every drop of warm blood in his noble heart he would freely spill, to protect or make me happy."

George never turned his eyes from Susie's sweet face while she was speaking, and when she paused, he put his arms around her, saying :

" You little angel."

What George did may be inferred from what Captain Waters said, who was standing at an open door near them, but out of sight, and heard all that Susie said of the Bo'son.

"Hold on, George, don't take 'em all, leave me some," and seizing Susie in his arms, heartily finished what George had so affectionately commenced.

Susie, though her eyes were moistened from the well-spring of a warm heart, overflowing with love and gratitude for the Bo'son, was not in the least disturbed nor flustered because grandfather had caught George in such an interesting occupation. The confidence and love existing between her grandfather and herself, was too great for any fear or distrust to exist. Susie was fully able, with all her tender feelings, to command herself, and say what would have relieved them from embarrassment, if they had been embarrassed. She said :

"It is well that I inherit a good constitution from my grandfather, and am not easily smothered."

Captain Waters and George both laughed, and the Captain said:

"I am glad, beauty, that you have inherited something besides a good constitution, from your grandfather. You are not afraid nor ashamed to express a good opinion of one worthy of it. I knew Bill the Bo'son before you were born, before your father and mother were acquainted, and will endorse all that you have said of him. What he would do for you, Susie, he would do for any of our family, and often spends hours in doing a favor for a stranger."

"I have known him since I was a small boy on the ship," said George, "and all that I know of seamanship, I learned from the Bo'son ; and on the ship he showed, whenever there was an opportunity, the same noble traits of character, that he now exhibits here in the country."

"He always seems pleased when I express to him my good opinion, but it does not change him in the least, otherwise than to make him more anxious to do something for my interest, which he considers his own. It was, George, for him and the others, that I bought the farm."

"I fully appreciate your kindness, and thank you for it; I must give him a call this morning at the 'midship-house, or he will feel neglected," was George's reply.

Captain Waters left the room, and Susie gave George a

brief account of Julia's marriage, and the condition of Mr. Livingston on that evening, and for the following two weeks,—also of Julia's disappointment and sickness.

George merely said, "poor Julia," and left to visit the Bo'son.

George found the Bo'son not in his house, but at the shop, shoeing a horse for one of the neighbors. Mr. Wilson was a little surprised to find the Bo'son at such work, and witness how handy he was at it, and after watching him for a time, said:

" Bo'son, that is a business you couldn't have learned at sea."

" No, sir, but I soon took to it after coming aboard the farm."

" Is that one of the Captain's horses?"

·' No, sir, this horse belongs to a poor widow, with four children, and not money enough to spare for having him sharp-shod. I heard of it last evening, and this morning I went there and asked her to let me shoe him, and next year I would take some early apples from her orchard for the pay. I said that so as not to hurt her feelings. Neither her horse nor her children shall want shoes while Captain Waters and his Bo'son live in this part of the world."

" Bo'son, you are always doing good to somebody."

" That is the way, Mr. Wilson, we should live, in helping one another; then more people would be happy than now are. It costs me nothing but a little time and iron to shoe this horse, and it will be a great benefit to the poor woman. If I was not doing this, I might be doing nothing, but pitying the poor woman, as the men do who are idling away their time in the store. I pity and help; they pity and do nothing."

" Bo'son, you are right; if the hours which men spend in idleness were devoted to assisting the poor, much distress would be relieved, and much good done."

When the Bo'son had finished shoeing the horse, he went with George to his house, and there the two had a long conversation of the past and future.

When the time came for George and Susie to leave for

New York, Captain Waters made Susie promise that she would return soon after the holidays.

Captain and Mrs. Waters had all their lives been accustomed to partings with family and friends, but in parting with Susie, even for a short time on that occasion, was a severe trial of their philosophy. Susie had entwined herself around their hearts, and it was a struggle for them to part with her.

When George reached the city with Susie, he accompanied her in a carriage to her father's, spent a short time with her mother, Mr. Morton being from home, and when leaving, remarked that he would have the pleasure of calling in the evening.

George Wilson called that evening, and asked an opportunity of speaking with Mr. and Mrs. Morton. It was granted, and George, sailor like, in plain language, stated his case. Mr. Morton, in a very kind manner, replied:

"Mr. Wilson, in the few past months my views and opinion on Susie's marriage have undergone a great change. Could I then have had my way, I should have wrecked her happiness. Wiser counsels than my own judgment dictated, prevailed, and Susie was saved. My life has been devoted to commerce, and the accumulation of money. I had false notions of a father's duty, and of the best means of securing the happiness of an only daughter. Circumstances lifted the veil which darkened my vision, and I clearly saw my error. I have since concluded that domestic happiness depends on affection, congeniality of dispositions and habits, and not on wealth and position in society. We know you, Mr. Wilson, from childhood, and if Susie loves and accepts you, our consent will be freely given for your union, when the proper time arrives."

"I fully unite with my husband in his consent, being willing to trust Susie's happiness with you," was the response of Mrs. Morton.

"I thank you both for your sanction of our engagement, and promise you, as I have promised Susie and her grandparents, that if she is not happy, it will be no fault of mine," was the reply of George.

George then stated to Mr. and Mrs. Morton what his plans were for the future, and what Captain Waters had promised in regard to a ship.

Mr. Morton approved of the arrangement, and said :

"After I was satisfied of the great mistake I had made in wishing Mr. Livingston to be the husband of my daughter, and learned how much better Susie could judge than myself who should be her companion through life, I concluded to let her make her own choice, without any influence on my part ; and I am satisfied with her choice."

"You have been over-kind, my dear father, and give me more credit for good judgment than I deserve. It was George who chose me."

"We will not argue the question, Susie, of who was first in the choice, as it appears that each was the first choice of the other. The world is before you, my children ; love each other, receive a father's blessing, and be happy."

Mr. Morton went to where Susie and her mother were sitting, kissed first his daughter, then his wife, and returning to George, shook him cordially by the hand.

After a little general conversation, Susie asked her mother of Julia's health and prospects of happiness.

"Julia has been restored to health, but her prospects of happiness are not bright.   Mr. Livingston is very irregular in his habits, and is, your father thinks, making great inroads on his property; but that is so ample it may take some time to waste it all. Julia lives in splendid style, has but little of Frank's society, and is far from being happy.   It is sad to see one so endowed by nature, and so blessed with the treasures of this world, wreck and ruin himself. He and Julia were educated with false notions of life and their duties, and acting on their convictions, will long seek, without finding, the sources of true happiness."

"Mother, I think that my cousin has not yet drunk her bitterest cup of disappointment and sorrow. There are dark and dismal days in the future for poor Julia."

"You made a very fortunate escape, Susie," said the father, "and are indebted to your own firmness, backed by father and mother Waters, for being able to convince me of my great error in wishing to match you with wealth and position, unaccompanied by worth and manhood."

" Your great and only wish, dear father, was to see me truly happy. You mistook the road which would lead to happiness, and willingly left it, when you found that you were wrong."

" And in doing so strengthened the cords of love and affection which bind our family closely together, and learned a valuable lesson, that I would leave as a rich legacy to those who come after me," was her father's reply.

"William," said his wife, "we were both in error. I thought that Susie should not know how to do the least thing about the house. Mother Waters convinced me of my error; took Susie, a simple girl, just out of a boarding-school, and not physically rugged, and in a few months, returns her to us improved in strength, and an accomplished house-keeper. Mother always took a common-sense view of every subject; and had she not been at sea with father, and been able to attend to my education, I should have had less to learn after we were married."

"Well, Laura, as we have both been wrong, both seen and given up our errors, we can impart some lessons of wisdom to our children, which may assist them in their journey through life. Now let us say good evening."

The parents and children separated, mutually pleased with the meeting and its results.

CHAPTER XLIX.

HARDENGRIP KILLS HIS HOGS AND LOSES HIS SAUSAGES.

AFTER George Wilson and Susie Morton left the Waters Snug Harbor, those remaining on the farm, and especially the Captain and Bo'son, appeared for a few days very lonely. The captain used his horses on the road in pleasant weather, and was generally accompanied by Mrs. Waters. When the weather or roads were unsuited to riding, the Captain was occupied with reading, and conversing with Mrs. Waters, in the house, or with the Bo'son at his shop.

Bill Thomas managed to find something to occupy himself with all the time. He took particular pride in keeping the family carriage and buggy wagon clean, and in order for use; also all the harness. The farm wagons were washed, painted, and put under the sheds. The wood-work of the plows, harrows, and other farming implements, was painted, and they were put away in their places.

The leaves, as they had fallen from the trees, were raked up, and taken in a wheelbarrow to the compost heap, to be used in the spring in fertilizing the land; and all the withered vines in the garden were gathered up and disposed of in the same way. The grounds around the house were kept in perfect order by the Bo'son; not a chip nor straw was allowed to rest unseen, or not removed by Bill Thomas.

Mr. Harrowell was in the habit of saying to the neighbors:

"There is no difficulty in managing a farm, when there is such a man around as the Bo'son. He keeps everything in order, and knows where everything is."

The Bo'son surprised the old farmers, by the facility with which he would shackle together a broken ox-chain, or couple a broken trace-chain, with shackles and couplings brought from the ship.

At killing time, the Bo'son also surprised the farmers with his knowledge of curing meats. He had obtained it on board of ships when on whaling voyages.

Bill had made a set of meat casks, sufficient to hold all the meat, both beef and pork, which the Captain wished to put down.

When a farmer is through with his fall work, his cellar filled with the products of the soil, the orchard and stock-pens, his barn filled with hay, and his granary well supplied; then, if there is an independent and happy man, it is the farmer.

Such was the case at the farm of Captain Waters, and all there were prepared to enjoy a country life, made cheerful with an abundance of good things to eat.

When all that was to do on the farm had been done, the Bo'son, one pleasant afternoon, was in his shop, engaged in fitting up an ox-sled, when he received a visit from Mr. Hardengrip. The Bo'son was civil to everyone, but he had few compliments for a man he so despised.

Hardengrip looked at the Bo'son for at least two minutes after receiving his good-day, and then, without returning the compliment, said :

"I call, Bo'son, to see if I could get you to help me kill hogs to-morrow."

"It is out of my line, Mr. Hardgripe."

"Hardengrip is my name, Bo'son ; and if it is a little out of your line, you might, in hog-killing, be handy to give a lift here and there."

"It is impossible for me to go, Mr. Hardergripe. There are men about here who make a business of going out at such work, and you can get as many of them as you want."

"They all want wages, Bo'son, and want cash. I thought you might come and help me a day, and some-time I could come and help you a day ; so, by changing work, I should save paying the money."

'I don't think we can trade in any way. Our work is all done that you could assist in, and the Bo'son don't go out killing."

"I shall have quite a number of people to provide a dinner for; do you think the steward would be willing to come over and cook for me, and that Lizzie would assist for one day about the house-work, sasage-meat, cases, and other things? As I have no one but myself to feed this winter, I thought I should make a large quantity of sasages, and sell 'em all. They are bringing a high price, and will turn to considerable cash, if I can only get them made, without having to pay for it."

"We are short-handed at present, Mr. Hardergripe, and there is no chance for you to get a single man out of the ship."

"Well, how is it about the women, Bo'son ? They tell me that Mrs. Waters is a great worker, and quick at such matters, and that when she does visit a poor neighbor, always takes with her a large supply of good provisions,—pies, cakes, and the like."

" Mrs. Waters is quick and handy at all work, and her 'lockers' are always full of good stores; they are well cooked, and she is never afraid to empty the ' lockers' on proper occasions, but she has other arrangements for to-morrow, and can't go."

" She is just the person that I most want, one that brings a great deal, does much work, and wants no pay,—not even a small piece of fresh pork to take home with her. I can put the killing off for a day or so, if she would come."

" I don't think, Mr. Hardestgripe, that you could put off your killing until Mrs. Waters would be sufficiently disengaged to be with you."

" I want such a person very much, and would put the killing off for a week to have her. I don't think there is another such person in this part of the country. It isn't every day that they are met with."

" If you put the killing off for a month, you would have no show for help here."

"Are you sure, Bo'son, that I have no chance of having Mrs. Waters and Lizzie? It would be such a saving."

" You have no more chance of having them, Mr. Hard-grampers, than you have of being struck with lightning."

" Then I may as well go and get Anna Moores; she will help me."

" Yes, you may as well go." And he did go.

Captain Waters was in a small room of the shop, and there, unknown to the Bo'son, having entered it through a side door, he heard all the conversation between the Bo'son and Amos Hardengrip. When Hardengrip left, the Captain appeared in the shop, and in a serious manner asked the Bo'son why he declined helping him.

" He is not worth helping, sir ; he is too mean to live, and the only man about here the Bo'son wouldn't like to help."

" Bo'son, as a christian and a good citizen, you should be charitable to all, and do good whenever you have an opportunity."

"If a man is in distress, and has his colors half-mast, or is overboard and wants help, the Bo'son and his dog will be on hand ; but when a chap like that, who would squeeze a half dollar until he made the eagle on it scream, and who would pocket the cents from a dead father's eyes, wants the Bo'son, he can't get him in tow."

"I don't blame you, Bo'son. The man has property, but it is of no good to him, or any one else."

Hardengrip, as he proposed when he left the Bo'son, went directly to the house of farmer Moores, to arrange with Anna. He found Anna in the kitchen, engaged about as when Ruth Goodwin made her a visit.

"Mrs. Moores, I want you to come to my house and assist me, to-morrow; I am going to kill hogs. Can you come ?"

"It is a little difficult, Amos, but thee being alone, I can't refuse. Will there be other help in the house ?"

"Yes; two Irish women to do the heavy work ; but I want you to take charge of everything. I want you to come early and make some bread and pies for dinner and supper, as there will be seven or eight men to eat ; and people when they go out always eat twice as much as they do when at home."

"I will be there, Amos ; thee can depend on me."

"Will you go by the way of the store ?"

"Yes."

"Well, stop and get a quarter of a pound of pepper; I am nearly out, and it will be needed."

"I will remember it, Amos; and be there bright and early."

Anna fixed herself and children,—her way of fixing,— and prepared to leave home for a day. She was in fuller dress than on the day that Ruth Goodwin made her a visit. She wore a brown worsted dress, made to button at the back, but she reversed the sides, because it was easier to button it in front. It didn't fit very well, but answered the purpose just the same. She wore shoes that laced up, but the tops of the blue yarn stockings,—as usual with Anna,—were not in their places.

When nearly ready to leave home, she filled her large

box with snuff, and debated with herself whether it was best to take a tow-apron which she had used, or a clean one. Anna finally decided that the work would be dirty, and she might just as well take the apron that had been used, as the clean one.

Anna stopped at the store for the pepper, and thinking it might be late before she returned home, and that she might possibly get out of snuff, got a quarter of a pound of that also, and put them both in her pocket.

Anna reached the house of Hardengrip, and declared that she was ready for the day.

"Anna, I want you should be very careful that nothing is wasted. Everything costs money, and money is hard to get, and hard to keep. Make only two pies for dinner, and cut them in as many pieces as there are persons to eat; and make some very plain ginger-bread for supper, and be sure and not put too much shortening in it, or in the pie-crust. Put no butter on the table for dinner, for we shall have good gravy with the fried inwards.'

"I'll attend to it all, Amos," was Anna's reply.

Anna was pleased with the appearance of things in the kitchen, saying to the women that were with her:

"Everything is handy here; one don't have to go from kitchen to closet for what is wanted to use, and it saves a great many steps. If we drop a little grease, or spill a little dirty water on the floor, it 'll never show. I don't like these kitchens that are so nice you are afraid to dirty them. Every place should be just fit for the use made of it."

Anna put on the tow-apron, took snuff, used the apron to wipe her fingers and nose, and then commenced making bread, cake, and pies. The hogs were killed, and portions brought into the kitchen, to prepare for sausage cases and sausage meat. Anna took snuff, used the apron, and kept to work on her pastry. The other women prepared the sausage cases and meat. Pepper was wanted. Anna emptied what she had brought from the store into a large tin pepper-box, gave it to one of the women, to season the sausage-meat, took snuff, used the apron, and continued the bread and cake business.

When dinner was about ready, Anna had worked so hard at the baking business, and been so often interrupted, each time having to take snuff, that her box was empty. She filled it from the paper in her pocket, took a pinch, threw back her head, snorting and sneezing, without being able for an instant to stop, or have any control over herself.

Anna had put the snuff into the pepper-box, and nearly the whole of it had been used on the sausage-meat and hogs' inwards, frying on the stove for dinner, and had filled her own box with pepper, and taken a full pinch of it.

The commotion in the kitchen called Hardengrip there, and when he found what had taken place, he was very wrathy. "Ten dollars worth of meat 'spiled' with snuff." He called Anna hard names, ordered her out of his house, and told her if she didn't hurry about it, he would kick her out.

The Bo'son was passing along the road near the house, the dog a little ahead of him, when Bose looked back at his master, gave one bark, leaped the fence, and went into the house. The Bo'son understood the dog, and quickly followed him. When Bill Thomas reached the kitchen, the dog had Hardengrip by the back of his trousers, holding him from going any nearer to Anna Moores. The Bo'son soon learned what the difficulty was, and that Hardengrip had much abused Anna. He told the dog to give him a good shake, and let him go. The dog obeyed.

Soon as Anna found that she had some one besides herself to depend on, she said:

"I'll tell my husband what thee has said to me, and he will come over here, and horse-whip thee."

"He needn't take that trouble, for I would just like no better fun than to ropes-end him on the spot," said the Bo'son, at the same time taking from his pocket half a fathom of "eighteen-thread rattling stuff."

"You can't touch my father to hurt him while I am here."

"Young man, I am sorry you have such a father; but I can't help it. Bose and I are good against any number of people who call themselves men, and stand by and see a lone woman abused, by such a chap as that."

The Bo'son took off his jacket, and what the result would have been is difficult to tell, but one of the men seeing Captain Waters riding by, called him in.

"Bo'son, what is the matter, and what has so excited you? This is unusual."

" This lady made a little mistake, sir, and they put snuff in the ' sasages;' and then because the lady couldn't take pepper for snuff, old skinflint was going to kick her out of the house. The dog got on deck before I did, fastened to him aft, and spiked his guns. The lady was going to send her husband to horse-whip him for calling her bad names, and I thought I would save her the trouble by using this on his shoulders," showing the rattling stuff.

" Bo'son, you are wrong for once."

" For taking a lady's part when she was being abused ?"

" No, not for that, but for offering to whip such a man as Mr. Hardengrip."

" He deserved it, sir; but if you say I was wrong, I will beg his pardon."

" Captain Waters, there is ten dollars worth of meat ' spiled ' with snuff, and another dinner to be provided, all at my cost. I knew I should miss Betsy at this time. Her death has cost me twelve or fifteen dollars this day. Why couldn't she consent to live until after killing-time, and then she might have died in welcome."

" Neighbor Hardengrip, accidents will happen in all families, so make the best of it. That is the way to get along smoothly," was the Captain's reply.

Anna emptied the pepper from her box, and found there was some snuff left in the pepper-box; she took a large pinch, used her apron, and left the house.

The Captain, Bo'son and dog soon followed her example. What Hardengrip did with his well-snuffed sausage-meat, who cooked his next dinner, and how many nights he laid awake bemoaning his loss, must remain unknown to the world, for he was alone, and has left no record of it.

CHAPTER L.

THE BO'SON TELLS A WHALING STORY.

THE Bo'son and his dog were known for miles around the Waters' Snug Harbor, and wherever they went, they were welcome visitors. Bill Thomas spent some of the long, pleasant winter evenings at the different farm-houses in the neighborhood, and interested the people living in them, with a history of the countries he had visited, and the manners and customs of people in foreign parts. He also related his adventures, and what he had witnessed when engaged in the whaling business. The farm-house of Welcome Goodwin was visited more frequently than that of any of the other houses, because there the Bo'son felt more freedom, and more at home.

Mr. Goodwin was the first of the neighbors who visited the Bo'son, and the first to invite him to his house. In that family Bill Thomas was always welcome, and his narratives listened to with attention, and full credit given to them.

The Bo'son never told a tale unless invited to do so, and one evening, when at the house of Mr. Goodwin, that friend asked Bill to give them an account of the death by drowning of his shipmate when on a whaling voyage.

THE BO'SON'S STORY.

" In June, 1823, I sailed in the ship ' Phebe Ann,' from New Bedford, bound to the coast of Brazil, on a whaling voyage. The ship was owned by Samuel Rodman, and fitted out by Captain David Coffin, as agent. The ' Phebe Ann ' was a small ship, only two hundred and twenty tons burthen, but for her size well adapted to the whaling business, being a ' weatherly ' ship and a fast sailer.

" The officers of the ship were: Charles Rawson, master; Charles Barnard, first mate; Peleg Ray, second mate; William Barker, third mate; Benjamin F. Gardner and Thomas Barnard, boat-steerers,—all belonging to Nantucket, excepting Mr. Barker. His home was at Newport,

R. I.   The crew consisted of William Cary, Zebulon Morslander, Paul B. Macy, Alfred Swain, Daniel Hussey, Henry Gardner, Charles Pitts, Edward P. Coffin, John Boss, Charles F. Swain, and the ship's cooper, whose name is not remembered,—all white men, and all belonging to Nantucket, excepting John Boss and the cooper. Boss belonged to Newport, but had lived some years on the Island of Nantucket, and there learned a cooper's trade. The cook and steward were colored men, and two natives of the Sandwich Islands completed the whole crew of twenty-one men. All of the men before the mast, who belonged to Nantucket, were on their first voyage to sea, excepting Morslander and Cary. The oldest of the green hands was not twenty-one years old,—the youngest only sixteen. They had been playmates and schoolmates from early boyhood.

"After sailing from New Bedford, and the young men had recovered from their sea-sickness, we had a pleasant, but rather long passage of four weeks, to the Western Islands (Azores), where we recruited the ship with potatoes, onions, apples and hogs.

" Leaving the Azores, we passed near some of the Cape de Verd Islands, and shaped our course for the whaling ground of Brazil.

" Near the island of Trinidad, in latitude twenty, south, just at sunset, we sighted a large sperm whale. The ship was under full sail, with studden-sails out 'alow and aloft,' the wind being light and well aft. The ship was 'brought to the wind,' the studden-sails hauled in on deck, 'courses' hauled up, main-top-sail 'aback,' and the larboard and waist-boats lowered; the captain stopping on board to take care of the light sails and the ship.

"The whale was 'close aboard.' Mr. Bainard, the mate, went in the head, instead of the stern of his boat, and by the time he could get his harpoons up and line bent, Gardner, the boat-steerer, had carried him alongside of the whale; he threw both irons well in, and the whale, in her first motions after being struck, filled the boat half full of water; then sounded, taking out about fifty fathoms of line, and coming again to the surface to spout. Mr. Ray pulled up and put two irons into the whale, but before Mr. Barnard could get in his fifty fathoms of line, the whale sounded again, and supposing it was going to be a deep sound, Mr. Barnard directed Mr. Ray to cut his line, in order to bend the two lines together. The whale took out only about one hundred fathoms of line, and in some way the line got in the whale's mouth, and the whale bit it off. It was dark, and there was no chance to strike the whale again, and we lost her.

"Two of Mr. Barnard's boat's crew, and four of Mr. Ray's, were green hands. It was the first time they had been alongside of a whale, but they showed no white feathers."

"Bo'son," asked Mr. Goodwin, "how many fathoms of line are taken in a whale-boat, and how is it carried?"

"One hundred and eighty fathoms, sir; and it is coiled in a tub, sitting between the after and second thwarts."

"What is the size of the line, Bo'son?"

"It is about the size of a man's second finger. At that time, whale-line was made only of the finest of Russia hemp, selected for the purpose, and so manufactured as to be always limber. Now, whale-line is also made from manilla hemp and cotton."

"Go on, Bo'son, with thy story, if thee pleases; for we are all interested in it."

"Had Captain Rawson been able to lower his boat with the other two, Mr. Ray would not have had to cut his line, and we might have saved the whale. A whale seldom takes more than two lines (three hundred and sixty fathoms) out, in sounding, though sometimes three lines are put together, making five hundred and forty fathoms. Whalemen think, that when a whale takes out two lines going down, she will take the most of the third line, by sagging of the bight, when coming up; for a whale does not go straight down, nor come straight up."

"How long, Bo'son, can a whale stay under water?"

"A large sperm whale, when not disturbed, will remain

under water one hour and a half, and then stay up the same length of time, spouting once a minute,—ninety times. If such a whale is disturbed, after being up half an hour, and goes down, it will not remain down more than half an hour. Other than sperm whales are up and down, from twenty minutes to half an hour each time, when not chased nor disturbed."

"Bo'son, thou hast given us more information about whales and their habits, than we have heretofore had opportunities of acquiring, and we shall all continue to listen, receiving much instruction from thee. Thou canst proceed at thy pleasure, and I will endeavor not to interrupt thee again with questions, though that is the only way to fully comprehend a subject matter which is being spoken of by one fully understanding it."

The Bo'son continued :

"When we first got on whaling ground, we had hard luck in having our boats stoven, and the captain injured by a whale ; so that he was unable to go in his boat for three months. The ship was run into, on a foggy night, by the ship 'Thorn,' Captain Post, of Sag Harbor, and by that accident we lost two boats, and all the cranes and davits on the starboard side. A short time after that, we lost the mate's boat in a gale of wind, with the cranes and davits used for that boat.

"The twelfth day of January, in the year eighteen hundred and twenty-four, will never be forgotten, while there is one man living who was on board of the ship 'Phebe Ann' on that voyage. It was a dark, cloudy day, the wind blowing fresh from the northeast, causing a rough sea. We had whale on board, and were 'boiling,'—the ship under easy sail.

"Immediately after breakfast, whales were seen near the ship, and the two quarter boats were lowered, headed by Mr. Barnard and Mr. Barker,—first and third mates. The crew of the starboard-boat, headed by Mr. Barker, consisted of William Cary, boat-steerer ; Paul B. Macy, at the bow ; Jock, a Kanaka, at the midship ; Daniel Hussey at the tub, or second ; and Charles Pitts at the after oar.

" The whales came up nearest to Mr. Barker's boat; he went alongside of one, called the harponeers-man up, and before Cary could throw his harpoon, the whale struck the boat, knocking Mr. Barker overboard. Mr. Barker, supposing that Cary had fastened to the whale, held on the steering oar, till the whale struck the boat again, cutting her in two pieces. The whale went a short distance, 'milled' around, and attacked the boat a third time, knocking her into small pieces, and leaving only the bow with one thwart, and a little piece of the stern.

" The mate's boat was only a short distance from the one that had been stoven. Mr. Barnard and his crew saw what had taken place. The boat was headed for the wreck, and the mate called on his crew to 'pull for life.'

" They had often, at his call, sprung to their oars when after a whale, but were now pulling for life, and at every stroke the boat seemed to be lifted from the water, and sent ahead with the speed of a race-horse.

"The men were picked up as fast as they could be reached, Cary being the last man taken into the boat. The bow of the stoven boat had 'righted,' and Cary had swam to it, and taking the place where he was standing when the boat was first struck by the whale.

"The men were counted, and only five out of six were in the boat. The names of the crew were quickly called, in the order in which they had been seated in the boat; and when the officer called the tub-oar, Daniel Hussey was missing.

" All eyes were turned again among the floating pieces of the stoven boat, but he was nowhere to be seen. Mr. Barnard remained on the spot until there was no longer any chance of finding him, and then headed for the ship, the men pulling long, slow strokes.

" When the boat was near enough to hail, the captain through his trumpet, asked :

" ' Is anyone hurt?' and no answer was give. He repeated it, and Mr. Barnard answered :

" ' Hussey is lost.'

" The captain said : ' Come alongside.'

" The crew of the stoven boat were taken on board, and

the mate returned to the wreck, picked up the oars, boat and lantern-kegs, line-tub and boat-bucket, and towed the largest piece of the stoven boat to the ship. It was taken on board, and given to the cook for kindling wood; the mate's boat was hoisted up, and no more boats were put in the water that day.

"Having whale on board, and boiling, every man had his station, and knew his duty. The ship's duty was carried on during the day, almost in silence. In one watch there was one station without a man to fill it. Death had made it vacant.

"Our little band of sailor brotherhood was broken, our shipmate had died, and while dying was buried deep down in the ocean, where the resting place of his remains could not be marked. Fifteen minutes after taking breakfast with the crew, sitting on the same chest, and dividing with me a portion of his meat, he was in an ocean grave. His shipmates, who had grown up with him from boyhood, felt his loss more keenly than the Bo'son, who had known him only for the voyage, and the sad impressions made on my mind that day, and the following night, will never fade entirely away. It was with me, as with them, the first death witnessed at sea.

"Before returning home, we visited St. Catherines, on the coast of Brazil. On our arrival at that port, we found the ship Improvement at anchor in the harbor. On board of that ship Daniel Hussey had a brother, who immediately came along side of our ship to see Daniel. Judge, Mr. Goodwin, if you can, the feelings of the brother. In a strange land, far from home and friends, expecting to meet a brother, he heard only of his death. The iron-nerved and hardy seaman was softened and subdued by affection and sorrow, and sympathized with, by all the shipmates of Daniel Hussey."

Here the Bo'son wiped a moisture from his own eyes, and Ruth Goodwin asked:

"Bo'son, had Daniel Hussey a mother and sisters living at that time?"

"Yes, Mrs. Goodwin; he had father, mother, brothers, and sisters. They all belonged to the same society that you do, and were esteemed members of it. I talked with his father after arriving home, and gave him a full account of the sad affair, softened only by telling how well his son had conducted himself as a seaman, and how high he ranked in the brotherhood of his shipmates."

"Thou wert then a young man, Bo'son," observed Welcome Goodwin.

"Yes, sir. That was over thirty years ago; but all the circumstances are as fresh in my memory as though it occurred only yesterday. I can see before me even now the sad faces of the captain, officers, and all the crew, as they stood around the deck of the Phebe Ann, after the death of Daniel Hussey."

"Bo'son, we are all obliged to thee for thy story; though a sad one, it is full of instruction to the living, to be always ready," said Mr. Goodwin, and the Bo'son left for his home.

NOTE.—There is not a word of romance nor fiction in the Bo'son's last story. Every word is true, every date correct, and every name genuine. The writer was one of the crew of the " Phebe Ann," and at the loss of Daniel Hussey pulled the after-oar in the mate's boat, and assisted in saving those of the stoven boat who were saved.

As a tribute of respect to the memory of the departed, and one of esteem for the living, composing the crew of the " Phebe Ann " on that voyage, the story is given as one of the Bo'son's, and in that character is not out of place in the book.

My shipmates, now living, I trust will not think unkindly of me for placing their names before the public without permission, for could I here give a full history of their lives and acts, they would lose nothing in the good opinion of the world. The surviving relatives and friends of Daniel Hussey can attribute no motive to the writer, in giving an account of his death, which occurred nearly fifty-four years ago, but to preserve in his own, and refresh in others, the memory of a loved and lost shipmate.

At the present time (December, 1876), nearly fifty-four years after the sailing of the ship on that voyage, there are living eight of the seventeen white men comprising the crew,—a remarkable circumstance. There are also living three of the crew of Mr. Barnard's boat, and one of those picked up from the stoven boat at the drowning of Hussey. Paul B. Macy, one of the crew of the stoven boat, died December 24th, 1874, and the writer was a pall-bearer at his funeral, fifty-one years after he was one of a boat's crew, that rescued him from drowning in the South Atlantic Ocean.—AUTHOR.

CHAPTER LI.

THE BO'SON AND HIS SLEIGH.

THE Bo'son saw and thoroughly examined sleighs of the different kinds used by the farmers, and concluded that he could build one, and make some improvements on those he had seen. The people had told him about the fine sleigh rides which they enjoyed during the winter, and that the first snow falling, some winters, remained on the ground until spring. Bill determined to build and have a sleigh of his own. He had a plenty of good timber, brought with him from the ship, and he set about it.

He had assisted in steaming and bending planks to different portions of a ship's bottom, and of timbers for boats, and well understood the process. He got the runners out of Delaware white-oak, split one end of them in two places with a saw, steamed and bent them to their proper form, and bolted together the parts split, so that they would hold their shape.

Before building the sleigh, he made a model of it, so as to know, as he said, "when the keel was laid, what the craft was to be when built and launched."

Bill wanted what he called a "top-gallant forecastle," under which he could "stow cargo to trim ship," and on which "he could stand and give directions when running through a narrow passage."

Immediately back of the dash-board, which was so constructed and arranged as to prevent the possibility of snow or splash being thrown from the horse's feet into the sleigh, he constructed his top-gallant forecastle, by raising it one foot above the bottom of the sleigh, with sides nine inches above that, reaching nearly to the front of the sleigh body proper, and then extending in a curved form to the top of the sleigh. This top-gallant forecastle was built entirely separate from the body of the sleigh, with a back of its own. Under it could be safely put away, whatever small articles were carried, and on it the Bo'son could stand and drive when the sleigh was filled.

The body of the sleigh was as much in the form of a ship as it could be, and answer the purpose for which it was to be used.   It was intended to carry four persons,—two in each seat, each couple facing the other,—but often had eight in the sleigh, and one on the forecastle, with the Bo'son.   Bill, when using his sleigh, was in the habit of saying:

"The amount of my freight depends on the assortment of my cargo, and how it is stowed."

The pole and whiffle-trees were made of seasoned hickory, that had been many voyages in the "Neptune" with the Bo'son.

The whole structure was very light in appearance, but made of such seasoned timber, and so ironed and braced in every part, as to be capable of carrying a heavy load, without being strained or injured.

The painting was as novel as the sleigh itself.   The running portion was black, then a red streak four inches wide, and above that a dark brown on the sides, also on the top-gallant forecastle.   The back of the sleigh was a bright yellow, the inside flesh color.   On the back of the sleigh was painted a whaling scene of two boats chasing, and a third boat fast to a whale.   The steward had the credit of painting that, but whether it belonged to him or not, is unknown, as the painting was all done in the private room of the shop.   The Bo'son placed sleigh-bells of different sizes and tones on the under side of the pole, in such a manner that they could not be removed.

While building the sleigh, the Bo'son had a set of double harness, silver mounted, made at the village, and purchased two strings of small silver-plated bells, to go around the horses necks ; also a full set of lined and trimmed robes, to be used with the sleigh.

Bill Thomas would have purchased horses, but the Captain had all that were necessary, and during the winter assigned one pair to his especial use.

Bill was well supplied with money, having taken a considerable to the farm with him ; and by direction of Captain Waters, the steward paid the men monthly, and money had been accumulating on the Bo'son's hands.

The steward was not only the Captain's financial agent, but on the farm acted banker for Bill and Lizzie; having an iron safe, where he could securely keep money and valuables.

Having a large supply of clothing, boots and shoes, all made in Europe, he had no use for money on the farm, excepting for such things as pleased his fancy, and his new sleigh was his first lavish expenditure.

The sleigh, when finished and painted, was as much of a wonder to the people, as the Bo'son and his dog had been.

By constant observation and practice, Bill, in the seven months that he had been on the farm, had become a safe and good driver. He could harness, handle and drive a pair of spirited horses with the best horseman around the country, though he met with many mishaps and adventures in that line in his early experience on the farm. In the business of driving, as in all other matters, the Bo'son, by patience and perseverance, backed by good nature, eventually succeeded.

When the sleigh was finished and ready for use, it was taken out of the shop ("launched," as the owner would have it), and christened the "first cutter;" and that name was lettered on both sides of the forecastle; and on the back of the sleigh, in gilt letters was " First Cutter, Waters' Snug Harbor," in two lines. The name above, and the port " hailing from," under it.

A light fancy cutter was called the " Captain's gig; " the family sleigh, bought with the farm, the " long-boat; " the farm sled, the " wood-barge."

The Bo'son said :

" It is necessary to name all the boats, and then they can be ordered to duty without having the wrong one ' manned.' "

It was not long after the " first cutter " was " launched," that there was a fall of nine or ten inches of snow, falling without being disturbed by wind, and on ground hardened with frost, making sleighing good.

The " first cutter " was got ready immediately after breakfast. The Bo'son had got his dark brown horses in fine condition, and with the new harness and silver-plated bells on, and hitched before the cutter, made a good appearance.

It was the trial trip, and Bill wanted the old crew, with one extra hand ; and so invited the steward, Lizzie and Mr. Harrowell, the farmer, to go out with him on his "first cruise."

When they were about "to sail" out of the yard, Captain and Mrs. Waters went on the piazza to witness the sight, and appeared to enjoy it and be as much gratified as the Bo'son or any of his party.

The old sea captain and his wife loved the members of their family who were in the sleigh, as though they had been their children, and did more for their comfort and happiness than many parents do for their children.   No child ever did more for a parent than either of the three would have done for Captain or Mrs. Waters.   Whatever pleased the "family,"—as Bill, Lizzie and the steward were always called, when spoken of collectively,—always gratified the Captain and his wife.

It was a glorious sight, the new sleigh, harness, silver bells, and fine horses ; the Bo'son, with the long ribbons attached to his tarpaulin-hat, streaming in the wind, and he standing on the "top-gallant forecastle" of his sleigh, lines and whip in hand, driving out of the gate and up the road, wearing such a pleasant and satisfied countenance ; while the old dog that was not to be left behind, was cutting all kinds of antics, rolling and tumbling in the snow, running alongside of the sleigh, and joining his cheerful bark, with the merry tinkling of the bells.

The Bo'son drove his party up the road through Shepherdville, passed the old Friends' Meeting and school-house went to Quaker Springs, Coveville, down the turnpike, and home.

It was such a turn-out as was never seen in that, or any other part of the country before, and was the admiration of all who saw it.   Not a boy belonging to the District School, no matter how mischievous he might have been, would have presumed to throw a snow-ball at the Bo'son's new sleigh, nor at the party in it.

After returning, the Bo'son looked at his chronometer watch, and without saying where he was going, drove out of the yard, and up the road. He drove to the district school, timeing it so as to be there at recess, and in turn gave all the boys and girls a ride in the new sleigh, and so becoming a general favorite with the children, and furnishing them something new to tell when they went home.

Returning home, he unhitched and unharnessed his horses, rubbed them dry, put their blankets on, and when they had stood sufficiently long at hay, for it to be prudent, he gave them grain and went to his own dinner.

After dinner, he invited Captain and Mrs. Waters to "take a sail in the first cutter." The invitation was accepted, and the Bo'son drove them to Stillwater village, where the establishment was inspected by a committee, composed of all the inhabitants that could be out of doors, and pronounced a perfect success, that should be patented.

When first introducing the Bo'son to our readers, we stated that personal cleanliness and careful dressing were fixed habits of his, and living on shore had not weakened or changed them. He wore a dress peculiar to his early calling, and differing from that worn by the people living around him; but it was clean, and suited to his character, and proper to be seen in the best society.

The Bo'son and his sleigh were the general talk of the neighborhood, and no parties or frolics were considered fashionable unless they were included in it. There was not a young lady for miles around who did not have a ride in the "first cutter."

Bill was so well known, and his character so well established, that parents felt safe in trusting their daughters to him and his cutter, and he always had a full freight when there was a gathering of the young people, and in such gatherings Lizzie was generally included, she also being a favorite with the young.

When a letter was received, informing the family that Susie Morton would be at the depot on a certain day, the Bo'son asked the honor of bringing her "on board" in the "first cutter."

It was arranged that the Captain, Mrs. Waters, and Lizzie should go with the Bo'son in his cutter to meet Susie, and take her to the farm. The dog, of course, made one of the party, and arrived at the depot a little in advance of the cutter. When Bill drove up, he found Mr. Morton, Susie and the dog standing together, the dog having immediately recognized his friends. After the usual greetings, Mr. Morton informed them that business made it necessary for him to return to the city without going to the farm.

Susie looked at the beautiful, but strangely constructed sleigh, and asked the Bo'son who made it.

"I did, morning-glory."

"What strange thing will you do next, old shell-back?"

The Bo'son laughed, knowing Susie had applied that name to him in return for his calling her morning-glory, and that she had learned it from her grandfather, and said it in sport. He whispered the answer in Susie's ear.

"Marry Lizzie, honeysuckle."

"It will be the wisest and best thing you ever did, though you have done many wise and good ones," was Susie's reply.

The party waited at the station until the train arrived, going south, saw Mr. Morton off, and then drove home.

CHAPTER LII.

A VISIT TO THE FAMILY OF WELCOME GOODWIN.

SUSIE Morton was a desirable acquisition to the farm, and also to the neighborhood; and the remainder of the winter was passed in receiving and making visits among the neighbors and friends.

While the sleighing lasted, the "first cutter," in charge of the Bo'son, was constantly in use, conveying the different members of the family around in making their visits, and in attending on all the parties within a circle of many miles.

So pleasantly did the winter pass, with all the members of the family, that spring-time came before they seemed to be aware that it was coming ; but notwithstanding that, it was welcomed by them all. Who can remember when spring wasn't welcome, with its spirit-giving air, feathered songsters, and blooming flowers ? Yes, even the aged look for it, and greet it, as do the young, because spring's balmly breezes and warming sun, give them new life and increased energy ; besides bringing back to them the feelings and scenes of the spring-time of their own lives. The memory of the past, when the past was pleasant, is ever sweet, and the longer past, the sweeter to be remembered.

The coming spring had brought with it the duties of the farm, and the Bo'son said :

"We must bend sails, and be ready to leave our winter harbor."

No member of the family rejoiced more than Susie Morton did, that the winter had passed, and spring had come. Susie loved the open air, and loved to exercise in it ; and there was another reason which gave her cause for rejoicing,—George Wilson would return before the spring months had passed, visit the farm for a few days, and then accompany Susie to New York.

The Bo'son and Susie had freely talked together about the future, and it was agreed, when George and Susie were married, that at the same time the Bo'son and Lizzie were to be married, though such an event as the Bo'son being married never entered the minds of Captain nor Mrs. Waters ; and it was determined to keep the matter a secret until the proper time came to divulge it. Susie and Lizzie had talked as freely with each other as had Susie and the Bo'son, so there was a perfect understanding between them all.

The Bo'son had succeeded in acquiring such knowledge of farming, and having so strong a desire to be doing something all the time, that he was as useful on the farm as he had been on the ship.

All in good time, George Wilson arrived at New York, and a few days later made a visit to the farm. His coming was expected, and a warmer or more sincere welcome could neither be bestowed or received. Every member of the family greeted him so heartily, that it would have been difficult to have told who rejoiced the most at his coming.

Susie had promised Welcome and Ruth Goodwin, that when George was again at the farm, they would make them a visit together. Susie was an equal favorite with the Bo'son, at the Goodwin farm, and always a welcome visitor in the family. In compliance with that promise, Susie invited George to accompany her to the house of Mr. Goodwin.

George had heard so much from Susie, the steward, and Bo'son, about Welcome Goodwin and family, that he felt a strong wish to also be acquainted. Captain and Mrs. Waters had frequently spoken in such favorable terms of the Goodwin family, that George was really anxious to see and know them.

When the Bo'son drove the family carriage to the door of the Goodwin farm-house, the good Friend and his wife gave George and Susie such a welcome, as pretended friends never give, and George soon felt as much at home as he would have done at the house of Captain Waters.

No language can fairly deceive, no well put on veil completely cover, a cold reception of the heart. If the heart is in rebellion against kind words spoken, there is a tell-tale in the eyes, around the mouth, or on the brow of the speaker, that no dissembler can hide from a close observer. Dissemblers may deceive themselves on such occasions, but not their visitors.

The Bo'son declined an invitation to have the horses put up, and also make a visit, saying :

"I am wanted at the harbor, but will call again in the evening, to take Mr. Wilson and Beauty home."

The Goodwin family were so accustomed to hear Bill Thomas call Susie pet names, that none of them offered any remark on that occasion; nor did Susie herself chide the Bo'son, as it seemed to come natural for him to do so.

After some general conversation, in which all were engaged, the good man of the house said :

" George, thou hast, I apprehend, like the Bo'son, visited many parts of the world, seen the people of many nations, observed their manners and customs, and gained much valuable information of a very different kind from what is within the compass and reach of a plain farming community."

"Yes, Mr. Goodwin, that may in part be true, for though still a very young man, I have been ten years sailing about the different oceans and visiting distant ports; but seamen are not always fortunate enough to possess themselves of much valuable information, that isn't connected with their calling."

"I fully comprehend thee, George, that the duties of the ship claim and receive the most of the time of captain and officers, when in foreign ports."

"Yes, sir, and to know a country and people, a traveler must go inland.   At seaports, we have to know and deal only with merchants, and they do not always reflect the character of the nation under whose government they are doing business."

"That must be so, George, and thou hast been a close observer in that respect; and now let me ask thee if thou hast ever seen a living king?"

"Yes, sir, I have seen William the Fourth of England, Nicholas of Russia, and Dom Pedro, the first emperor of Brazil."

"Seeing them, thou wert convinced that they were only men, high in authority."

"Yes, sir, but the three whom I have seen belong to the family of nature's noblemen, and would have been great men, if they had not been heirs to thrones. William was a sailor before he was a king, and though the son of one king, and brother of another, he served with distinction in the navy, commencing as a midshipman; and when called to reign over a nation, proved a wise and good king. Russia has not had a wiser nor a better emperor than Nicholas. Dom Pedro had a kingdom and an empire. He gave the kingdom of Portugal to his daughter, Dona Maria, and when that throne was usurped by another, he bestowed the crown of Brazil on his son, went to Portugal, placed his daughter on the throne, and there lived and died as Duke of Braganza."

" Well, well, George, thou art a good historian, and must have found much time to read, and been blessed with a good memory. Now let me ask thee of something thou art certainly familiar with. I have heard that, in a gale of wind at sea, the ocean rolls in mountain billows; is it so ? "

" No, sir, and such descriptions are only figurative. In a heavy, steady gale, there is on the ocean a long, rolling sea that ' combs ' and breaks, but is rarely over twenty feet high, and seldom that. They are not dangerous to a ship which is properly managed; but when a heavy gale suddenly shifts, and continues to blow, there comes up a cross sea, meeting the old sea, and then a display of the best seamanship will not always save a vessel from loss of spars, and sometimes of the craft herself."

" Why is it, then, that we have so many descriptions, and from different persons, of such mighty rolling mountain billows? Canst thou tell me that, George?"

" Those descriptions are written by landsmen, from the representation of others, or from having seen only one gale, and that when sea-sick and well frightened,—and what did not exist, was furnished by the imagination."

" I can now understand all about it; but we are having all the conversation to ourselves, without giving the women folks an opportunity to talk. Thou, too, Susan, hast been to sea."

" Yes, sir ; a number of voyages with grandfather Waters, and the Bo'son."

" As friend Waters has given up his ocean life, I apprehend that thou hast also given up all idea of going again on the great ocean ? "

Susie had her suspicions that friend Goodwin, with all his plainness, kindness and friendship, could relish a little joke, and she was correct in her opinion, and answered by saying :

" It isn't everyone who sails the ocean, that I should have sufficient confidence in, to trust myself at sea with."

" Shouldst thee meet some one in whom thou couldst

repose the same confidence, that thou reposest in thy grandfather, and he should invite thee to make a voyage to sea with him, what would be thy answer?"

"That," said Susie, laughing, "would depend on a great many circumstances; such as where he was going, how long the voyage was likely to be; the character and disposition of the man; whether I liked him, or not; who was his first mate; and if he was going to take the Bo'son along."

Before Susie had finished her answer, all had joined her in laughing, and the Bo'son appeared at the door with the carriage. He went in, and joined the happy circle, and remained with it until it was time to leave for home.

We have given only a small portion of the conversation, which was on many subjects, and all united in it. Welcome Goodwin and his family discovered that George Wilson was a man of good general information, possessing great conversational powers; and George was charmed with every member of the family, and especially with Mrs. Goodwin, as all were, who enjoyed an acquaintance with her.

On the way home,—as was very natural,—the pleasures of the afternoon and evening were talked over, and when it came the Bo'son's turn to speak, he said:

"Mr. Wilson, there aren't any other people like these Quakers, and the Goodwin's are among the best of them. I liked that man the first time I saw him, and I like him better every time that I do see him. He is all truth and goodness, every inch of him; and I would trust him, and put as much confidence in him, 'as I would in my dog Bose,—and that, you know, is a great deal."

"I think you are right, Bo'son," said George and Susie, at the same time."

"I have seen many men, Mr. Wilson, who pretended more, but were less than Mr. Goodwin; and I have heard him preach so many plain, good sermons, that I believe in the doctrine of Quakerism, and wish we had more such men; and here we are at home, with the Captain on the look-out."

Captain Waters was on the piazza, when they drove into the yard, and hailed them with "Sail ho! what ship is that?"

"'Neptune;' Wilson, of New York," answered the Bo'son.

"Welcome to port," replied the Captain. "Where are you from?"

"Goodwin Sound," again answered Bill Thomas.

"Come to anchor, and furl your sails," said the Captain, which the Bo'son understood was to unharness, and put up the horses and carriage.

CHAPTER LIII.

A NEW SHIP AND ANOTHER VOYAGE.

THE morning after the visit to the Goodwins, Captain Waters called the family together,—that is, Mrs. Waters, George, and Susie, saying:

"I wish to have a little talk with you about the future, and will commence by asking George, if he thinks that he will be competent to command a ship in another year?"

"Yes, sir; fully competent by that time," was George's answer.

"Then I must be looking about me, and arrange for the building of a ship for you to command."

"You are certainly very kind, and very considerate, Cap'n Waters, and I am greatly obliged to you."

Without appearing to notice what George had said, the Captain continued:

"A good ship can't be properly built in less than a year,— that is, if expected to last; and no other kind of a ship should ever be built."

"Do you intend to own the whole of the ship?" asked Mrs. Waters.

"No, mother; only five eighths of the ship,—the controling and commanding portion. My old friend and consignee will take the other three eighths."

" Where will the ship be built ? " was asked by George Wilson.

" In New Bedford, where the ' Neptune ' was built, and by the Hillman Brothers."

" How large a ship do you contemplate building ? "

"Only a small one, George; about one thousand tons. Very large ships are not profitable for trading voyages, though they do very well when freights are high. Now tell me what are your plans about being married."

At that question, George was a little embarrassed, but it was only for a moment, for he saw in the bright and beautiful face of Susie, an expression which gave him confidence, and he answered :

" It is our intention. still, to be married just before I sail in command of a ship, and for Susie to make the first voyage with me."

" If that is the case," said Mrs. Waters, " we shall have to let Lizzie go with them, for Susie might be lonely at times, when duty called George on deck in stormy weather."

" Yes, mother, that is true; and I have been thinking very seriously of letting the Bo'son go one voyage with George, to put the new ship in perfect order for him. There is no other man who has ever sailed with me, who could be so useful on board of a ship, when making her first voyage."

" If you could spare Bill, I should much like to have him, and another voyage would be pleasant to the Bo'son."

" Grandfather," said Susie, " I have a secret to tell you and grandmother, and you mustn't scold me for not telling you sooner. The Bo'son and Lizzie are to be married at the same time that George and I are."

" Whales, chain-lightning, pitch-forks, and threashing-machines ! " shouted the Captain.

" China tea-sets, chicken-soup, the land of Goshen ! Joseph Waters, do hold your tongue. What makes you use such unheard of expressions ? "

" Now, Nancy, how much have you improved on my exclamations ? Well, well, mother, never mind ; we haven't either of us said anything very bad ; but the news was so sudden, and so unexpected, that it took us both aback. The Bo'son is going to be married ! The very funniest thing that could happen. Sly-puss ! how long have you had this important secret stowed away in your noddle ? "

" Ever since the ' first cutter ' brought me on board."

" So you are trying to talk sailor, because you are to become a Captain's wife. I understand ; you received that information from the Bo'son, when he brought you up from the station."

" Yes, sir ; and inherited my propensity to talk sailor, from my grandfather; and if it was a fortune, I should not have to marry for it."

" Susie, did the news shock you, as it did your grand-mother, and cause you to say bad words ? "

" No, sir; I was not shocked any more at the news, than my grandfather was, and only said, ' It will be the best thing you ever did, Bo'son."

" Well, Susie, I begin to think that you have more com-mand over yourself, than your grandparents have ; and now let us ' call all hands,' and talk this whole matter over, in a ' seaman-like ' manner. Susie you call the stew-ard, Bo'son and Lizzie."

It was not an uncommon occurrence for the Captain to call the family together, on the farm, as he had often done on the ship ; and neither of them, when called, con-sidered it strange, expecting only to spend a pleasant hour with the family, and George Wilson. The Bo'son was the last of those called, to make his appearance, and he brought the dog with him.   As he entered the room, Captain Waters, who was standing, walked to him and laying his hand on the Bo'son's shoulder, said :

" You old barnacle! what do you mean by shipping for a long voyage, without letting me know about it ? "

The Bo'son fully understood his Captain, and being satisfied that he wasn't displeased, answered :

" I haven't signed the articles yet, and can give up the voyage, sir, if you don't like it."

" A fine Bo'son you would be, to promise that you

would go a voyage, and then give it up.   Who put it into your head to think of being married ? "

" You did, sir."

" When, Bo'son, did I ever say a word to you about marrying ?   If I did, I have no recollection of it."

" It was on board of the ship ' Neptune,' sir, the evening that you agreed to let me come to the farm, and bring Bose with me.   You said ' who knows but you may get married, and have a farm of your own ? '   After we left the cabin, Lizzie laughed about my marrying a rosy-cheeked, corn-fed, country girl, and I told her, that ' if ever Bill Thomas married, the woman would have to know something about salt water.' "

" I remember it very well, Joseph," remarked Mrs. Waters.   " Don't you, steward and Lizzie ? '

The steward didn't remember it, and Lizzie made an effort to forget it but couldn't succeed, and was laughed at for her failure.

Susie Morton, seeing that the Bo'son and Lizzie were both a little embarrassed, concluded to " pilot them out of danger."

" Grandfather, there is no use in your trying to play mad with the Bo'son, for there are too many warm and kind feelings in that great heart of yours ; and you are so pleased to know that Bill and Lizzie are to be married, that if it couldn't be accomplished in any other way, you would compel me to break my engagement with George."

" No, no ; I wouldn't do that, by thunder I wouldn't; I might do some strange things, but not break up your arrangements "

" Joseph Waters, why will you use such expressions ? "

" O, mother ! I can't always stop to select soft words, when I am in a hurry.   Now, Bo'son, hear what is to be your fate, as a punishment for your folly. You and Lizzie are going to be married, and I mean to send you both away from the farm."

" Where in the name of —— "

" Mind what you say, Bo'son."

" Where, in the name of a gun-tackle, will you send us, sir, and who will go pilot ? "

"I have not made up my mind where I shall send you, but surely from the farm."

The Bo'son and Lizzie began to look very serious, believing the Captain had determined on breaking up the family, which had so long been together. Susie couldn't bear to see the Bo'son in trouble, even for a few minutes, and said:

"Bo'son, don't be alarmed; where you and Lizzie are sent, George and I will be going."

"Stop, stop; you little soft-hearted tell-tale," said the Captain. "I am the Judge to sentence the Bo'son, and mustn't be interfered with. Bill Thomas, late Bo'son with Joseph Waters, for, and in consideration of your having promised to marry Lizzie Jarvis, without the knowledge and consent of your late commander, you are sentenced to make another voyage to sea, in a new ship, under the command of George Wilson, and to take your wife and dog with you."

"Capt'n, Capt'n, do you mean that?" said the Bo'son. much excited.

"Yes, Bo'son; I do mean it." And the Captain briefly stated the arrangements, which seemed to bewilder the Bo'son for a few minutes, as it was unexpected; but recovering himself, he shouted in a loud voice:

"Cap'n Wilson! Cap'n Wilson! My little George Cap'n of a new ship, and Bill Thomas his Bo'son! Hurrah! hurrah! The Bo'son makes another voyage, and takes the dog with him! Speak, Bose, speak!"

The dog did speak, and speak loudly; and the Bo'son, taking George Wilson in his arms, hugged and tossed him up, as though he was only a child. The Bo'son then took Susie in his strong arms, but handled her as delicately as he would have handled a child. He tenderly kissed her, and received one in return, after which he bestowed the same favor on Lizzie and Mrs. Waters, without giving offence to either. Captain Waters and George Wilson were not idle, and there appeared to be a general kissing game played, in which the dog took an active part, for his paws were in turn on the shoulders of everyone. Then the Captain and Bo'son took each other by the hand; but for a moment neither spoke, though the Captain hammered his Bo'son over the shoulders with his other hand, striking such heavy blows as would have injured a less solid frame. Bill Thomas was the first to speak, saying:

"Cap'n Waters, this is more than I had ever expected to live and see. Your boy George, whom I helped to make his first splice, stood by him when he steered his first trick at the wheel, and was at his side the first time he went aloft; now to have him for my Cap'n, and to sail under him as his Bo'son, is glory enough for Bill Thomas. God bless you, Cap'n Waters, and God bless George, Cap'n Wilson."

"God bless us all, and bless you, as He has blessed me with such a Bo'son."

The Captain and his Bo'son were both nearly overcome with the warmth and earnestness of their feelings. After a short silence, the Captain, still holding the Bo'son by his hand, said:

"Bill, I never meant to part with you, and I only do it now for a short time, because George will be a new Cap'n, and the ship new, and I know that on the first voyage, you can be very useful to him; but it is only for one voyage, mind you, Bo'son."

"Yes, sir; and Mr. Wilson is the only man who could have your Bo'son."

"Susie is the only woman who could have my chambermaid," said Mrs. Waters.

"What is to become of me?" asked the steward.

"You must stay here," answered the Captain. "I can't do without you, to keep all my money affairs and farm accounts correct. It will only be a few months that we shall be separated, and that will not take place until next year. You, steward, I hope, will always remain with me, and after one short voyage, the Bo'son and Lizzie will be with us; and we shall not again be separated, until one after another, we end the voyage of life. I shall be happy in seeing others happy, who have long been around me."

Susie Morton, perceiving that the Captain was deeply

exercised in feeling, changed the current of his reflections, by saying :

"Grandfather, let me name the new ship, if you please, and I will furnish a set of colors for her, of my own making?"

"You can name the ship, Susie. Now, what will you call her?"

"I will name the ship 'Joseph Waters.'"

All clapped their hands, and said "Joseph Waters."

The Captain could make no objection, and that name was determined on; which pleased them all, and especially the old Bo'son. The new ship and her first voyage furnished the little family party subjects for conversation, until a late hour in the evening, when they separated for the night, each to remember the past, and contemplate the future.

CHAPTER LIV.

THE CAPTAIN BUILDS A SHIP, AND HARDENGRIP WANTS A WIFE.

WHEN George and Susie left the farm for New York, Captain Waters also left, going to the city, and stopping there a few days, and then to New Bedford, where he contracted for building the new ship. The frame was to be put up during the summer and fall, but not to be planked until the following spring, as the Captain wished the frame well seasoned.

The arrangements for building the ship did not keep the Captain long from his home, as he and the builders were old friends, and could depend on each other, and the ship was to be built by day's work, and not by contract. Captain Waters wanted a ship equal in goodness to the "Neptune," and was willing to pay for every day's work done in her construction.

The Hillman Brothers inquired about the Bo'son, and were informed that he would rig, but not assist in building the ship. They expressed some regret, as they would have been pleased to count him in their gang of carpenters.

Captain Waters returned by way of New York, and took Susie with him to the farm, where they were both, as might have been expected, received with joy and satisfaction.

Mrs. Waters asked after Mr. Livingston and Julia, and from Susie learned that Frank was constantly going from bad to worse; that although Julia lived in splendor and had all that money could purchase, she was by no means happy, and admitted that fact to her cousin. Susie could sympathize with, but was powerless to aid her.

Spring work on the farm commenced in earnest, about the time that Captain Waters, George and Susie left for New York, and when the Captain returned, all the spring crops were in the ground.

The good neighbors had ceased to offer advice or suggestions about crops on the Waters' farm, having learned that Captain Waters, with the assistance of Mr. Harrowell and the Bo'son, could manage his own affairs.

Anna Moores, who had long wished, at last paid a visit to the Snug Harbor, as the farm was now generally called. Before doing so, she asked Ruth Goodwin to her house, to assist her in preparing herself for the visit. Ruth cheerfully consented, and when Anna left home, she was really in a presentable condition, and realized the change in herself. Ruth said to Anna:

"Thou art, truly, a very goodly-looking person, when clean and properly dressed, and though I have often seen thee with that dress on, thou hast never looked as comely dressed as now."

"O, Ruth! I see it is in knowing how to put things on, and in future I will bestow more time and labor in attiring myself; but thee must remember that my Jonathan, is not like thy Welcome, pleased to be neat himself in his personal appearance, and to see others so."

"I know it, Anna; but thou canst change thyself, and that may, in some degree, change thy husband. Husbands and their wives often grow to be alike in their habits, and if they strive to do so, can improve each other."

"I believe thee, Ruth; thank thee for thy assistance and advice, and will now go."

Anna was driven to the Harbor by a boy, and cordially received by Mrs. Waters and Susie. They had all met at the meeting-house, and knew each other. Anna visited every part of the house, not excepting the kitchen and steward's room, and was agreeably astonished at all she saw. She remained to tea, and wasn't "pisened" by eating victuals cooked by "a nasty man." On her return, like the Queen of Sheba, she said, "The half had not been told me."

The summer and its work were over, fall at hand, and winter soon to follow. Everything on the farm, and in the family of the Captain, had been pleasant and satisfactory. The Bo'son had met with no ship-wreck, because he had become a good navigator; nor had he been engaged in any act which furnished special amusement for his Captain.

Amos Hardengrip, after losing his sausage-meat, by a mistake of Anna Moores, and being nearly whipped by the Bo'son, improved every occasion to be reconciled with him; and the Bo'son, having no unkindness in his heart, could forgive, but never respect the man. They were soon on speaking terms, and Hardengrip more than commonly sociable. The Bo'son suspected there was some design on the part of the old miser, and determined to watch him closely. After a time, Mr. Hardengrip began to ask Bill questions about Lizzie, and then the Bo'son concluded that he was after another wife, and thought he could see some fun ahead, and decided to be free and communicative the next time they met. It was not long before they did meet, and Amos, after wishing the Bo'son good morning, more pleasantly than usual, said:

"Bo'son, I've been thinking a good deal about that Lizzie at your house, since we last talked about her, a few days since. Do you think she would like to have a home of her own?"

"Certainly, sir; did you ever know a woman that didn't?"

"Do you think she would like to be married?"

"Yes, Mr. Hardengripe, if she had a chance; for I have often heard her say so."

"She is a nice kind of a woman, I think, Bo'son; and knows something of cooking and housekeeping."

"Yes, sir; she can cook equal to the steward, keep house equal to Mrs. Waters, and make butter equal to any woman in the county."

"I suppose, Bo'son, that she receives wages where she is?"

"Yes, sir; and always has, for more than twenty years."

"And spends it all in buying clothes?"

"Not a bit of it; her wages would clothe a queen."

"What becomes of her money then?"

"She puts it in the bank."

"Ah, oh, that is it," said Hardengrip. "She must have as much as a thousand dollars."

"Yes, sir; more than five thousand dollars."

"Is that possible,—and you think she would like to marry?"

"Oh, yes, certainly; and the man than gets her will have a treasure."

"She must have a good stock of clothes, Bo'son."

"Enough to last her ten years."

"And do you think, if she married, that she would let her husband have her money to use, and make more with?" asked Hardengrip.

"Every dollar of it, as freely as she would give him a glass of water."

"I should like to call on her some time, when the Captain, yourself and the dog were not at home."

"It is possible that we may be from home to-morrow; and if we are you will know it, as we shall drive by your house," said the Bo'son.

Hardengrip had made up his mind to have Lizzie Jarvis for a wife, and the Bo'son had made up his mind to have some fun, and so went home, and first told Lizzie what was coming; then told the Captain, leaving Lizzie to inform Mrs. Waters and Susie.

That night Hardengrip dreamed of Lizzie, bags of

money, snuff, sausages, and coffins made of old boards, taken off the fence ; and felt in the morning that he really needed a good and careful wife.

The next day, after dinner, he saw Captain Waters and the Bo'son pass his house in a buggy wagon, followed by the dog ; and Hardengrip immediately said to himself, " This is my time,—now, or never."   But it will require another chapter to tell how he sped in his wooing, because his first visit was out of the usual order of such calls.

CHAPTER LV.

HARDENGRIP GOES A-COURTING.

AMOS Hardengrip was so anxious to visit Lizzie, while those he most feared were absent, that he did not wait to properly dress himself, but just as he came out of the field, where he had been digging potatoes ; he left his house to offer himself in marriage to a woman who had traveled constantly for over twenty years, and had lived with refined and educated people all that time.   Hardengrip had neither coat nor stockings on ; wore a well faded, and well soiled brown flannel shirt ; a pair of dark pants, with a black patch on each knee ; an old straw hat, with a portion of the brim gone ; an old pair of shoes ; and was without a necktie of any kind.   He didn't wash his face and hands after leaving the field, but mounted his old yellow, bald-faced horse, without saddle or bridle, using only a rope halter to ride him with, and rode to the farm house of Captain Waters.

Hardengrip had never been inside of a well furnished and well-kept house, had very little education, and had never mingled in good society, or he would not have gone on such a mission, in such a manner.   His anxiety to get and keep money, was so great, and his knowledge of the world so limited, that after talking with the Bo'son, he entertained the idea that Lizzie Jarvis was so anxious to marry, that she only waited for an offer, to become a wife;

and his only fear was that some more fortunate man would make the offer before him.   He had actually decided in his own mind, how he would invest the five thousand dollars, and that after it once came into his possession, Lizzie Hardengrip should never again handle or control a dollar of it.   Saying to himself as he rode down the road : " I know how to manage money and women, when I am in full charge of either."

"Mrs. Waters, Susie and Lizzie were in the sitting-room when Mr. Hardengrip rode up to the gate, dismounted, secured his horse by tying him, and then walked to the kitchen door, and into the kitchen, where he found the steward and two young Irish women, who belonged to that part of the house.   Without passing the compliments of the day, or any ceremony, he said :

" I want to see Lizzie Jarvis; is she here ?"

The steward knew Hardengrip, and in his quiet, mild way, answered :

" Mr. Hardengrip, Lizzie is in the sitting-room with Mrs. Waters and Miss Morton; will you please walk around to the front of the house, and to the room on the left of the hall."

Hardengrip was disappointed, and a little disconcerted, but was dreadfully in earnest.   He had never been in such a kitchen, and did not feel at home even in that part of the house.   He mustered resolution, and said :

" Steward, you show me the room."

" Certainly, sir, with great pleasure; come this way if you please."   And passing through the dining-room to the main hall, he went with the visitor into the sitting-room, and bowing, said : "ladies, Mr. Hardengrip," and immediately retired.

Mrs. Waters left her seat, and in an easy, pleasant manner, walked to Mr. Hardengrip, offered her hand, and then invited him to be seated, the other ladies rising at the same time, and acknowledging his presence.   Hardengrip, without walking, running or hopping, crossed the room in a peculiar style, and took a seat with his back to an open window, wearing all the time the old straw hat, which he did not appear to think necessary to remove, and his pantaloons being short, showed a large proportion of his legs below the knees, and they were well covered with the soil of the potato-field.

It being in the forenoon, the women were plainly but neatly dressed, and were all engaged with some light sewing work. In re-seating themselves, as an act of courtesy, they all faced the visitor, and were at the back of the centre-table. Hardengrip, to use a nautical phrase, was "hard and fast ashore," as everything was so different from what he expected, but he was making great efforts to float himself. He kept the soil-colored legs in full view, and constantly moving by crossing, uncrossing and re-crossing them, and the first words which he uttered were:

"Lizzie Jarvis, I want a wife."

"That is not strange, and I presume you will have no difficulty in getting one."

This answer, though a proper one, so encouraged Hardengrip, that he immediately said:

"I don't expect any difficulty, for I want you for a wife, and you will marry me."

"No, Mr. Hardengrip, I am not disposed to marry any one at present."

"Don't you want a home of your own, where you will be mistress yourself?"

"No, sir; I am at present very pleasantly situated, and have a good home."

"But it isn't your own, and you have to do as others tell you."

"Mr. Hardengrip," said Mrs. Waters, "Lizzie has been with us over twenty years, and while we have a house, she will never want one."

"That may all be; but she wants a home of her own, and wants a husband, as every woman does."

"I certainly don't wish you for a husband, Mr. Hardengrip, and again say no."

"What is the matter with me, that I aren't the man to be your husband, and why will you not marry me? I insist on your doing so, and am determined to take no refusal."

"I am afraid, sir, that if I married you, and should die, that you would bury me in a coffin made of old boards, and then sell my clothes and sweatmeats."

"In the first place, there is no fear of your dying, and if you do you shall be properly buried."

"Mr. Hardengrip," said Mrs. Waters, "there is no chance of Lizzie's marrying you, even if she wished to marry. You are not such a man as would suit her, and you should be satisfied with her answer."

"Woman, I don't want anyone to interfere in this matter; I know Lizzie Jarvis, after thinking over the matter a little, will marry me, and I shall have her for my wife before next killing time."

Lizzie was a little disturbed and a little riled, and answered:

"I know that she will not, though your sausage meat should again be seasoned with snuff."

When that subject was alluded to, Hardengrip was provoked, and used expressions unsuited to the place and company, and wound up by swearing that Lizzie Jarvis should be his wife, if it cost him fifty dollars. As he concluded the last expression, the Bo'son blew some shrill notes on his silver call, close to the ear of Hardengrip, who jumped from his chair, and without ceremony left the room and the house, and hastened to the gate, where he mounted his horse and started up the road.

For some minutes before the notes were sounded at the open window, and close to the ear of Hardengrip, the Bo'son had been seen by the ladies, who were facing that way, and he had been making telegraphic signals to Susie and Lizzie, which were also observed by Mrs. Waters. Had Hardengrip understood the notes of a "Bo'sons call," he would have known that the Bo'son was "piping all hands to mischief."

Hardengrip was in a great hurry,—as the Bo'son would have expressed it,—" to leave the coast;" and Bill let him get a short distance on the road, and then said to the dog: "Go for him, Bose."

The dog did go, at the bidding of his master, and when Hardengrip saw the dog coming, he did his best to get his horse on a run, but failed, and the dog took the horse by his tail, and hauled that end of him first over one side of the road, and then over the other side.   Hardengrip all the time whipping the horse with the end of the halter rope, and shouting "get off dog ! get off dog ! go along jack ! get up jack !" while his own long legs were swinging about, within a foot of the ground ; the whole forming as ludicrous a spectacle as could have possibly been gotten up to order.

The Bo'son called the dog back with his whistle, and when Mrs. Waters and the others went to the door, the Bo'son was rolling on the grass, nearly choking with laughter; but contrary to his custom, uttered not a word, and soon disappeared.

Late in the afternoon of that day, Captain Waters and the Bo'son passed the house of Hardengrip, on their way home, followed by the dog ; the horses and dog appearing to have made a long journey.   Hardengrip was again digging potatoes near the road.   The Captain spoke to him, and so did Bill, but he wasn't in a talking mood. The dog took not the slightest notice of him.   Hardengrip was never able to satisfy himself, in his own mind, whether there were two Bo'sons and two dogs, or whether he was so frightened that he couldn't tell what happened.

How the Bo'son managed to be at the farm with his dog, and return with his Captain, none but those two knew, and they both pretended ignorance of what had taken place in their absence, but failed to convince the family that they were ignorant.

Hardengrip was treated with more courtesy than his manner and motive deserved, but he was in the company of refined and educated ladies, who had no motive nor desire to treat him otherwise.

Captain Waters had a number of choking spells, that evening, in laughing over the affair ; and Mrs. Waters, as usual, cautioned him ; but he said :

"Nancy, it is no use; let me alone this time, and let me have it out.   The Bo'son didn't tell me what he was up to, but I have laughed enough to last me a month."

Mrs. Waters, Susie and Lizzie enjoyed themselves over

the affair, which was not allowed to slumber for many months, and each time when it was mentioned, it furnished a source of amusement to them all.

CHAPTER LVI.

JOE WESTERN GOES TO THE FARM, AND THE SHIP TO NEW YORK.

THE Bo'son's face wore a funny appearance for a number of days after the visit of Hardengrip, but none of the family ever mentioned the circumstance, outside of their own circle; consequently the neighbors knew nothing about it, as Hardengrip was not likely to speak of it himself.

After the fall work of the farm was all done, and everything prepared for winter, Captain Waters and the Bo'son visited New Bedford, to inspect the frame of the new ship. They found all to their satisfaction, and the Bo'son was much pleased, as the ship was modeled after the "Neptune," and as a figure-head was to have an image of his old captain. There was no favor which could have been granted the Bo'son, in this world, that would have been so highly prized, and so gratifying to him, as that of sailing in a ship called the "Joseph Waters," carrying on her prow the image of his old commander.

Returning by way of New York, they spent a number of days in the city, and the Bo'son visited the Sailors' Smug Harbor, and there met his first friend, Joe Western, who aided him to run away from the brig, at Fayal, thirty-four years previous to their meeting at the Harbor. The Bo'son recognized his friend, though time and hard service had somewhat changed him. Great was the joy of Joe Western, when he found, in the old Bo'son, what was once his little boy friend, Bill Thomas. They spent the day together, and communicated to each other a thirty-four years' history of their lives. Western, like too many seamen, had saved nothing to supply his wants in old age, and though hale and hearty, for a man sixty-seven years of age, was unfitted for active sea-service, and had anchored at the Snug Harbor. He was as pleased to hear of the Bo'son's good fortune, and comfortable circumstances, as he was to again see him. There is a tie which binds seamen together, stronger and more lasting than the ties which bind any other class, or clan of men. When they parted, the Bo'son promised to see his friend again, before he left for the farm.

That evening the Bo'son asked the Captain if he could spare a few minutes to talk with the Bo'son.

"Certainly, Bo'son, always time to talk with you. Any accident, Bill? Let me hear what it is."

"No, sir; no accidents,—but I have found my old shipmate, Joe Western, whom I have often told you of."

"I remember all that you have said about him, and that he assisted you to run away from a brute of a cap'n, or I should never had you for a Bo'son. Where is he, and what can we do for him?"

The Bo'son stated all the particulars of Joe's whereabouts, age, health, and circumstances, and then said:

"I am going out in the new ship, and you will want some one on the farm, and around the house, to take care of things, and keep all snug. Western is just the man, though he can't carpenter and blacksmith. I should like to take him up with us."

"That's right, Bo'son, you do it. There is plenty to eat on the farm, and he shall not want clothes nor money. Never forget a friend nor a favor. He shall have all he needs to make him comfortable in his old age, whether he can work or not, and I will take care that he don't hurt himself with hard work."

"Thank you, Cap'n, thank you; I'll attend to him, and glad enough he'll be."

The next day the Bo'son went to the Harbor, and arranged with his shipmate to go with them to the farm. Western obtained leave of absence from the Governor of the institution for six months, which could be be renewed if required.

The Captain, Bo'son, and Joe Western returned to the

farm, and when the family learned who the third person was, they all gave him a warm and hearty reception. Bill took him to the midship-house, gave him the spare berth, with a privilege of the whole establishment. Western was pleased with his change from the old to the new Snug Harbor. After Western had been a few weeks at the farm, he appeared to renew his age, and said :

"I am happier, and better situated now, than I have been since I left my father's house, over fifty years ago."

When Captain Waters heard him make the remark, he took his hat off, and reverently said, "Thank God."

The winter was spent at the farm, as the preceding one had been. Susie Morton visited the city during the lolidays, and was accompanied back to the farm by Gecrge Wilson, who had returned from his voyage to Europe, and was granted a leave of absence of ten days from the ship, previous to his preparing for the last voyage which he would make, before taking command of the new ship, " Joseph Waters."

The ten days spent by George Wilson at the Waters Snug Harbor, were ten days of real, rational enjoyment. Bill Thomas the Bo'son was in his glory. Sleighing was good, the weather fine, with a moon near the full, and Bill's sleigh, the " first cutter," in perfect order. It being a gala season, the Bo'son a good and careful driver, and having extra road service to perform, the Captain said to him :

" Bo'son, you can drive my carriage-horses, when Fayal and Pico need rest. You have become such a good driver, that I can trust you with my fancy team."

" Thank you, sir; Fayal and Pico, that you put in my charge, are good horses, and I have taken extra good care of them; but while Mr. Wilson is here, there will be double duty for horses, and when I drive Whalebone and Grampus, will be very careful of them."

George Wilson was pleased with Bill's novel sleigh, and the manner that he handled and drove the horses, and enjoyed the many rides given him by the Bo'son. In speaking of it to Captain Waters, he said :

"I believe there are but few things the Bo'son couldn't learn, and do well."

"George, Bill Thomas is a remarkable man, and every year appears to grow younger and smarter. Only let him have some innocent fun, and for the time he will be a boy; and when there are duties to perform, he is more than a man. Hardengrip's coming here after Lizzie will furnish Bill amusement all his life-time."

"Bill has told me all about it, sir, and I have never known him to enjoy any sport so heartily."

Captain and Mrs. Waters, George and Susie, would fill all the seats in the body of the sleigh, and as they wished to have Lizzie make one of the party, Bill arranged a seat for her on the top-gallant forecastle of the sleigh, saying:

"Lizzie is soon to be a Bo'son's mate; her proper place is at his side."

All their friends in the neighborhood, and on the other side of the river, in Washington county, were visited; the sick and needy called on, comforted and relieved, and all that would give comfort to others, was enjoyed by the family at the farm.

The last day of George's stay at the farm was a bright, sunny one, and the Bo'son, accompanied by the family, drove him in the sleigh to the depot.

When the winter was over, and spring-time came, Bill prepared to leave with Captain Waters for New Bedford; the Captain to superintend the finishing of the ship, and the Bo'son to rig her, and see that everything was in order for a voyage.

As this was likely to be the last ship that Captain Waters would be an owner of, and was to bear his name, and to carry his image as a figure-head on her bow, extra work was done on every part of the ship. After the name was decided upon, the size of the ship was increased one-third, and when finished she was fifteen hundred tons burthen, instead of one thousand tons, as originally intended. The increased size may have been caused by a little pride on the part of her owner, and if so, it could be pardoned in one of his character.

The ship was finished, rigged "hove down," re-caulked and coppered, the captain saying:

"I know that there is no port in the world where the work on a ship's bottom can be so faithfully and effectually done as at New Bedford. The long voyages which their whale ships make, have taught them the necessity of doing their work well."

After the bottom of the ship was prepared for sea, the last coat of paint was put on the hull and spars, the sails "bent," and the ship ready to proceed to New York.

George Wilson had not arrived from his last voyage as first officer of a ship, but was daily expected; continued westerly winds had lengthened his passage from Liverpool beyond the usual time.

Captain Waters shipped a crew, and took the ship to New York, arriving off the Hook, the day that the "Neptune" did from Liverpool, and the two ships sailed up the Bay together.

Well might George Wilson be proud of the ship that he was to command, for after arriving at the dock, and being examined by nautical men, she was pronounced to be as fine and perfect a ship as had ever been built. A freight for London was engaged for the ship, officers placed on board of her; and Captain Waters, George Wilson and Bill Thomas left for the farm, there to attend to some very important matters.

———

CHAPTER LVII.

A DOUBLE MARRIAGE, AND COSTLY PRESENTS.

PREPARATIONS for the double marriage had, for a long time, been making at the country home of Joseph Waters. The Captain and his lady were determined that nothing should be left undone to render the occasion an interesting one, not only to those that were to be united, but to all who might be present.

Lizzie, after a little opposition on the part of the Bo'son, succeeded in persuading him to dress differently from common, on that occasion, so that he might look a little like other folks, when they were married.

"I will do it for you, Lizzie, but I wouldn't have done it for any other live woman."

"Except Susie," was Lizzie's reply.

"Yes, yes; I would do anything for black-eyed Susan, but I'll not have a claw-hammer coat; it shall be a frock coat, made of navy blue cloth, with white trousers, white waist-coat, white shirt, with a turndown collar, blue necktie,—and if you insist on it,—gloves for the occasion; but I can't wear gloves all day."

"That isn't necessary, Bill; but you will have a shore-hat, because we shall visit some in the city, before we sail?"

"Yes, Lizzie; I'll do that too, and then I shall hardly know myself, and don't believe the old dog will know me, I shall be so changed."

"You will remember, Bo'son," continued Lizzie, "that two and a half years on shore, has changed us all in habits, though not in character; and now we are about to change our relationship to each other, and notwithstanding that you are going Bo'son of the ship, you are to live in the cabin, and eat with the Captain and officers, as I also shall; being more of a companion for Susie, than stewardess of the ship."

"I know it all, Lizzie, and will do whatever you wish while ashore."

Cards of invitation had been sent to the neighbors whom the family were accustomed to exchange visits with, including Welcome and Ruth Goodwin.

The cards stated that the marriages would take place at ten o'clock in the forenoon; and reception until one in the afternoon.

Susie's father, mother and brothers were there, also many friends from the city, including Julia Livingston, who left the city with her father and mother, to be present at the wedding of her cousin. Frank sent his compliments, and an excuse that his illness prevented his being present. The family fully understood the excuse.

The Bo'son was indeed a changed man in his appearance, when dressed in a suit so different from what he had always been accustomed to wear. A finer, nobler appearing representative of the family of " Neptune," never led a blushing bride to Hymen's altar.

Susie and Lizzie were dressed beautifully for the occasion, and looked as lovely and happy as brides could possibly look.

At the hour appointed, the family and invited guests were arranged, standing around three sides of the front parlor of the family house, the good minister and his friend standing in the middle, but nearest and facing the folding doors.

The company was not kept waiting long, as George Wilson soon appeared in the back parlor, with Susie by the hand, and the Bo'son following him, hand in hand with Lizzie Jarvis. George passed through the folding doors with his lovely companion, and stood before the minister; the Bo'son and Lizzie took their places at the left of Susie. They were unaccompanied by groomsmen or bridesmaids. A more lovely sight could not have been presented to the gathered friends. A brief but appropriate prayer, a simple ceremony, followed by a benediction, and George Wilson and Susie Morton were united for life, and so were Bill Thomas and Lizzie Jarvis.

The usual congratulations and kisses were bestowed, and the company invited into the back parlor, to see and examine the bridal gifts.

These presents were rich and beautiful, that were bestowed upon Susie, consisting mostly of silver ware, valuable books and articles which would not only be keepsakes, but also useful in life. It being known to all the friends of Susie Morton, that she was not fond of jewelry, nor accustomed to make much display of it, she received only one set, and that of great beauty and value to her, as it was made in Europe, brought across the ocean by George Wilson, and presented before her marriage. She wore it at her wedding. Lizzie was not forgotten, but received a present from all who were acquainted with her.

It was noticed that Susie's presents from her grandfather, father, brother and uncles, though they were all beautiful, and calculated to be lasting, were not of great value, and some present were surprised at it, knowing their ability to make costly ones.   Mrs. Waters quickly expressed her surprise to Susie's father, and he walked to the table where the others were standing, taking at the same time a package from his pocket, and saying :

" Susie, my dear child, I am so pleased and satisfied with your marriage, that I present you, as a bridal gift, the deed of a house and lot in the city, which I paid ten thousand dollars for ; also a bond of three thousand dollars, bearing interest, which you can convert into cash, when you wish to furnish the house."

The rich gift was so unexpected, that Susie, with all her self-command, could only kiss and simply thank her father, but her joy and thankfulness was pictured in every liniament of her face.   Her uncles, the two sons of Captain Waters, each presented a government bond for two thousand dollars, and her brother a similar bond for one thousand dollars.   They each received a grateful acknowledgement of their kind remembrances and valuable presents.

Mrs. Waters went to the table, and taking up a package of silver forks and spoons, marked " From grandfather to his pet, Susie," said :

" Joseph Waters, your heart must have been opened very wide, when you made that present to our Susie, as a bridal gift.   It isn't like you, and I fear you are not well."

Captain Waters looked like anything but a sick man. His face was cheerful, and his eyes sparkling with delight ; he had shaken the hands of the whole company a number of times, and kissed Susie every time he could get near enough to her to do so, petted the old dog, and pulled his ears, while he was watching, with pleasure, the others as they bestowed their gifts on his darling grandchild.   In answer to the remarks, he said :

" No, mother, I am not sick, nor exactly like myself. I haven't been present when any of the children were married before, and now four of them are 'spliced' in a single day ; but they shall have something to remind them of the old man of the ocean ; " and walking to Susie, he

also handed her a package, saying: "There, my darling, is a bill of sale of five eighths of the ship 'Joseph Waters,' cash value of fifty-seven thousand, four hundred and forty dollars. Accept it as a bridal present from grandfather, and may she always have good freights and fair winds."

It was a surprise to them all, and Mrs. Waters could not conceal her pleasure and satisfaction. Susie put her arms around his neck, saying, after kissing him :

"Grandpa, what can I say or do? You are such a good man."

"Nothing, my child, nothing; only continue to be good and be happy."

The Bo'son could stand no more; his heart was full, and he shouted:

"Hurrah! hurrah! for everybody and everything!"

Captain Waters said :

"You, Bo'son, close that upper gangway of yours, and come here."

"Aye, aye, sir," was Bill's response.

"Here, sir," continued the Captain, "is a deed of thirty acres of land, on the opposite side of the road, together with the buildings and all the improvements, as a present for you, and a home in your old age."

"Cap'n Waters, what makes you do so ? I thank you, but don't deserve such treatment, and haven't any cargo of words to hoist out."

"Close your hatches, then, Bo'son, and stand by for dinner, for I am hungry and dry," replied the Captain.

A bountiful dinner was partaken of by all present, over which they had no time to waste, but enough to fully enjoy it, as the whole family were to leave that afternoon for the city, including the old dog.

The guests living in the neighborhood were pleased with the entertainment. Welcome Goodwin and his wife were utterly astonished at the display of wealth, and the lavish freedom with which Captain Waters and his children bestowed it upon the newly-married people. When parting with George Wilson, the Bo'son and their wives, Mr. Goodwin said, while shaking hands with them:

"May you be blessed with corn and with oil; the fat of the land be yours, and Heaven's richest and choicest blessings be scattered all around you. Farewell, friends."

The Captain, when he and Mr. Morton were by themselves, said:

"What do you think, William, about George Wilson having no rich relations nor powerful friends?"

"Father, I am satisfied; you have been very generous, and we all are blessed."

Julia was sad and very sorrowful, and in congratulating her cousin said:

"You will be happy, and I miserable. You endeavored to save me, but I would not, and I must suffer through life."

Late that afternoon, the whole family left for New York, all but Julia happy and joyful, and all of them pitying poor Julia Livingston.

CHAPTER LVIII.

CONCLUSION.

CAPTAIN Waters had bestowed a rich bridal gift on his pet grandchild, but in doing so, had not displeased any member of his family. Years before he had furnished each of his two sons with a sum greater than the cost of a new ship, as a capital for them to do business with, so they had no cause to complain. Mrs. Morton, the Captain's only daughter, and mother of Susie, was not likely to complain at the good fortune of her only daughter. Mr. Morton remembered that he had once objected to having George Wilson for a son-in-law, because he had no rich relations, and he also remembered the reply: "If he marries our Susie, he will have one powerful friend, one rich relation; for he will have Joseph Waters for a grandfather." Mr. Morton fully realized the truth of that remark in the rich dowry bestowed upon his daughter by her grandfather. Only Mrs. Waters and the

one.   Captain Waters had given his special attention to the cabins, and his long experience in that line of business, enabled him to fit them up with great taste, and with every convenience to make them pleasant and convenient.

It was very difficult to determine whether Captain Waters or his Bo'son felt the greatest pride and satisfaction in seeing George Wilson master of such a ship, and of addressing him as "Cap'n Wilson."   Mrs. Waters, when on board, and observing the manner of her husband and the Bo'son said: "I believe you are both growing childish about George and his new ship."   But there was something in the sparkle of her eyes, and the brightness of her face, which plainly told there was no disapproval of their conduct on her part.

When the ship was loaded and ready for sea, Captain Waters engaged the steamer "Goliath," to tow her outside of the Hook, and if wished, to the Light-Ship; and invited the family and some friends to go down in the ship, and return in the steamer.

It was a beautiful bright day, with a moderate wind from the north-west.   At ten o'clock in the forenoon, the family and friends embarked on the steamer, at one of the piers, and went alongside of the ship, at anchor in the harbor.

As the steamer went alongside of the vessel, the Bo'son's call was heard.   The crew manned the rigging, and gave three hearty cheers, to welcome their Captain, his wife, and their friends on board.

Captain and Mrs. Waters went first on board, followed by Captain Wilson and his bride; and the four received their friends, as they landed on the deck of the noble ship.

The crew had been shipped with the understanding that no liquor was to be furnished by the ship, nor used on board; consequently they were all sober, neat in their appearance, and ready for duty.   Some of them had sailed with the Captains and with the Bo'son.   The ship was in perfect order, and clean in every part, as ships always were, where Bill Thomas was Bo'son.

The anchor was taken to the bow, the steamer went

ahead, and the ship moved down the Bay, and through the narrows. No sail was made on the ship, till she was in the Lower Bay. The friends were invited into the cabin to partake of a lunch, which might have been dignified with the name of dinner, had it been later in the day.

Before the ship reached the point of the Hook, she had set her top-sails, top-gallant-sails, and royals, her courses hanging in the brails.

The wind was still light near the land, but was blowing a good breeze a .few miles at sea, and the steamer continued to keep a good strain on the tow-line. When about five miles out, the wind had so increased, that the ship, under sail, was going nearly as fast as the steamer. Orders were given for the steamer to "let go the line," the ship to be brought to the wind, with the main-top-sail aback, and the steamer to come alongside.

The leave-taking was tender, sincere, and affectionate; but with none of them, foolish. They were seamen, or the families and friends of seamen; had parted often, and met again. None of them expected this was their last meeting and parting.

When the others had exchanged adieus, Captain Waters took George by the hand, saying :

"Cap'n Wilson, you have a fine ship, good officers and crew, and now a fair wind. It gladdens my old heart to see you so situated. May you always have fair winds. As you now have a leading wind, after we leave the ship I want you to put every yard of canvass on her. I must see her under full sail, and then I shall be satisfied."

"You shall be gratified, Cap'n Waters; but that will be a small consideration for what I owe you, and thank you for with all the warmth and earnestness of a sailor's heart."

Mr. Hurlbut, the first mate, and Mr. Preston the second mate, with the Bo'son and their young captain, were standing with their hats off, around their old commander, looking upon and loving him like a father. He shook them all by the hand,—Bill the last, and as he did so said: "Only this voyage, Bo'son, and then you stay with me for life." The Captain again kissed Susie, and with Mrs. Waters left the ship.

As the steamer left the side of the ship, and dropped astern, the rigging was again manned, and the departing friends cheered, the old dog on the taffrail barking hard and loud enough to have bursted the throat of any common dog. The cheers from the ship were returned from the steamer, Captain Waters leading.

As requested, Captain Wilson made all sail. The wind being from the northwest, and the course of the ship east, southerly, the lee clew of the mainsail, studder-sails and outer jibs would draw to advantage. The steamer was on the weather-quarter of the ship, not going quite as fast as the ship, but so situated as to allow all but the head-sails of the ship to be seen.

When all sail was on the ship, and the old Captain could have a full view of her, he swung his hat, and hurrahed until he was hoarse in the throat, very red in the face, and appeared greatly delighted. Mrs. Waters went to him, saying :

" Joseph, be moderate ; I fear you will injure yourself, and be overcome with excitement."

" I can't help it, if I am. Let me alone, mother, for this time, and let me enjoy it. I have held in all day, and now let us hurrah for the children. You, Nancy, have seen many ships at sea under full sail, but did you ever see a more lovely sight than that ship presents ? "

" No, Joseph, I never have ; and it has been a very happy day with me."

" It has been one of the brightest, happiest days of my life, mother. There goes a ship-load of our children, whom we have brought up. Every officer, and some of the crew, have sailed with us. George is Captain, Susie is his wife, and the two have enough wealth to give them a fair start in the world. Susie will be very happy. The Bo'son and Lizzie are with them." The Captain took off his hat, raised his eyes, and reverently said, " May Heaven greatly bless them all."

There was a moisture on the face of the old sailor ; the good wife wiped it from his cheeks, and led him to a seat from which he could still see the ship sailing on her course. After watching the ship for a time, he turned his pleased and cheerful face to his wife, saying :

" Nancy, yonder goes some of the fruit of your prudence and economy in early life. When we were first married, you carefully used or saved the money which I earned, and what you then saved has been accumulating and being added to, until now we can assist those we dearly love. You could always calm my hasty, angry passions, and hold me in check."

" In all things, I have only done the duty of a wife, and with you rejoice in the happy results."

" You have nobly done your duty, and with the assistance of others, we have saved our Susie from the fate and misery of Julia; and now let us return to the farm, and there contentedly await the return of those from whom we have just parted. Whatever may happen, we need not fear that George Wilson will die a drunkard. When only a youth, he pledged himself to temperance, and has kept the pledge. He and Susie will be happy.

www.ingramcontent.com/pod-product-compliance
Lightning Source LLC
Chambersburg PA
CBHW020942120726

47905CB00008B/2638